1964

❧

GIDE

❧

GERMAINE BRÉE

GIDE

Rutgers University Press
New Brunswick · New Jersey

Foreword

In a vigorous article on André Gide, Gaëtan Picon, perhaps the foremost contemporary French critic, spoke of the "actuality of André Gide."[1] In no sense did he intend this merely as a brilliant paradox. When we have pushed to its limits our present concern with "man's fate," with each man's responsibility within our social and historical situation as well as our preoccupation with man in the mass, we shall, Picon suggests, some of us at least, "return to André Gide." For Gide's most enduring concern, one which cannot long be overlooked in literature, was each individual's growth as he journeys through that single, precious life allotted him.

Since his death in 1951, Gide has moved away from us, of course, as all writers must. But the short span of years that have gone by has already begun to serve him well, stripping both the man and the work of the more superficial or less admirable characteristics that struck his contemporaries sometimes all too forcefully. Nothing now comes between us and a work unusual by its urbane resistance to the onslaught of criticism which followed Gide's death. Less noisy but more lasting scholarly criticism has slowly been accumulating in those last ten years, and we now can appraise better the man who, for a period of approximately sixty years, never faltered in the task he had set himself: to fashion his life and his

[1] Picon, Gaëtan, "L'usage de la lecture" (The Uses of Reading), Mercure de France, 1960.

work by means of a constant intellectual discipline of a very personal kind. To his very last breath Gide was still seeking to clarify what he truly was experiencing in the particular situation in which he found himself. It was his means of preserving his freedom of thought in a never-ending battle against others and, most of all, against himself. His work allows us to follow the sometimes devious paths which always led him to "obtain," as he liked to say, from himself his own integrity.

The year after Gide died I started to work on a book which was later published in France, *André Gide, l'Insaisissable Protée.* Since then a number of stimulating studies on André Gide have appeared. They have been of help to me in revising my original book for this English-language edition. The more important of these are Justin O'Brien's *Portrait of André Gide* and Dr. Jean Delay's two volumes *La jeunesse d'André Gide,* a psychoanalytic study of the first twenty-odd years of Gide's life. An abridged English edition of this work will be available in a translation by June Beckelman for the Chicago University Press. Other studies, and many articles which are not all listed in my short bibliography, also proved interesting, and yet my basic approach to Gide's work has not greatly changed. When I came back to his work I found that it was, rather, reaffirmed.

I am greatly indebted for all quotations to Gide's translators listed in the bibliography. Very often I have offered my own translations, not because I think they are necessarily better but because frequently a more literal, if less eloquent, rendering made my critical appraisals clearer.

In this revision of the original textbook I was helped considerably by June Beckelman, an experienced translator and editor, and by Ellen Conroy Kennedy, whose innumerable and helpful suggestions vastly improved the text. Mrs. Edna Dahl and Eric Schoenfeld gave generously of their time in the preparation of the manuscript. But most of all I feel in-

debted to André Gide himself who, after ten years, proved
to be a writer still slightly aloof, still quite as tantalizing and
rewarding as before.

GERMAINE BRÉE

Madison, Wisconsin
December, 1962

Contents

Contents

GIDE

André Gide: *Fact and Legend*

> *Il m'importe avant tout de pou-*
> *voir penser librement.*
>
> Above all, I must be able to think
> freely.

∿∿∿∿∿∿∿∿∿∿∿∿∿∿∿∿∿∿∿∿∿∿∿∿∿∿∿∿∿∿∿

"My ideas do not naturally follow each other logically," Gide wrote in 1900. "They come all together or not at all." [1] Gide is no logician; nothing is less systematic than his thinking.

> Take things for what they are.
> Play with the cards one holds.
> Insist upon being as one is.

This does not keep one from struggling against the lies, falsifications, etc., that men have imposed on a natural state of things, against which it is useless to revolt. There is the inevitable and the modifiable. Acceptance of the modifiable is in no wise included in *amor fati.*

This does not keep one, either, from demanding of oneself the best, after one has recognized it as such. For one does not make oneself any truer to oneself by giving precedence to the less good. [2]

These few lines offer the sum total of Gide's wisdom. It had already been at work underneath the maze of confused speculation, personal anxiety and inhibitions of the early *Journals*. It took Gide many years to free his thought from the purely disquisitional and present it directly without excuse or justification. His convictions, slowly come by, do not obtrude upon the reader, persuasive rather by their singularly unpretentious air. Gide's Theseus found that the greatest danger he encountered was not the Minotaur, but the labyrinth. Gide steadily fought against the lure of all labyrinthian speculation.

When stated as above, Gide's thought may seem limited and rather sibylline. To what "things" is he alluding? What does he mean by the "cards" we hold? What is the "natural state of things"? What Gide really requires of us of course is that we reformulate all the great questions, a healthy state of mind all too rare at the turn of the century. But how and on what grounds? Gide's pragmatic ethic is founded on two basic precepts: we must refuse to compromise our "becoming" either by failing to see beyond the present moment or by yielding to the attractions of the many-faceted mental lie. One can be grateful to Gide for stubbornly warning against all forms of doctrinaire contagion and for pointing out the dangers we run when we fail to think and decide for ourselves. There is a commitment to noncommitment in Gide that is a welcome contrast to the noisy and questionable commitments of partisan thought. Yet this would not be a sufficient reason to take his works seriously. Gide's wisdom proposes a dynamic form of individual opportunism kept within bounds by a sense of human dignity: one should follow one's inclination, but, he insisted, upward. His innate optimism led him to trust that each human being would sift out for himself what was best, given the circumstances. His art of living is addressed to individuals and brings a warning rather than direction to an age whose vital preoccupations and deep-seated anxieties concern collectivities rather than individuals. But Gide attracts because behind the precepts one always finds the man. His ethic was formulated by him, for himself, and he worked at perfecting it to the very end—a fine example of intellectual vigor and moral dignity. Almost from the outset he fashioned his works with a boldness of thought absent in his life, spent on the whole within the protective precincts of the intellectual grande bourgeoisie: "I was braver in my writing than in my life," [3] he admitted regretfully. Gide was never a coward. It is rather that, like his friend Valéry, he distrusted the rigidity of all forms of intellectual dogmatism. Of a speculative bent, an intellectual himself by temperament, he preferred to try out his ideas and push them to their limit in literature rather than in life. It was his manner of testing their value without himself losing contact with the world of reality.

Gide's personal ease and fine sense of balance, quite rare in the often crass brutality of our own time, may temporarily, perhaps, hide the firmness and integrity of his critical approach and its value as example and discipline. In the long run it will emerge as the very foundation of his reputation. From *Fruits of the Earth* to *New Fruits of the Earth*, Gide eliminated all direct messages from his work. His extraordinary ability as author was to probe and reveal indirectly the devious ways of human consciousness in relation to everyday existence. And in this chosen realm Gide concentrated upon a topic of no small consequence: the struggle of human beings with truths compulsively followed.

True, Gide's excursions into the labyrinths of the subconscious are limited when compared to the audacities of the surrealists who came after him or the revelations of psychoanalysis. But he did not write merely to liberate himself or to express his new insights. Gide is first and foremost a disciplined artist whose distinguishing mark is the control he achieved of form and language. He was gifted to an extreme degree with the ability to develop complex and very finely structured narrative patterns. Whether "récit," "sotie" or novel, all his work reflects the same artistic conscience and ability. In this respect Gide has influenced the course of the French novel more than Proust. Seeking to expose certain forms of self-deception, Gide posed the deeper-lying question of the limits of the mind at grips with the actual experience of life. Yet as an artist he was committed to mold experience into form. This struggle of Gide's with himself as an artist gives his works their particular dynamism and humor. Each mold is set aside in turn as the artist watches, with elation, life spilling out of the form he had tried to impose upon it while he as an artist inevitably seeks another mold. Gide's ideas are always ideas of form, aesthetic in nature and not political or ethical. To keep form and content in strict equilibrium is an artistic discipline which Gide untiringly imposed upon himself. Hence the fundamentally restrained, or classical, understatement and objectivity of each work.

At one stage in his life Gide felt with some violence that several centuries of civilization had set up between himself and the world of reality a screen of beliefs and rules that was fast proving dangerously inadequate. This was the true scandal to which the discovery of the world of homosexuality had awakened him. His first step was to dare to appraise and liberate his desires; his first advice to others was of the same order. But this brought him face to face with moral chaos. From this perplexity arose the supple Gidian game of thought and experience by means of which Gide fashioned himself and his work in terms of the reality he grasped. He felt that the culture of which he was an inheritor need not be bankrupt, if only it was willing to come to terms with the modern world. A cautious heir of that culture, Gide was not a revolutionary. His was a warning voice, intent on revitalizing gestures and formulae so that they might become acts and living expressions of belief.

"I believe that what most pushed me to write was a pressing need for sympathy." [4] This attempt to establish contact with the reader is perhaps the weakest part of Gide's work. It explains the more superficial, artificial mannerisms in which he indulges. But it was also one of the sources of his creativity. In a sense Gide uses a "proposition" as a starting point for his work, such an intellectual proposition as might come up in casual conversation. Gradually he shapes a concrete fictional situation which has this proposition as its momentum and orientation. The story establishes the relation between reality and the character's conceptions of reality, and then reveals the dangers lurking behind the proposition, however plausible it might seem. This is Gide's way of conversing, through art rather than abstract debate.

A book or a fictional situation for a book begins for Gide where there is a break in the "balance . . . between the real world and the mind's creation." [5] In the course of his stories, the original proposition—"the mind's creation," in other words—is little by little limited, qualified, reduced and finally demolished, as all of the mind's creations in a Gidian world must necessarily be. This seems to have imposed upon Gide's novels the "strangulation" which he sometimes deplored.

Gide's work was bound to change in the process of creation, tracing as it did the modifications of an idea in contact with life. The change of direction always takes place at the very center of a Gidian work, as the story reaches its peak. The general movement of each story thus seems to have depended not on a decision arbitrarily made but on Gide's inner sensitivity. There Gide's evolution was unusual. Because he knew how prone he was to letting himself be carried away by emotions, he reacted by imposing a strict self-discipline on his writing. Temperamentally inclined toward torment, resolutely he pursued the happiness which comes from equilibrium, a Goethean happiness, the kind of happiness his *Theseus* achieves. Emotion and discipline were combined in

Gide's search for the new forms of expression he developed with a "sort of musical logic" [6] that in the case of *The Counterfeiters* he compared to a fugue. The conflicts between intelligence and sensibility, characteristic of many French postsymbolists, became, for Gide, powerful incentives to create subtly balanced, carefully modulated works. The "adversary," whether Claudel, for example, or simply the "other" within himself, played a really essential part in the genesis of the best of his works, more as instigator than as foe. Since Gide's ideas came all at once, sometimes giving him the impression that his entire lifework was alive in him and had been from his youth on, the impetus needed to start work on any one idea had to come from outside. The Mephistophelean outer suggestion is then taken in hand, and Gide sets up the mechanics by which it can go into action and through which its weaknesses are uncovered. Where Michel and Alissa sink into tragedy, Gide, like his Theseus, moves on. Gide's elusive humor, a rarity in our emphatic age, makes it clear that art, after all, simply plays with the substance of life; it "proposes" whereas life "disposes."

Gide is one of the rare French writers since Rabelais for whom humor is one of the mainsprings of creativity. On the whole, critics seem singularly blind to the peculiar modalities of Gidian wit and the unique corrective they bring to his more easily recognized and less original use of irony. The mechanism of the sotie, with its ludicrous characters and burlesque debates, travesties we quickly recognize, is the most patent form of Gide's humor. But a gentle amusement underlies the tragic ironies of the récits and suffuses the atmosphere in which the counterfeiters in the novel go about their dastardly work. Humor rescues Gide's work from pathos and moralizing, giving it its particular air of lightness and fantasy.

"But a special joy," said Gide, "comes from the discord between the real and the imaginary." [7] Gide's humor is a form of that special joy. He could not take tragically as does a

Sartre the discrepancy between his Zeus and Prometheus—
Zeus representing the natural order, Prometheus man's consciousness—prone though he is to take Prometheus's side.
Zeus' tranquil disregard of Prometheus's grandiose schemes
and consequently the ludicrous scaling down to size he in-
flicts on the best of these, seemed to Gide both moving and
grotesque. The double perspective that this sense of discord
introduces determines the subtle play of light and shadow in
every Gidian work. To attack Gide on the ground that he
evades all issues is absurd. Writing, for Gide, was not a form
of demonstration. A book embodied the play of idea and
sensibility peculiar to Gide in contact with certain facets of
his own experience. Situations and themes are used over and
over again, but serve only as might the seven notes of the
scale. Each work echoes the others, refers to them, yet they
never interpenetrate; each is closed to the others and in itself complete—"full as an egg," as the baffled protagonist
of *Marshlands* had dreamed. Many readers think they have
drained the liqueur from a Gidian work when actually they
have scarcely sipped. Gide requires the reader to penetrate
the meaning of his works. He does not explain them.

There is nothing superficial about Gide's thought, but its
real expression lay in the creation of literary forms, almost
as difficult to explain verbally as are musical forms or abstract
paintings. Gide was right to claim that his works could be
sanely evaluated only from the point of view of art, "a point
of view never taken by the critic, or almost never. Besides it
is the only point of view that excludes no other." [8] The end
of his remark suggests that Gide did not propose to divorce aesthetic value from all others. So far as his work was
concerned, he knew that its significance would appear only
through an understanding of the forms he had fashioned.

Language, for Gide, was strictly subordinated to the intent
at work in the form. Word by word, sentence by sentence,
it had to reveal a dynamic structure. Gide, a natural virtuoso

with language, did not reach perfection by an easy path. In *André Walter* he had wallowed in an apparently spontaneous patchwork of borrowed rhythms and imagery, to say nothing of imitative rhetoric. But under the aegis of Mallarmé he soon learned to lay aside oratory and hackneyed metaphor in favor of more subtly suggestive rhythms and a new complex imagery. His "secretly musical" [9] side also presented great temptations, however. For Gide had little visual imagination, and the blend of vague imagery with facile musicality is one of the royal paths to preciosity. He therefore imposed a demanding discipline upon himself. At the time he was writing *The Immoralist* he described the process to a friend:

> The ever more stringent demand I make upon myself obliges me to go back to the same sentence eight times, and keep at it half a day, often only to scratch it out the next day; all that because of subtleties touching upon propriety, order, or clarity, and rhythms so tenuous that I really believe I am the only one sensitive to them—but it can't be helped. At least afterwards, I rest and often feel keen joy in rereading what I have written and rereading it again in print. [10]

Not until Gide succeeded in separating his heroes from himself was he able to fashion his style, his language, in relation to the musical logic of each individual work. *Strait Is the Gate* is a fine example of Gide's control of language, with its two carefully differentiated registers for Jerome and Alissa. After *Strait Is the Gate* Gide was in search of an unobtrusive variety of tone, a carefully controlled spontaneity approximating the modes of spoken language without adopting its loose syntax and vagaries. Narrative gave way to dialogue in an attempt to create an entirely self-sustained four-dimensional world which the reader might approach from every side. The autonomy sought by Gide required an increasingly demanding control if the work was to convey what he wanted to say. He used all the resources of a language he had thoroughly mastered to shape a new, subtle and personal register. But in a sense his very subtlety in the use of a term, the slight twist he gave by an imperceptible change in the place of an adverb, and the tight control he kept over each word give his work its rather mannered, dated clothing. Gide's works are like the man. They are newer, more powerful, more imaginative than is at first apparent under their rather fastidious garb.

Gide's works are so deeply rooted in a fast-disappearing culture that a whole re-education may be necessary before they again find a large reading public. Like Vergil's works, so dear to Gide, his own may find a place only on the library shelves of a few subtly sensitive individuals. Gide's freedom from grim disillusion or revolt, his humor and optimistic enjoyment of life seem more compatible with less harassed times than our own. To relate and reveal is a modest ambition, less dramatic than to denounce or explicate. The discovery of the "other" in us is now a worn-out theme; the fight against the closed world of deterministic materialism, though still with us, has long since gone beyond the simple forms it assumed at the turn of the century. The grain of folly Gide instilled in his characters, which carried them to the extremes he himself carefully avoided, seems very mild today. Yet in its solitary independence, the work of André Gide remains unshaken. In its entirety it is one of the outstanding literary achievements of our time.

By the time of his death, in 1951, André Gide had attained a unique position in the world of letters. It had not come to him easily. Sixty years earlier, at the age of twenty-two, he had published his first work: *The Notebooks of André Walter*, an adolescent, autobiographical novel. But it was not until the nineteen-twenties, when he was over forty, with the bulk of his work behind him, that he achieved fame —a fame consecrated, to the indignation of some, by the Nobel Prize in 1947. Until well into the twenties he seemed to live almost exclusively among a coterie of cultivated friends. Although the coterie steadily grew to include most of the better-known literary figures of Europe, it kept the characteristics of a closed circle of men of letters homogeneous in interests and tastes. Through the literary magazine *La Nouvelle revue française,* founded by Gide and his friends in 1908-1909, the group slowly came to exercise a determining although not exclusive influence on French letters. For about a quarter of a century Gide, the most prominent writer in the group, seemed to be at the very center of French letters and of controversies which disturbed the literary world, sometimes reaching out beyond the borders of France. Though the seventy-year-old writer seemed strangely out of place in the war-torn world of the early forties, remaining on the periphery of events even when he felt their impact, his gaunt figure, battered hat, and tight-lipped, masklike face never failed to elicit interest and respect.

Gide's friends—both real and so-called—published a rash of essays after his death. Intimates who had lived in his shadow sought, so they said, to unmask the man beneath the "role." For years he had been a controversial figure: to "defend" André Gide, "denounce," "justify" or "condemn" him, "analyze" him or "converse" with him had even before his death become a popular literary game and a source of revenue for many of his acquaintances. After his death a steady attempt was made in some quarters to discredit the work along with the man. His works were put on the *Index.* Yet there was no massive indictment, no violent attack; merely the reiterated suggestion that Gide's work was sinking into oblivion, losing the favor of a younger generation indifferent to his personality, to his intelligent sophistication and optimistic humanism, and to his prime concern with literature. The once much-discussed "problem of Gide" receded into the background, for it had in fact been closely connected to the petty squabbles of an obsolete literary milieu.

The assumption that Gide was a minor figure seems true today only in a limited sense, however. In spite of his sincere good will, it is probably true where his social activities are concerned. One need only compare the inept and artificial "trial" held in 1935 by the "Union for Truth," at the time of Gide's adherence to communism,[11] with Zola's trial, forty years earlier, at the time of the Dreyfus case. Zola's intervention was really dangerous for him and it was effective, as demonstrated by the violence of the passions it released. Gide obligingly participated in the 1935 discussion, but his temporary and distant flirtation with communism, like the discussions it raised, remained strictly an affair for intellectuals and had no further repercussions. The same ineffectuality was apparent when Gide, along with other intellectuals, attempted to oppose fascism, as well as in his later criticism of the U.S.S.R.[12] Gide's social concerns and activities are not really significant, nor for that matter were the anecdotal exterior aspects of his personality that so fascinated, disturbed or annoyed his acquaintances.

It seems difficult now to understand the violence of the discussions about Gide's personality that agitated the restricted milieu of literary Paris, and their lack of common sense. Yet these disputes helped considerably to distort the significance and true originality of his works. The fact that Gide, a Protestant, withstood trends that made converts to Catholicism of some of his closest friends; the peculiar circumstances of his private life: a married man, admittedly devoted to his wife and yet an avowed homosexual who, more and more unashamedly as time went by, drew upon homosexuality as a literary theme; the flirtation with communism —all these peculiarities provoked emotions and indignations which now seem childish. After all, Gide is not the only writer never to have been converted; whose private life is not

above reproach; who was attracted by communism in the
thirties, only to express his later disappointment.[13]

Perhaps all the vehemence can be traced to his paradoxical position: he openly participated in the rites of a social
class—the well-to-do bourgeoisie to which he belonged—and
benefited from its traditions only to discard them with perfect equanimity. To the scandal of some, Gide was at one
and the same time permeated with the gospel and an atheist;
the head of a tightly knit family that included in-laws, cousins, nephews and nieces; and also an impenitent homosexual;
a grand bourgeois, hailed for a time as an intellectual leader
by the communists, and later a critic of the communists, yet
a critic who never became a militant "anti-communist." Consequently, part of the commentary that Gide inspired might
be classified under the heading: "The ethical impossibility of
being André Gide." To placate some of his contemporaries,
Gide should have ended like Don Juan, by disappearing into
hell. At times he seems to have enjoyed this role, but he carefully avoided the fate. His death, on February 19, 1951, was
exemplary in its serenity. In truth Gide's temerities in themselves seem inconsequential. Their value is wholly intellectual
and fully evinced only in his works. Gide played along with
his critics willingly, in fact delightedly, often deliberately pro-
voking them. His careful publication of a great many personal documents, from *André Walter* to the profoundly disturbing *Et nunc manet in te* (*Madeleine*) (1947), describing
the intimate tragedy that had linked him to and separated
him from his wife, certainly contributed to the legend about
him. To the cult of the written word inherited from Mallarmé he added the cult of what he called "sincerity." A true
literary Midas, throughout his life he transformed all that
affected him into literature. His *Journals* (1889-1948), at one
time so greatly admired, often give a disconcerting importance to the innumerable small incidents of his daily life:
the meticulous count of his nights of insomnia, for example,

or the insidiously veiled allusions to passing hours of furtive pleasure taken with some unnamed adolescent.

Where his own life was concerned, Gide never attained the detachment, freedom of mind or humor of Montaigne, one of his favorite authors. The earnestness characteristic of his social manner seems also to have hampered somewhat his relations with himself. As a writer he was often able to use to good effect a peculiar, very personal form of humor. But it never seemed to act directly upon the self-image which, under the guise of sincerity, he sought to impress upon his readers. This painstaking and lifelong self-portrait is, however, only one aspect of Gide's work, and it is marginal to his literary achievements. But it had some rather surprising effects. In attacking Gide as a person—for his "pernicious influence," his "poses," his "attitudes," his "revelations," some few pompously moralistic critics thereby attacked individual freedom and the freedoms of speech and judgment. The "problem of Gide" became a kind of touchstone which brought to light forms of concealed intolerance in the world of letters. More perhaps than he deserved, and with the unwitting aid of his critics, Gide became a champion of individual freedom.

Both in his *Journals* and in his partial autobiography (1920-1921), *If it die . . .* , Gide revealed a great deal about himself. Yet the documentary value of these accounts can be challenged. A brutal little book initiated by a young man [14] Gide had treated pretty badly in his *Journals*, shows the wide margin left to myth in Gide's "sincerity." It is more than likely that Gide's fictional works disclose more of his real personality than do his *Journals*.

When Gide, along with many of his contemporaries, discarded the trappings of symbolism he sought to base his art on an experience personally and authentically lived. But for him life was really subsidiary to literature. An avid reader and sensitive critic, Gide led a pre-eminently literary life.

More than Normandy or Languedoc to which he claimed he belonged, literature was his true province and the literary milieu his true milieu. If he considered that his whole life must serve as foundation for his writing it was because, at the turn of the century, he had clearly discerned the esoterism that was undermining much "fin de siècle" writing. In a sense, he deliberately made his life the sole subject matter of his work. But, unlike his more directly autobiographical books, his fictional works are free from personal beatification. His autobiography, *If it die* . . . , was written when Gide was nearing fifty. Is it any more revealing than his earlier fictional works: *The Notebooks of André Walter, The Immoralist* (1902), or *Strait Is the Gate* (1909)?

At the time of *If it die* . . . , Gide was less interested in himself as a whole than in two aspects of his personality, the homosexual and the writer, both of which fascinated him. The portrait he draws of himself as a child, honest though it undoubtedly is in intent, is strongly colored by what he imagined were inevitable psychological characteristics of his sexual deviation, a debatable point of view in the light of present knowledge.

Many of the suggestions that Gide put forth about himself in the course of his self-portraiture were all too eagerly seized upon, systematized and repeated. The two sides of his personality, for example: the "Norman" temperament that was his mother's and the southern "Languedoc" temperament of his father; or the Protestant-Catholic conjuncture. Gide made use of them when he wanted to combat Barrès's racial theories or to draw Claudel out when Claudel attempted to convert him. But can one consider seriously these facile pseudo-psychological antitheses based on the now outmoded theories of Taine? How many people today in the Western world and more specially in France can really trace their ancestry back to a single province? Gide was, in fact, of pure French extraction, "crossbred" only within the limits of France. He was so unadulteratedly French that with the exception of his first two trips to Algeria (1893-1895) as a young man no journey made by this perpetual traveler ever left a mark upon his works. Even the psychological crisis precipitated by Gide's Algerian sojourn had little to do with Africa. Apart from a few exotic settings and an enriched vocabulary Algeria brought nothing to Gide's works.[15] He was impervious to anything foreign.

Gide's contact with Algeria merely hastened a transformation that had already begun. His convalescence after a first attack of tuberculosis and a first and belated experience of sexual fulfillment opened up new perspectives, intensifying his reaction to the austerity of his Protestant milieu. His knowledge of Africa, however, did not go much beyond the circle of the adolescents he frequented, in whom he saw Vergil's shepherds, Mopsus and Amyntas, Menalcas and Corydon. What he brought back from Algeria was a sense of the relativity of the values of his French bourgeois heritage and what he thought he had discovered was a real counterpart of the bucolic settings of Vergil, whom he read all his life.

Gide achieved a position where he could throw open to French literature doors through which ideas from abroad could enter. He had an ability to absorb and appreciate large doses of foreign literature. Yet in his own work he assimilated and developed only those very rare ideas which corresponded to the needs of his own acute and limited sensitivity. Only certain carefully isolated elements of the authors he most admired, violent authors like Blake, Nietzsche and Dostoevsky, filtered into his own writing. Gide naturalized everything he touched and nothing too vigorous, turbulent or bizarre ever slipped into his works.

The antithetical Gide dear to many critics was born of still another Gidian pronouncement by now so hackneyed that it cannot be overlooked. "The need for dialogue defines me." From dialogue to duplicity is a short step. The "duplicity" of André Gide soon became a stereotype for his critics. It was in 1894 that the twenty-five-year-old Gide first used the term "dialogue" to describe his new mood:

> I have arrived at the fortunate state in which one no longer has personal faith. This state, which for the philosopher would be skepticism, is, for a man of letters, what one might call the state of dialogue. It comes from a continually greater and, especially, deeper insight or understanding of the beliefs and ethics of others; from the possibility of becoming as sincerely and passionately moved in turn by one as by the other; and finally, from the complete disinterestedness of one's personal opinion.[16]

The state of dialogue here defined is not a dialogue of Gide with himself; it is an objective "availability," an "unbiased" curiosity, to use Gide's favorite terms, in regard to all points of view. "People like you and me," Gide is supposed to have said to a friend, the critic Du Bos, "critical minds, more particularly auto-critical . . . are people of dialogue and not of affirmation." For Gide, dialogue opposed to dogmatism opens the way to polyvalence rather than mere dualism of thought. The Gidian "dialogue," therefore, is not simply an oscillation between conflicting tendencies. It is rather a perpetual state of open-mindedness.

Another obvious road to the misunderstanding of Gide is the widespread idea that his works are nothing but thinly disguised autobiography. Yet no works are more meticulously executed, more deliberately situated in the realm of literature considered as an art. After his first work, *The Notebooks of André Walter*, Gide, who had come to know Mallarmé, never confused the realms of art and of life as did the surrealists. His works have no ultraliterary aim. He considered literature and life as united by a complex and often obscure network of exchanges, each realm supporting the other, yet each remaining clearly distinct from the other. It was not the facts of his experience that seemed important to Gide, no matter how unusual, but rather the aesthetic use he made of them. His life served merely as a starting point for his art. The resolutions of the conflicts it proposed to him were in his case always aesthetic, inherent to the work, to the medium and techniques by means of which he elaborated the initial suggestions. They did not carry over to his life as such. To seek in all Gide's works the "psychology of André Gide" is a dangerous exercise and a rather useless one. Like a conjurer, one extracts from the hat the rabbit carefully furnished for that purpose by oneself.

To a combination of all those trends in Gidian criticism, but more particularly to the religious, we owe the "diabolical," "demoniac," "dionysiac" Gide, the "possessed" and "tortured" Gide which, it must be admitted, a candid reading of his works fails to uncover. Gide nurtured many doubts. Yet from the time of *Fruits of the Earth* (1897) most of his work is characterized by a certain luminosity and by a polite, sometimes ironic, distance from reality. Gide accentuated the distance within his stylized—or, as he said, "unburdened"—world. Persons and themes are closely attuned, meeting in a limpid "Gidian" space, where the diabolical has little or no place. In fact it would seem that this very lack explains why Gide's work had so precarious a hold during the 1950's over a generation just emerging from World War II. His work, pre-Freudian and pre-Marxist, is free from existential anguish, complex symbolism, sophisticated or primitivistic uses of imagery and language. Armed to the teeth with psychoanalytical, political or philosophical theories, the critics turned toward more obviously chaotic and difficult works. The deceptively simple surface of Gide's writing had succeeded in hiding from them the complex inner play of forces at work in each book. Gide, the decadent aesthete, was scorned.

Gide himself contributed a good deal, as always, to another, diabolical, image of himself.[17] Enigmatic, seductive when he pleased, he sometimes rather fancied himself in the role of a Mephistophelean perverter, a moral perverter to be sure, ultimately concerned with "higher" ethical values than those he challenged. Perverters appear frequently in his works but they are always ordinary human beings endowed with no diabolically supernatural powers. Particularly after *Corydon* (1911), his attempt to justify homosexuality made his transformation into a prince of darkness complete. His Catholic friends and, more especially, his Catholic enemies saw him in the perspectives of their own faith. "As for Satanism," Gide commented, "let's not bother with it now. I fear it's just a matter of words." [18] "Were I capable of anxiety, I should not be capable of writing books," [19] he added. "They blame me because I am not unhappy." [20] And in fact Gide's essential theme is not torment but happiness, whether hard-won or thrown away, with its virtues, dangers and limits, the "direct realization of happiness and harmony."

Not that Gide was free from concern with others or with himself. Throughout his life he participated in social and political activities. He served as mayor of La Roque, the small village in which he owned an estate. He worked hard from 1914-1916 to help the Belgian refugees in Paris. At the time of the Dreyfus affair, he was pro-Dreyfus although without much conviction. He took positive stands on most of the issues that stirred France, during the eventful first half of the twentieth century, and always on the side of freedom, justice, tolerance and generosity. Yet the courteous tone of his voice, the careful ponderation of his arguments belong to the nineteenth century, to the liberal traditions of the cultivated grande bourgeoisie he still represented.

Recollections of the Assize Court (1914), *Journey to the Congo* (1927), *Return from the Tchad* (1928), *Return from the U.S.S.R.* (1937), some pages of the *Journal*, particularly between 1929 and 1935, the writing collected in the volume entitled *Littérature engagée* (Literature of Commitment) all testify to Gide's social good will. Nonetheless, his voice lacked resonance and his interventions were amateurish. Social problems never really touched Gide deeply. By 1914 he was already too old to be drafted and it was more as a spectator than as a participant that he considered the events that weighed so heavily on the destiny of his country: they saddened or surprised him but never really disturbed him. Having passed the age of sixty, he seemed to realize what this indifference had cost him:

There comes a time in life—and I believe that this time must come if one merely lives long enough—when the things which one scorned in one's youth take their revenge, just as in Greek tragedy Aphrodite or Dionysos takes revenge for the disdain of Hippolytus or Pentheus. Yes, today I am paying for my refusals of the past, of that long time when everything I knew to be transitory and belonging to politics and history seemed to me unworthy of real attention. Mallarmé's influence was responsible for this. I came under his influence without being aware of it, for it merely encouraged in me a natural tendency and I did not then yet realize how important it is to be wary of what flatters you and that the only real education comes from what goes against your grain.[21]

Gide's regret is an artist's regret. He is already elaborating it; it might produce, after all, another *Hippolytus* or *Pentheus*. In spite of all his efforts, at sixty he still believed what he had believed at the turn of the century when he was in his thirties: "It is his own works that the artist must put in order, not the world which surrounds him." [22]

Chapter II

A "Man of Letters"

> . . . *si j'examine ma vie, le trait*
> *dominant que j'y remarque, bien*
> *loin d'être l'inconstance, c'est au*
> *contraire la fidélité.*
>
> . . . when I examine my life, the
> major characteristic I note is not
> lack of constancy, far from it, but
> rather fidelity.

~~~~~~

Between Gide's first work, *André Walter* and his last, the posthumous *So be it* (1952) stretch sixty years of publication. Though he was neither a facile writer nor prolific in the Balzacian manner, Gide wrote a great deal and one can smile at the epithet "sterile" sometimes used to describe him. In his *Journals* Gide often insisted on his difficulties as a writer, on the paucity of his imagination. As usual, there came a time when he qualified his previous statements:

If my journal is published later on, I fear that it will give a rather false idea of me. I did not keep it during the long periods of equilibrium, health, and happiness, but instead during those periods of depression when I needed it to get hold of myself, and I show myself as whining, whimpering, pitiable. . . . As soon as the sun reappears, I lose sight of myself and am completely absorbed by work and life.[1]

Actually Gide's work is abundant and astonishingly varied. The nonfictional portion comprises autobiography, whether in the form of memoirs, journals or travel notes; essays on literary and other subjects; prefaces, letters, translations and anthologies. His fictional works are just as diverse: there are treatises; plays; poems written in free verse, in prose or in a combination of both; récits, soties, all appearing under unusual labels. For some there are no fitting labels: *The Return of the Prodigal Son* (1907) or *Theseus* (1946). In any event, many of the separate works slip easily from one label to the other. A "poem" such as *Urien's Voyage* (1893), which is really not a poem, started as a novel or a treatise. Of the three soties, *Marshlands* (1895) began as a treatise and *Prometheus Illbound* (1899) as a novel. The play *Philoctetes* (1899) began as a treatise and the récits at one time were all novels. *Proserpine* (1934), a novel, eventually became a dramatic symphony. Gide adopted the present classification of his fictional writing only in 1910, and later, in the thirties, was inclined to give it up. After stating that he considered *The Counterfeiters* his only novel, what was he to call *André Walter* or the *Pastoral Symphony* (1919)? Gide's works change labels and remain as they were. Their diversity points to the experimental nature of his aesthetics. At the time he first began to write the symbolists had made fashionable indefinite fluid forms that combined literature, metaphysics, music, and irony in varying degrees. In search of his own instrument of expression, Gide, although in a different mood from the symbolists, continued to experiment with new literary structures and techniques. Naturally enough there is a certain consistency in the patterns he developed. His works fall into two large groups: those which tend toward the novel and those which tend toward drama. He had begun as a novelist and always remained primarily concerned with the problems of novel writing. He was never greatly drawn to the theater, as his friend Copeau remarked and as he himself admitted: "I do not often go to the theater which often bores me to death; I can seldom bring myself to stay to the end of a performance." As he saw it, drama was a musical rather than a scenic medium which could combine a variety of voices diversely modulating common themes, a medium which he used in many guises.

But Gide, like his works, cannot easily be classified under any heading, whether as novelist, essayist or playwright. He was, of course, not alone at that time in his search for new forms, all the arts were on the move. Yet perhaps he alone managed to baffle his readers through an apparent simplicity rather than complexity of form. While a young writer in the wake of Mallarmé he sometimes attempted to formulate general aesthetic theories. Later, as in the *Journal of the Counterfeiters*, for example, he merely presented a set of documents and a few details of technique. But, different though they are in scope, Gide's major works, like those of his friend Valéry, are never spontaneous productions. Each is the carefully controlled realization of an aesthetic idea from which it draws its originality.

As a result, Gide's writing is related to poetry, organizing language and image as it does from within, molding them according to a highly individual mental vision and to the emotional demands of the writer's sensitivity. Gide was a highly emotional person. His immediate reaction to any situation came in the form of emotion rather than as image, fragrance or sound. "Not the landscape itself," wrote his first hero, André Walter, "but the emotion it arouses." Gide feared the sentimentality to which this tendency might lead and often took refuge in humor or irony. A contrapuntal play of emotion and irony marks such works as *The Return of*

the Prodigal Son and *Theseus;* emotion sets the tone of the
first, irony of the second. Both are, in fact, parables in which
emotion, irony and idea achieve a subtle equilibrium. With
the exception of *André Walter*, all Gide's works are in a sense
parables.

Chronologically, the work as a whole seems to have developed in three stages: the rich creativeness of the first years
from *André Walter* (1891) to *Saul* (1903), which then slows
down and to which *The Return of the Prodigal Son* (1907)
is a sort of epilogue; then, with *Strait Is the Gate* (1909) a
vigorous, fertile maturity reaching its peak in *The Counterfeiters* (1926); last, a steady decline in creative power which
Theseus (1946), serene, gentle, ironic and somewhat coquet-
tish in its mannerisms, nonchalantly brings to an unexpectedly brilliant end.

Gide often said—and friends in this case have corroborated
—that he had all his more important works in mind before
1900. Although he published *Oedipus* in 1931, he spoke of
Oedipus in his *Journal* as early as 1896. Theseus, a character
to whom he was always partial, made his first apparance in
1897, in *Fruits of the Earth*, but came into his own only
some fifty years later. Gide often complained that it took
him far too long to move from conception to execution, but
this appears to hold true only after *The Immoralist*. As a
young man, Gide seems to have written with ease, and, although as he grew older he was greatly to evolve in his point
of view and techniques, he never went much beyond the
terrain explored in his early work, content rather to cultivate
it more diversely. *The Immoralist* is the last of the works in
which Gide revealed large fragments of himself. The loss of
his initial facility seems to have been the price he paid for
a greater objectivity, and mastery of style.

Gide's literary universe is limited from a social point of
view to a small section of the French bourgeoisie before
World War I, and reflects some of its qualities and limita-

tions: its basic austerity and formality, its naïveté and the undercurrent of optimism that was characteristic of the precarious golden age of the early 1900's. But Gide does not write social novels. He uses the bourgeois milieu as a setting for his work only because he was born within its confines and never, however hard he tried, really escaped from them. Within that milieu, he never suffered from economic or political pressures, the difficulties he encountered were entirely personal in nature. Perhaps that is why, on first reading, his works seem narrow in scope and rarefied in atmosphere. Only a careful reader will see that these sharply defined boundaries do not really circumscribe Gide's world.

Et nunc manet in te (*Madeleine*), which was widely accessible only after Gide's death, revealed the one circumstance in his life which seems to have affected him deeply: the complex relationship with his wife, Madeleine. His homosexuality and his abandonment of the Christian faith appear to have troubled him only in regard to her. He loved her, but their marriage was never consummated and from the outset it never prevented him from taking his pleasure as he wished. He had the child she desired, but with another woman. Between them, perhaps because Gide, consciously or not, so wished it, the subject of their strange relationship seems never to have been broached. In *Et nunc manet in te* Gide has told the story of his wife's silence, and of the stubborn resistance with which she met his attempts to re-create the spiritual intimacy he needed, which at first she had readily given. Almost all his books before *The Counterfeiters* were written for her. In the later years she refused to read them, aware no doubt that Gide was insidiously attempting to break down her defenses under rather easily penetrated disguises.

The misunderstanding between them never flared out into the open, and Gide's writing profited greatly from their strange relationship. Much of the richest substance in his work he drew from this personal situation. Without Madeleine Gide, his disconcertingly successful life might have lacked that part of shadow which alone could give significance to the Goethe-like serenity he wished to emulate.

Gide's homosexuality, on the other hand, seems to have offered him an inexhaustible source of freedom and adventure. To others, especially as Gide grew older, it sometimes seemed closer to monomania. It led him to take many risks, the least of which perhaps was the publication, at first covert and then open, of *Corydon* (1911; 1920). But the society which had looked askance at Oscar Wilde was as casual about Gide as Gide's Minotaur was about his Theseus: "Facing me, stretched at length on a flowery bed of buttercups, pansies, tulips, jonquils, and carnations, I saw the Minotaur. As luck would have it, he was asleep . . ." [2] On the whole, Gide was respected at the time of his death as the "man of integrity" that he was. "Oh, Lord," he wrote in 1916, "grant that I not be among those who cut a figure in the world, grant that I not be among those who succeed." [3] In spite of the aura of scandal surrounding Gide's private life, God, thoroughly Gidian, did not grant his request. Yet, unlike Proust, he was never able to give his erotic experience an adequate literary expression. Except in his memoirs, he never touched upon the subject without a rather fatuous self-consciousness and a didactic earnestness which greatly diminished the aesthetic value of the theme.

Gide's religious evolution, however, had real repercussions on his work and even molded it to a certain extent. Like many of the intellectuals in his generation—Claudel, Jammes, Ghéon, and Copeau among them—Gide soon found it impossible to accept the spiritual values of the past. But, whereas most of Gide's friends reacted against the rationalistic deterministic materialism of the nineteenth century in favor of Catholicism, Gide was in a very different position. At twenty he was a fervent Christian who practiced his religion with conviction, carrying his Bible everywhere, even into the most esoteric symbolist salons. Among the better writers of his generation he is almost the only one to have had a genuinely Christian adolescence. The austere faith of his mother and the warmer faith of his wife, the two people who influenced him most deeply, suffused his whole life. That Gide was a Protestant is important of course, but secondary.

Gide considered Christianity and the ethical problems it poses an integral part of the psychological make-up of most people. He was not, like Maurice Barrès, primarily interested in its aesthetic values; nor did he see in Christianity, as Paul Bourget did, mainly a desirable and powerful force for moral and social order; nor was it for him the disquieting force at work in Joris Karl Huysman's life. Though Gide's own beliefs changed, he always considered that the Christian faith played a major role in shaping modern characters and destinies. His fictional characters, therefore, quite naturally set their goals and examine and judge their actions according to Christian values.

Gide was in his middle twenties when, around 1895, he began to drift away from religion. So far as he was concerned, however, the absence of a God did not necessarily lead to a nineteenth-century scientific vision of the universe as ordered by an implacable mechanism of natural laws. In spite of his lifelong interest in botany, Gide never showed any interest in the sciences as such, or in scientific theory. Increasingly he came to think in terms of a world in which human life had meaning only in human terms. The Christian God played an active role in this world only in so far as, believing in Him, people lived according to a law given as His. What struck Gide was the alogical, "absurd" quality of life. He was neither a mystic nor a philosopher but rather an observer at war with dogmatic systems. People and situations interested him less for what they were than for what they might become. Hesitant at first, he became more and more fascinated with this idea, whereby, because of a chance interplay of forces, some one event happens to occur rather than another just as amusingly improbable and quite as possible.

Within its own boundaries Gide's conception of life paralleled some of the scientific theories of the period, anticipating new and major literary themes: human life in a purposeless universe raising the problem of man's freedom and responsibility, the problem of ethics and morality, the questioning and testing of all accepted values through action.

Unlike the future existentialists, Gide was delighted rather than disturbed by the notion of the absurd. The absurd often invades his fictional world in the form of strange characters and improbable situations. Gide plays with his ideas, and though his fundamental point of view announced the then still latent tendency of the times, he himself, within this perspective, raised only a few quasi-classical problems. Life, as Gide portrays it, thus seems both unexpectedly new and yet detached from any particular period in time.

Gide attributed most of his good as well as his bad qualities to his Protestant upbringing: his inability to lie, his dedication to the search for truth; his capacity for self-discipline, but also the torments of his adolescent years. As a fatherless and only child, brought up by two austere women, he lived in a narrowly confined, puritanical home: "Ours was a sad upbringing which made us imagine voluptuousness, which is glorious and serene, as veiled in tears and anguished, or solitary and morose." Life always appeared to Gide in a kind of ambivalence, tempting and frightening like the Minotaur.

"I love life passionately," he once confessed, "but I have no confidence in it. And yet one should have." [4] This love and distrust of life responded to its enigmatic ambivalence. In one of his lectures Gide quoted a passage from Dostoevsky's letters:

Concerning my work here, you speak words of gold; you are right, I shall be left behind, not so far as the times are concerned, but rather because I shall no longer know what is happening in our country. . . . I shall lose touch with *the living flow of existence* . . . and how that does affect one's work! [5]

Gide always found it difficult to keep in touch with the living flow of existence. "I was fortunate to have fallen ill," he said at the time of his tuberculosis, "very seriously, it is true, but of a sickness which did not kill me—on the contrary—only weakened me for a time and had one certain result, it gave me the taste *for the rarity of life*." [6]

This taste for the rarity of life, *Fruits of the Earth* notwithstanding, is apparent in the more precious aspects of Gide's writing. The powerful vitality of the Bible, Shakespeare, Goethe, Dostoevsky, Browning and Blake, with whose works he was thoroughly at home, left no trace in his own.

The living flow of existence for Gide was, above all, literary. He spoke enthusiastically of the benefits of travel and adventure. But his journeys, when compared to those of men like Rimbaud, can hardly be called adventurous. Life for Gide was the book to be written: "that which others call a literary career," he said, "and which I call my life." [7] His interests, his anxieties, his problems all turned into literature. Small wonder that he was fascinated by the problem of sincerity. Long before he was aware of his homosexuality and the forms of dissimulation it generated he had already felt the dangers of literary counterfeit. With one sentence, "I'm afraid it's all a question of words," he later was to put a quick, ironic end to the discussions raised by *Numquid et tu* . . . , a religious meditation.

Though Gide distrusted literature, he came to terms with it, giving it the lion's share of his time but without letting it interfere too much with his own life. Never for a second does Gide seem to have doubted the value of his calling as a writer. Writing was more important in his eyes than any other activity. Anything connected with literature could lay claim to his time and energy. In this realm he acted decisively, with conviction, and with benefit for French letters as a whole. He believed in a free and broad exchange of ideas and literature and he facilitated it in every way. He countered the narrow provincialism of small literary cliques by his perceptive and enthusiastic essays on foreign writers and by his translations. He was dedicated to literature. "When I examine my life, the major characteristic I note is not lack of constancy, far from it, but rather fidelity. Such deep fidelity in both heart and thought I believe to be infinitely rare. Let those be named who, before dying, were able to see the accomplishment of what they planned to achieve, and I shall take *my* place among them," [8] wrote Gide in answer to those who reproached him for his elusiveness. He had accomplished his work as a writer and this, to him, was everything; the rest was not important.

The moralist in Gide was born of the artist. He had a demanding conception of the writer's responsibility toward his work. He believed, with Mallarmé, that a work of art worthy of the name must in a unique fashion elucidate some essential problem of human living. Gide was concerned with what use people made of the gratuitous and temporary gift of life. While he remained a believer, it was not ethics in themselves that he questioned but only the effect of their misuse upon people's lives. In his later works, those which arise from a concept of the world as gratuitous, the concern with ethics and their relativity is more complex.* He focuses on the

* Gide belonged to a generation that was just finding its way out of the closed mechanical world of nineteenth-century science and had not yet plunged into the tête-à-tête with the philosophies of history and of dialectical determinism which were so deeply to absorb their successors. He was just twenty in 1889 when Bergson published his *Essai sur les données immédiates de la conscience* which among other ideas raised the question of the "free act." The notion, divorced from its Bergsonian context, proved immensely stimulating to Gide, who was quick to see how it might renew the whole rather worn-out psychology of action and motivation in the novel and, in fact, the very

moral adventures of human beings which furnished him an inexhaustible, mysterious and ever-fascinating spectacle. Turning away from the novel of psychological analysis, the thesis or realistic novels, Gide created new forms better suited to his point of view. The problems he wanted to raise are close to those Sartre and Camus were to formulate. But where Sartre and Camus sought to achieve their ends by intentionally jolting the reader, brutally in the case of Sartre, intensely in the case of Camus, Gide accomplished his ends by much quieter and subtler means, through a skillful play of irony, a casual ironic humor, and by a certain quality of other worldliness in the whole atmosphere of the work. He was quite right when he suggested that his works yield their meaning only when approached from an aesthetic point of view, for this is the only approach which simultaneously reveals their intellectual content and their ethical meaning.

Each book, as it appeared, struck the slowly growing circle of Gide's readers with its newness. Though Gide never went far afield nor greatly varied his material, he never wrote the same book over again, its counterpart or its equivalent. Each book was shaped from a different point of view, ideas for Gide, as for most artists, appearing in the guise not of abstractions but of form. That is why a chronological study of Gide's work is of necessity also an account of his inner development.

---

technique of novel writing more or less immobilized in Flaubertian deterministic patterns. He wanted a word to designate precisely those acts that break with established patterns, revealing in an individual hidden complexities of which that individual himself is unaware: random acts, inexplicable acts, spontaneous acts, apparently unmotivated or inconsequential acts. Gide was on the track of a psychology of the irrational or subconscious self which psychoanalysis was just beginning to uncover. These apparently inexplicable acts he called "gratuitous." He saw in them the sign of the hidden forces at play in human lives which could raise havoc with the best intentions and the most carefully laid plans—a fertile field for the novelist.

Chapter III

The Early Works

J'attends toujours je ne sais quoi d'inconnu.

I am always waiting for something unknown.

~~~~~~

Gide's first works, from *André Walter* to *The Amorous Attempt,* have a fragile, sometimes fastidious charm all their own. André Walter's adolescent spontaneity has an engaging naïveté. *Narcissus, Urien's Voyage* and *The Amorous Attempt,* which derive from more sophisticated fin de siècle moods and the stylistic practices of Maurice Barrès, Jules Laforgue, Pierre Louÿs and Henri de Régnier, attract as might an art of the miniature. They are exquisitely finished works in which the young writer skillfully blends complex and highly artificial patterns of thought and feeling with the subtle ironies fashionable in his literary coterie. Gide's irony, directed against his own attitudes and stylistic tricks, and a latent skepticism hovering behind his most elegiac flights achieve a delicate balance in the writing. Though artificial, these early works are neither pretentious nor entirely derivative. Young Gide seems to have been fully aware that they were tentative and belonged only to the narrow "path of dreams" [1] he speaks of in *André Walter*. When in 1895, with *Marshlands*, Gide stopped to take stock of his recent literary efforts he violently satirized their themes, tone and ideological pretensions. Yet he never completely recaptured the freshness of these first, highly ornamented "treatises."

Among them *André Walter*, published in 1891, has a place apart. A son of the Romantics, Gide's hero has never heard of Mallarmé; Verlaine is the most avant-garde of his literary gods. Through Novalis and Sénancour he harks back to Goethe's *Werther*. André Walter is an egocentric and isolated hero entangled in a struggle involving his private fate, an ideal love, and his yearning for a state of mystical, religious ecstasy. The events he relates in a loose narrative take place between March and December of 1889, with flashbacks to 1886. André Walter is a moody, romantic double of his creator, and to fill out his story Gide drew heavily from his own diary.

The fictional chronology of the novel is simple and made explicit in a preface signed P.C.—initials hiding the identity of young Gide's friend and confidant, the future writer, Pierre Louÿs. In March, 1889, André Walter withdraws to Brittany to write a novel in complete solitude. His projected novel, "Allain," is to be "strange, scientific and passionate." Ten months later Walter dies, mad, leaving a novel and a diary. *André Walter*, Gide's novel, is purportedly Walter's diary. The "symbolic" (symbolic meaning)—as Walter would say—is clear: Walter dies, but what killed him lives on in a book.

The autobiographical content of *André Walter* is more complex, as Gide later explained in *If it die. . . .* The curiously fraternal and yet ill-assorted couple whose misunderstanding seals Walter's doom never ceased in one form or another to haunt Gide's work. Gide openly admitted they were a projection of Madeleine Rondeaux, his cousin and future wife, and himself. But Walter's story is not Gide's. Un-like Walter, Gide had no intention of giving up the idea of marrying his beloved. Even in so early a work Gide starts quite typically from his personal situation but develops it "scientifically," exploring latent possibilities which he him-self had no intention of trying out. Walter does what Gide refused to do: he renounces his love for Emmanuèle and consequently dies. The premise of the book is clear: an un-fulfilled love can prove mortal to the lover. Gide hoped his message would sway his recalcitrant family, Madeleine more particularly.

But beneath the surface of the book, veiled or smothered in ethical and metaphysical digressions, are other, more ob-scure preoccupations, yet unrealized by the young author him-self. Thirty years after he wrote *André Walter* Gide saw what had probably escaped him at twenty. Because of his austere upbringing, the solitary adolescent had found masturbation the only outlet for his sexual drives, but not without a deep sense of guilt.

And yet, as I had to admit to myself, the state of chastity was insidious and precarious; as every other relief was denied me, I fell back into the vice of my early childhood and despaired anew every time I fell. With a great deal of love, music, metaphysics and poetry, this was the subject of my book.[2]

The avowed aim of the book—to effect a marriage with his cousin might at first seem a natural and satisfactory so-lution to Gide's clearly defined and difficult problem. Theo-retically, Walter would have been saved had he married Em-manuèle. In fact, however, Walter's dilemma is far more complex: "Actually, I don't desire you," he writes. "Your body embarrasses me and carnal relations terrify me,"[3] a strange avowal, particularly since Gide at the time of *André Walter* did not as yet suspect his own homosexual tendencies. For Walter, Emmanuèle has two natures. When he thinks of her deliberately, she is noble and pure. But as the novel progresses, in his dreams her face becomes distorted. In Walter's imagination Emmanuèle is grotesque and threatening. Is she not in fact responsible for Walter's madness and death? *André Walter* is chaotic perhaps not only because, as Gide suggested, its subject was too personal but rather because the young author himself was confused about the real subject of his book.

Divided into two parts, a "white" and a "black," the story itself is quite straightforward. Before the story begins, at his mother's deathbed, André Walter, who loves his cousin Emmanuèle with a passion exalted and pure, had renounced the possibility of consummating this love. Why, young Gide never explains. He just happened to need that situation. Emmanuèle, who returns her cousin's love, then marries someone else and Walter's sacrifice is therefore complete before the novel starts. We never know anything more about Emmanuèle's feelings. She plays no part in the one-sided drama and Gide kills her off quite unnecessarily in the second part of his novel. The "white notebook" is a record of the first stages in Walter's solitary life. He concentrates upon his past, re-creating the story of his lost love in a series of flashbacks —interspersing the narrative with philosophical meditations, accounts of his struggles against forbidden sensuality, and his moments of ecstatic asceticism. Born of Walter's memories and struggles "Allain" begins to take shape. The white notebook ends in an atmosphere of peace and serenity with the firm resolution: "—now, I shall write my book."

With the "black notebook" we reach the real crux of the drama. What plunges Walter into death and madness has little to do with his love for Emmanuèle, a love nourished on books, shared prayers, spiritual exaltation and lofty emotion. Walter believes his soul—or "will to love," as he calls it—needs no other compensations than these. He is in love with the idea he has of his love. His sorry death, however, is really due to a hopeless struggle against the flesh.

Since young Gide seems not to have fully grasped the inner significance of his story, it is loaded with all manner of religious, metaphysical and ethical digressions: discussions of those problems which torment and delight adolescents and which he had debated in his diary. Consequently, Walter no more succeeds in making something out of his "Allain" than Gide did in imparting life to his ambiguous Walter. Walter's story is not Gide's and in a sense, as Gide later was to realize, his death freed the young author from certain obsessions. But his thoughts most certainly are Gide's own. Hence the extreme complexity of the form Gide chose seems quite unnecessary: a young man writes a novel about a troubled young man who is writing a novel concerning still another troubled young man. Just to embroil things further, Gide's novel purports to be the nonfictionalized notebook from which "Allain" was born, but actually it is largely Gide's own diary. The fiction of an intermediary character is weak to begin with; two of them are really more than the reader can put up with.

In any case, although he seems deliberately to have attempted to give his novel a new structure, Gide appears to have hesitated between two contradictory ideas. In the wake of the Romantics he was writing the story of a tragic spiritual evolution for which he had planned a thematic structure analogous to certain musical forms. But Walter nonetheless proclaims, "A novel is a theorem." [4] It demonstrates "not the truth of realism, necessarily contingent; but a theoretic truth, an absolute truth (at least from the human point of view), or 'ideal truth,' which reveals a pure Idea. . . . It is a demonstration." [5] In spite of the Platonic ring, Gide is still pretty close to Taine and Spinoza, both of whom he quotes. The theatrical side of his novel is weak. More interesting are his attempts at a thematic structure. Four years before the publication of *André Walter*, Edouard Dujardin's *Les Lauriers sont coupés* (translated as *We'll to the Woods No More*) had attempted the same kind of thing. Gide seemingly had not read it when, in *André Walter*, he made use of certain devices of the interior monologue. Yet Gide never again experimented with the techniques Joyce was to put to such brilliant use a few years later. In Gide's hands the monologue later developed into the récit, a purposefully organized linear narrative, doubly controlled, first by the narrator and then by Gide himself.

"When I reopen my *Notebooks of André Walter* today their inspired tone exasperates me. I was fond at that time of words that leave the imagination full license, such as 'indefinite,' 'infinite,' 'inexpressible.' " [6] Among the other pseudoromantic or decadent terms of which the young Gide was inordinately fond are: languor, ardor, fervor, weeping. The souls of his lovers tremble, leap, vibrate, sing. "Like two flames that blend, our two souls merged, but in a far distant space enharmonized with the palpitation of their wings." The writer never tires of his "enharmonizations." The air vibrates with whispers of love. Everything is suffused with febrile ecstasies. Intense emotions are intensely felt, and pain, painfully. Otherwise, there are few descriptions of the outer world. Shadows are dark, dew is fresh, fields are empty, woods sleep. At twenty André Gide was a young man for whom the outer world did not really exist. His style is rhetorical, vaguely lyrical, full of reminiscences from the Romantic poets and permeated with easily recognizable alexandrines and octosyllables. Often it turns hortatory, biblical, and piously moralizing. Occasionally a violent sensuous notation anticipates the future Gide of *Fruits of the Earth*.[7]

Yet in many ways *André Walter* is Gide's only spontaneous book in contrast to which the apparent spontaneity of *Fruits of the Earth* is in reality carefully calculated. "It was not only my first book, it was my Summa; it seemed to me that with it my life would be complete and brought to its conclusion. But yet there were moments when, leaping outside my hero as he foundered in his madness, my soul, at last free of him, of the moribund weight it had too long dragged behind it, caught glimpses of dazzling possibilities." [8]

These possibilities were suggested no doubt by Gide's new contacts with the symbolists and the fascination of Mallarmé's weekly salons. One of the subsidiary themes of *André Walter* was to become a central Gidian preoccupation: the relationship of the writer to his work, the "retroaction" of life upon a book in the making, of the book upon life in the making. In the next two years *Narcissus, Urien's Voyage,* and *The Amorous Attempt* were reflections of Gide's efforts to appropriate the moods and techniques of the "eminently esoteric and closed" coterie he had so recently come to know. Consciously symbolist in tone and atmosphere, they are charming minor works that cost Gide no very great effort and were not really anchored in his own personal experience.

But in these circles, and more especially through his contact with Mallarmé, Gide became a much more conscious artist, sensitive to the dangers of the pietistic moralizing and sentimental tone he all too easily assumed. The erotic and religious themes of *André Walter* disappeared as Gide explored more sophisticated avant-garde paths.

In those days, instead of heeding our own thought, we seemed to be more or less consciously obeying a vague directive. The movement in progress was a reaction against realism, with an accompanying backwash against the Parnassian school as well. Supported by Schopenhauer . . . I considered everything that was not *absolute*—that is to say, the whole prismatic diversity of life —*contingent*. It was very much the same with every one of my companions; and our error did not lie in trying to extract some beauty and some truth of a general order from the inextricable hodgepodge presented at that time by *realism*, but rather in deliberately turning our backs upon reality.[9]

Determinedly Gide turned his back on both inner and outer reality. But though he later extricated himself from some of the dead ends of neosymbolism, he was never to abandon the great principles he learned from Mallarmé. To Mallarmé, as Gide often said, he owed his high standards of artistic integrity, discipline, and the exigencies of style and form. Mallarmé's impersonality, the quasi-sacred respect in which he held works of art, the occult and mysterious meanings which he felt it must transmit made Gide forever suspicious of his own facile lyricism and emotional subjectivity. Mallarmé's influence was to go deep and it permeated all Gide's works. But in the early eighteen-nineties Gide first preferred the more ornate decorative arabesques of the literature in vogue.

In theory and form his *Narcissus* (1891) derives from the literary idealism advocated by Mallarmé:

An idealism which (as in fugues and sonatas) refuses natural materials, refusing also, as brutal, the precise thinking which would order them, so as to retain of all things only the suggestion. And establish among images an exact relationship, from which will arise a third aspect fusible and transparent offering itself to divination.[10]

As Barrès and Laforgue had temporarily done before him, Gide turned away from the "natural materials" of life, toward myth.[11] But not too sure perhaps of his reader's faculties of divination, he did not at first trust to mere suggestion; he gravely added footnotes explaining "the exact thought" behind the little tale he was writing.

Gide's Narcissus evokes at first the familiar Greek myth of the perfect motionless adolescent, captivated by his own unattainable reflection in a deep pool. But it promptly gives way to two others, first, to the image of an androgynous Adam, seated under the Ygdrasil tree, contemplating Eden; then more indefinitely to the image of a poet who, contemplating the unceasing flow of forms, distinguishes *the* form, the archetype, Paradise. In Gide's hands the myth becomes a Neoplatonic, semiphilosophical fable. Adam, in his Paradise, by breaking a branch of Ygdrasil, the tree of knowledge, broke the divine equilibrium; substance and idea became separated. The poet's task, Gide suggests, is to correct this evil by identifying each form with its prototype or idea, reaching the absolute beyond appearances.

The Greek Narcissus would recognize neither his Gidian counterpart, the landscape, nor the adventure:

> There is no longer either a bank or a pool; no metamorphosis and no reflected flower;—nothing but Narcissus, alone, nothing, therefore, but a dreaming Narcissus, isolated in the grayness.

Here, then, is no limpid pool, but the river of Time:

> A dismal, lethargic canal, an almost horizontal looking-glass; and nothing would distinguish this dull water from its colorless surroundings save that one feels it to be flowing.[12]

Lethargy, stagnation, grayness: mirroring perhaps young Gide's own subconscious mood and the dreamlike and baffled state of frustration in which, in part, he lived; perhaps, too, a mere reflection of the disillusioned, weary manner of the decadents.

"Narcissus dreams of Paradise" as he leans over the river where images flow rapidly by which await only Narcissus "to come into existence" and which, "under his gaze become clothed in color." He had set out in search of an image that would reveal to him the form of his own soul. What he sees is the androgynous Adam who, central and motionless, "meditates upon the perfect Forms" around him in the "garden of Ideas." Adam is a Narcissus too, and a bored Narcissus, "spectator perforce and always of a spectacle in which he has no part to play but that of an eternal watcher, he grows tired of it . . . everything is being performed for him, he knows it—but he himself . . . himself, he cannot see."[13] So breaking a branch of the tree in two, he shatters the harmony of Paradise, and terrified now, himself split in two and forever separated, Adam forever attempts to recover his lost unity. Here, in scholarly fashion, Gide inserted a doctoral lesson on the role of symbols:

Truths lie behind Form-Symbols. Every phenomenon is the Symbol of a Truth. Its only duty is to manifest that truth. Its only sin, to prefer itself.[14]

Human beings too are Form-Symbols; "we live in order to manifest," to reveal. And Gide's treatise has something to reveal, but what?—a rather obvious idea, at first reading: the poet

. . . plunges profoundly into the heart of things,—and when he, the visionary, has caught sight of the Idea, the inward and harmonious Number of its Essence, which sustains the imperfect form, he seizes it, and then, regardless of that transitory and temporal form which clothed it, he is able to restore to it an eternal form, its own veritable form, in fact, its fatal Form—paradisiac and crystalline.[15]

But when, like Adam, he prefers himself or, like Narcissus, becomes enamoured of his own reflection in the water, the ideal Form escapes him.

Is this orthodox point of view really Gide's? In his Paradise, Gide's Adam rebels, and from his willful and "scandalous" gesture all life devolves. Insidiously Gide seems already tired of his Neoplatonism.

Perfect harmony, always imaginable, appealed to me less than the disquieting deformation of that harmony according to a personality. Aesthetic will seemed to me to reside not so much in the choice of lines, tones or sonorities with a view to a harmonious work, as in the will to work in complete harmony, in order to deviate (deform) that harmony according to oneself.[16]

The conclusion of the treatise picks up the theme in a minor, ironic tone, poking gentle fun at the whole thing:

When Spring came this year, I was tormented by its loveliness, and because my desires made solitude painful, I went out into the country early in the morning.[17]

An anti-Narcissus, the narrator spends the whole day trying to escape from himself:

A secret and ecstatic joy could be felt rustling the branches. I waited. The nocturnal birds wept. Then all was quiet; it was the hush before the dawn; joy became serene and my solitude an ecstasy under the admonitions of night.[18]

Gide-Adam is ready for a definitive gesture. But what gesture? "And now what shall I manifest?"

That the work of art is a scandalous act through which the artist testifies to his discord with the world is an idea that derives from Mallarmé and which Valéry, later, was to make one of the pivots of his thought. But Gide shakes it off with a shrug of the shoulders. Fascinated by his own reflection he found it easier to contemplate his own image while waiting for the realization of his vague dreams. To wait and to dream are the two moods most familiar to his Narcissus' "soul," which surely must be "exceedingly adorable, if one is to judge by its prolonged vibrations." Gide's next works will be less pretentiously concerned with Truth, Form and Idea but just as deeply rooted in his still adolescent mood of dream and frustration.

Chapter IV

The Path of Dreams

"Madame, je vous ai trompée;
Nous n'avons pas fait ce voyage."

"Madam, I deceived you;
We never went on the journey."

~~~~~~

The Poems of André Walter, Urien's Voyage and *The Amorous Attempt* reflect Gide's temporary and frustrated attempt to escape from the world of dreams into a world of reality. Abandoning the introspective mood of his first two works, he cultivated the absorbing themes of tentative experiences that lead nowhere. The three thin volumes are melancholy and ironic in tone, closely related in mood, and suggest that, in those first years of experimentation, Gide had a genuine, though limited and never realized, poetic potential. All three works tell the story of a spiritual adventure, entangled in the story of two lovers, two sister souls, moving through seasons of love, shared walks along adventurous frontiers, in dim landscapes which the sound of the horn suddenly disturbs, where the Park is always closed and the Avenue leads nowhere. Gide, temporarily under the influence of

Laforgue and the minor symbolists, had adopted their more superficial trappings.

As Gide admitted when his *Poems of André Walter* was reprinted in 1932, he was always partial to this first and unique book of verse, an affection shared by few readers. Composed in both regular and free verse, his poems used a variety of meters culminating in a group of prose stanzas reminiscent of those with which the poet Paul Fort was then experimenting. But, although he had sloughed off the rhetorical lyricism of his first novel, Gide had merely substituted one set of conventions for another. The themes, rather than the expressions, are of interest, revealing a latent state of bafflement from which the young man was attempting to extricate himself.

Each group of stanzas relates an episode in a symbolic adventure, a departure involving two lovers. A somewhat indirect disillusioned Laforguian humor pervades the story, whose simple conversational tone and syntax and dreamlike sequences of lightly modulated evasive rhythms have a certain artificial yet suggestive charm, to which this new note of veiled humor greatly contributes:

> One night we raised our heads
> From our weighty books.
> A storm of wind rushed through the pines
> The moonlight shone like a strange dawn.
> You said to me: "It's time we set out
> We've been shut in for too long."
>
> I was bending once more over the book.
> But you, you cried ENOUGH
> Of this abstract dogmatism
> O! From so much reading,
> My head really aches [1]

The two sister souls stray in a vague kind of darkness, among shifting landscapes where they lose each other or meet in a strangely alogical yet continuous sequence of scenes. The subdued anguish in the atmosphere, the poet's detachment from the image of his own self moving from scene to scene, the obscure consciousness of resistance to an evil rhythm, all suggest the atmosphere of a bad dream. Were it not for the somewhat literary flights of fancy and the verse, Gide's poems would call to mind future surrealist or expressionist dream-techniques.

Certain images in the poems are persistent and seem really to come straight out of Gide's subconscious, intimate distress. Distress, in fact, pervades the boggy marshes in which the lovers flounder and envelops the icy peaks they try to climb. One senses a real fear in the young man, as he tells of the ill-starred adventure, a kind of apprehension that his vitality, perhaps his virility, is threatened at the very core. As they depict the two lovers, lost in mud or terrified by glacial waters, torn by the high and sharp summits of saintliness or mired in tedious monotony, unconsciously, it would seem, young Gide's poems reveal his growing, but carefully repressed anxiety concerning his love and his present life. Gide seems to have suffered acutely in his young manhood from what he was later to call "estrangement," an English term he used in its English form.

> Perhaps it's all a dream
> And we shall soon awake.[2]

The dream motif is contained and distorted by a current of subdued, realistic irony. Gide is playing with the discordant moods within himself, as had Laforgue and Barrès before him. The interplay of romantic melancholy, dream and common sense is droll rather than pathetic. Gide pokes fun simultaneously at himself and at the work he is writing.

The same skillfully manipulated ironic detachment adds an element of intellectual vigor to *Urien's Voyage* and *The*

Amorous Attempt, both otherwise rather effete exercises in which Gide deliberately organizes and exploits the dream-techniques used more spontaneously in the *Poems:* the equivalence of images or even of words merging one into the other in nonlogical sequences; the inexplicable appearance and disappearance of characters whose identity is interchangeable; the fusing together of disparate elements into a tonal unity of style—these are all characteristics of Gide's next two ventures along "the path of dreams."

Urien's Voyage recounts a spiritual odyssey involving three main symbolic stages: The Pathetic Ocean, with its tepid waters, its pernicious, "delightful" islands teeming with attractions, such as the Isle of Circe; the Sargasso Sea, whose stagnant waters and gray flat banks had haunted Gide since *Narcissus;* the deserted Glacial Sea, illumined only by the aurora borealis. The ship is the ship of the Argonauts, or perhaps Ulysses', manned by a group of indeterminate companions or "knights" with the curious mellifluous names reminiscent of Maeterlinck that were the fashion in those years, the narrator Urien, Nathanael, a name dear to Gide's heart, Alain, Mélian, Cabilor, Agloval, Paride and others, nineteen in all. To their common adventures the narrator adds his own incongruous encounters with a curious female figure called Ellis, no doubt after Dante's Elice or Helice (*Purgatory* XXV, 131; *Paradiso* XXXI, 32), the Arcadian nymph whom Artemis changed into a bear, a move countered by Zeus, who made of the bear a constellation: Ellis's misadventures and metamorphoses parody other more famous ones.

At first Urien's voyage was to have been *the* symbolist novel ("Mallarmé for poetry, Maeterlinck for the theater, and I for the novel," Gide had rather boastfully announced); instead it turned out to be a gentle caricature of symbolist attitudes dissimulated under a rich tapestry of image and rhythm.

The prelude to the *Voyage* picks up the same themes as

the *Poems;* the adolescent lassitude with regard to books, metamorphosis, and the need at last to come to grips with "real" life.

When the bitter night of thought, study and theological ecstasy was ended, my soul, which had burned alone and faithful since evening, finally sensing the coming of dawn, awakened listless and weary. . . . I moistened my brow with the dew on the windowpane and ventured out into the narrow valley of metempsychosis.[3]

The discarnate "unburdened" soul then glides toward a dream port of Oriental splendor, where, with his companions, Urien boards a fabulous dream ship, the *Orion.* "Now, having tasted in this one day the promise of all future adventures, no longer looking back at the past, we were to turn our eyes toward the future." [4]

The *Orion* puts in at seven ports of call in the Pathetic Ocean. The atmosphere of voluptuous languor increases as the companions pass sleeping sirens and a "miraginous" city fades away behind them. They venture into a dead plain and through a city where flies thickly buzz, while within its confines howling dervishes fascinate crowds. They go past heavily scented markets where women call and detain them. They visit a coral island and end in the royal city of Haiatalnefus, where they linger until a plague to which some of them fall victim drives them out.

Only twelve of the companions are left to run aground in the Sargasso Sea, where drifting down the River of Boredom, the *Orion* shrinks almost to nothing. And there, on the dreary seventh day of the voyage, Ellis suddenly appears:

On the seventh day, we met my dear Ellis who was awaiting us on the lawn, seated under an apple tree. She had been there for fourteen days, having taken the more rapid land route; she was wearing a polka dot dress and carried a cherry-red parasol; beside her was a small suitcase with toilet articles and some books; over her arm she had a plaid shawl; she was eating an escarole salad while reading *The Prolegomena to Any Future Metaphysics*. We helped her aboard the boat.[5]

Two days of gloomy stupor ensue, then Urien breaks the spell. Brutally he throws overboard all Ellis's books. Immediately the River of Boredom flows backward, the boat grows larger, and the companions sail out toward the open sea while Ellis, sick and delirious, lies at the bottom of the boat.

The *Orion* next sails into a glacial sea, in regions inhabited only by whales and birds, where one of the companions, Eric, suddenly wreaks havoc among the swans and guillemots. They next reach Eskimo country:

The Eskimos are ugly; they are small; their loves lack tenderness; they are not voluptuous and their joy is theological . . . as they have no reason to hurry, their thoughts are slow; induction is unknown to them, but from three small definitions they deduce a metaphysics; and the sequence of their thoughts, forever disconnected, descends from God to man.[6]

Here scurvy awaits them, not greatly to their surprise.

Every climate has its anguish; each land its ailments. In the tepid islands, we had seen the plague; near the marshlands, a state of languor. Now, sickness was born of the very absence of sensual pleasures.[7]

Only seven of the knights are cured, seven, a mystical number; like the seven stars in Orion. These seven knights now undertake an exhausting hike to the North Pole.

Once again Urien encounters Ellis, now really somewhat Dantesque, who appears to him alone, vehemently and piously asserting that "every road leads to God" before she "disappears into the heart of Paradise" in a burlesque apotheosis, a much easier path to heaven than the difficult one now taken by the seven weary companions. After a few more episodes the journey ends as the companions reach a small, perfectly circular lake:

If we had known before starting that it was this we had come to see, perhaps we would never have set out; and we thanked God for having hidden the goal from us and for having made it so distant that our very efforts to reach it had already given us some joy, the only sure one. . . . And kneeling down again, we sought, in the black water, the reflection of the sky I dream of.[8]

The "I" emerging from the "we" recalls Rimbaud. But the journey itself recalls many other voyages: Sinbad's, Ulysses', and Poe's Arthur Gordon Pym's, or even Flaubert and his *Salammbô* or Jules Verne. A complete homosexual symbolism can be and has been[9] extracted from what seems rather to be a fairly simple allegory to which young Gide himself handed us the key. The voyage is in fact a "pilgrim's progress."

The first temptations consist in the languors of the "chimerical isles," proposing every form of self-indulgence of which sensual voluptuousness is only one. Young Gide punishes the weaker knights biblically by loosing the plague upon them. Bodies fall to pieces, sweet scents turn into foul smells, and the tepid swimming pools become festering places of corruption. But the knights who resist gain a first victory, a sense of the power of their individual will. Thence they move into the still waters of introspection. "Psychology: psychology, science of the soul's vanity. May the soul renounce you forever." Introspection is responsible for a steadily shrinking soul and leads to stagnation. Yet, for those who refuse to succumb, something is gained:

Idleness on the gray lawns was not useless, for the vanishing landscape left our wills free; because of boredom, our souls, indeterminate in the countryside, were able to develop and become very sincere. And when we act, it will be most certainly according to our own ways.[10]

The knights have now gained self-knowledge. But of the twelve four remain asleep in the marshlands of introspection.

The others penetrate into the frigid kingdom of absolutes where the soul slowly dissolves and the taste for life fades away. Eventually the companions find the strength to go beyond even the nihilistic despair of a frigid corpse they encounter holding out a blank sheet of paper. What they seem to find at long last is the small, apathetic and perfectly circular sea of their own solitary, circumscribed and still vacant selves. The *Orion* disappears and all the companions merge at last into the solitary "I." At the outset of their journey, the knights may call to mind some of Gide's friends—Louÿs, Valéry, and others—but the final mystic figure, *seven*, seems to refer to the "I" alone. The adventure is Urien's only, and the voyage a quest for identity.

In this allegorical adventure what is the part played by the rather ludicrous Ellis? Meticulously prosaic, or ecstatic and Dantesque, she is always incongruous. To think of her in terms of Madeleine Rondeaux is easy but not convincing when one recalls Gide's veneration for his cousin. Something about Ellis—the inevitable books and notebooks, the need to moralize, the addiction to botany, the plaid shawl—makes one think of Gide himself, of his fastidious and old-maidish side, delineated by the small suitcase, the escarole salad, and the incongruous red parasol.

The concluding "Envoi," as in a ballad, writes the tale off as a mere exercise in words, a piece of literature. Urien's voyage now truly becomes "le voyage du rien," a journey for nothing, in fact no journey at all.

> Madame, I deceived you;
> We never went on this journey.
> Forgive me, Ellis, I've lied.
> This journey is only my dream,
> We never left
> The room of our thoughts,
> And we passed life by
> Without seeing it.[11]

The Amorous Attempt, or "A Treatise of Vain Desire," is more intricate in form and lighter in touch than *Urien.* Two lovers, Luke and Rachel, meet in spring, she coming from the fields, he from the forest. Their love grows as spring moves into summer, then starts to wane, until with autumn the lovers separate. "Two souls meet one day and because they were gathering flowers, both thought they were alike." [12] Their monotonous happiness derives from this initial misunderstanding, thrives on flowers, kisses and walks, and on Luke's descriptions of flowers, kisses and walks. It is, literally, monotonous.

But Luke begins to feel restless, vaguely filled with "an anguish and thirst for adventure." He now speaks of the forest and of high feats of chivalry. "On the sand, seated beside the waves, Luke looked at the sea and Rachel at the land." Then autumn comes:

. . . Tell me about Autumn, said Rachel.—Autumn, Luke answered, ah! it is the whole forest and the brown pool on its edge. The deer come down to drink and the horn sounds. . . . Did you see the palfreys? Let us go back to look at the quiet pool where the evening is falling.—Your story is absurd, said Rachel; no one says palfreys nowadays and I don't like noise. Let's go to sleep. . . . It was soon after that they parted.[13]

Luke's "vain desire" for adventure echoes Gide's own: "I have set down here a dream which had been disturbing my thoughts too much and insisted on coming into existence. A desire for happiness this Spring wore me out. . . . I longed to be happy as if there were nothing else I might be." [14] The narrator of *The Amorous Attempt* addresses a woman he loves, and their affair develops in contrast to that of the other two lovers, Luke and Rachel. When the fictional lovers part, the narrator proposes to his beloved a love fulfilled and flowering amid the winter snows. The contrapuntal move-

ment of the two situations, the fictional and the supposedly
real, conveys the sense of the subtitle "A Treatise of Vain
Desire." In his *Journal* Gide noted:

I wanted to suggest the influence of the book upon him who
is writing it, and during that very writing. For as the book emerges
from us, it changes us, modifying the course of our life. . . . So
I was sad because a dream of unattainable joy tormented me. I
narrated my dream and, separating the joy from the dream, made
the joy mine; my dream was thus disenchanted, and I full of joy.[15]

The story told, its author feels free again to act, free even
to love. "I am happy; I am alive; I have lofty thoughts. I
have finished telling you this story which we found so tedious; great tasks now summon us." [16]

Everything in the story, of course, is symbolic: the plain
and the forest, the seasons, the sound of the horn. But Gide
is not really involved in his symbols. What amused him was
to show how freely a storyteller can deal with a theme. As
the story takes shape, the narrator handles it more and more
dispassionately, from outside, boldly standing back from his
own work. Gide emphasizes this by punctuating the story
with asides, comments made by the narrator to the woman
he loves. At first the narrator is sad and decides that his
lovers will be happy: "Madam—This story is intended for
you. You know our melancholy loves went astray in the
plains, and you used to complain that I found it hard to
smile." [17] But the balance of emotion subtly changes: "This
story is for you: in it I have looked for what love brings; if
I have only found boredom, that's my fault; you have made
me forget the magic of happiness. Luke and Rachel loved
each other, so much the worse for them; for the sake of my
story's unity, they do almost nothing else." [18]

The work is slight, yet in *The Amorous Attempt* Gide is
playing with a basic theme, the ambiguity of the relations
that link an author's life and his works:

No action upon an object without a retroaction of that object upon the active subject. It is this reciprocity that I wanted to point to; in one's relation not with others but with oneself. The active subject is oneself; the object that retroacts is a literary subject one imagines.[19]

Gide's symbolic tales have sometimes been compared to the *Tales* of Novalis, whose *Heinrich von Ofterdingen* he was reading at the time. But Gide's stories are less obscure, less profound and mystical, closer to parable than myth. More detached from himself, Gide was moving away from an autobiographical type of fiction. Though he made use of some of his own moods, it was with deliberation. He isolated them, and manipulated them in order to create a specific atmosphere. He was experimenting with the new techniques of narration that were fashionable in his circle, but dealt only with fairly simple tonalities and moods.

Symbolic tales were then most popular. Gide was familiar with many forms of these: biblical parables, *The Arabian Nights*, Oscar Wilde's oral fables to which he had listened fascinated, and Laforgue's "legendary moralities." He was acquiring a certain technical deftness and sophistication. "At least," says the narrator in *Urien's Voyage*, "I have stopped screaming." To break the overmellifluous tone which plagued him in *The Amorous Attempt*, Gide had made use of an ironic commentator as intermediary between his work and the reader. The narrator's presence invites us to see in these oversubtle exercises in imagery an indirect form of parody.

Gide wrote his early works, from *André Walter* to *The Amorous Attempt*, before he was twenty-three. Understandably enough, they have a common theme: the image of the road to be followed, the goal to be reached. Ellis in *Urien's Voyage* insists upon it, and in *The Amorous Attempt*, certainly not a pious work, the voice of the woman asserts: "Our only end is God." But in counterpoint, each work tells of attempted evasions. They are all, as Gide called them, "deferred temptations," imaginary foretastes of a life where sensuous satisfaction and intellectual skepticism would be openly admitted.

They all speak of departures and quests: Walter's quest for purity, Narcissus' quest for his soul, Urien's quest for something undefined, Luke's departure for the sake of departure. The urge to break with the past becomes more imperative with each work. But the departures are only imagined. Gide's repressed inner tensions come to light rather pathetically despite the mannered arabesques of his writing. Recurrent symbols haunt the young writer's world: the face pressed against the windowpane and the many forms of sickness. Life eludes Gide's "doubles," but he himself would not long be satisfied with deferring life's temptations:

> It happened one day, as you know,
> That I tried to look at life;
>
> I turned away—oh! Madam—forgive me;
> I preferred to tell a lie
>
> Preferring still to lie
> And to wait—to wait, to wait . . .[20]

Gide was then reading primarily Novalis, Laforgue, Rimbaud, and Goethe. But the themes they may have suggested—theories of creation and execution, of form and idea, of the spiritual journey—seem of largely cerebral interest to the twenty-year-old writer, whose undeniable talent lends a certain effete and youthful charm to his ironic and melancholy fantasies.

"Our books will not really have been very truthful accounts of ourselves but rather of our wistful desires, our longing for other lives, eternally prohibited, and for all impossible acts," [21] wrote Gide with much acumen, at the time. Gide had not yet found the answer to the question he had formulated in *Narcissus*: And now what should I manifest?

Chapter V

Departures

> *Je crois que la route que je suis
> est ma route, et que je la suis com-
> me il faut.*
>
> I believe that the path I follow
> is *my* path, and that I follow it as
> I must.

Marshlands (1895)—a "satire of what?"—is an impertinent, rather contemptuous glance backward at the "path of
dreams," the "submissive gestures," and the limited horizons
of Gide's early work.

> I know that a soul implies a gesture
> From which a certain sonority radiates.[1]

In 1893 Gide had made the gesture. His first two trips to
North Africa, where he spent the winters of 1893-1894 and
1894-1895, were not merely touristic forays. His *Journal* and
writings show that by 1893 he had surreptitiously become detached from the strict tenets of religious and social orthodoxy
which his mother had so firmly instilled in him. These first

of many journeys released in Gide a streak of restlessness, a taste almost for vagabondage which was eventually to take him far afield: all over Western Europe, several times to Africa, from Algeria to the Congo, to Egypt, to Greece and to Russia. They did not entirely break the shackles of a certain asceticism in Gide's way of life, as reflected in his persistent indifference to any luxury or beauty in his surroundings and to the lack of concern for comfort, even for conveniences, which his acquaintances often mention. But in contact with the vitality of people living in primitive conditions Gide divested himself of the strait jacket of repression which had so hampered him. At last he succeeded in coming to grips with the outside world.

First his voyage, then a long convalescence in Algeria following his bout with tuberculosis, opened to him a larger vision of existence and new worlds of feeling. The new joys that beckoned him awoke a sensuous appetite which Gide indulged freely though somewhat self-consciously. Still with some posing, to be sure, he seems to have discovered that life was infused with inexhaustible delights. For the first time he appears to have tasted the irresponsible joys of a schoolboy on a long, sunny summer vacation. His new freedom, from both family and literary friends, and his convalescence seem to have introduced him to manifold phenomena of existence and accustomed him to thinking of the joys of the senses as a laudable source of pleasure rather than of sin. His long-repressed sexual desires began to seem legitimate: flesh and spirit then were perhaps not necessarily enemies? With alacrity Gide began to accustom his senses to pleasures he had hitherto reproved. The whole mood of his writing changes, illuminated, sometimes rather fatuously still, by these newly found pleasures.

With Gide, however, literature is never very far in the background. His African journeys could hardly have been better timed. The brilliant coterie of talented young men—

Valéry and Claudel among them—who had gravitated around Mallarmé were showing signs of restlessness. Although still respected, sometimes adulated, Mallarmé was not their only master. Symbolism was on the wane and its succession was open. The ephemeral school of "naturism" had appeared with its "back to nature" slogan. Whitman, Dostoevsky and Nietzsche were the new constellations in the French literary sky. Everything challenged an ambitious young writer—and Gide was ambitious—to try himself in new directions. Gide moved from his symbolic tales to the satirical *Marshlands* and to the direct lyricism of *Fruits of the Earth* with apparent ease.

"I had demanded from my mind such a denial of the reality of appearances," Gide wrote of his symbolist stage, "that the variegated pattern and diversity of the outer world and the veil of the Maya had lost all importance for me, which is extremely dangerous for an artist." [2] The veil of the Maya (the shimmering beauty of appearances) was greatly to preoccupy him in the next phase of his work. For a while he put aside problems of being and appearance, image, symbol and idea. With many of his contemporaries he turned to the living world he had previously scorned.

His emancipation favored the release of latent creative forces. Almost all Gide's later work took shape in his mid-twenties, between 1893 and 1896. Writing to his friend Marcel Drouin, during the winter of 1894-95, Gide outlined his program:

Aside from work add my correspondence with my mother, and you will see what is left for the terribly tough translation of Novalis, for *Marshlands* which isn't getting done, and for all the rest I'm trying to do at the same time: *Philoctetes*, which I finished *preparing* in Engadine, and of which some passages are written; *Proserpine* the novel I told you about in La Roque . . . the volume "of pure lyricism" on which I am working more particularly. . . .[3]

He referred here to *Fruits of the Earth,* and already he had in mind *The Immoralist, Strait Is the Gate,* and *The Pastoral Symphony,* and mentioned *Bathsheba, Theseus,* and *Saul* in *Fruits of the Earth.*

Returning briefly to Paris between his first two trips, Gide looked with dismay and detachment at the narrowness of the horizons that had previously encircled him:

I brought back with me, on returning to France, the secret of a man resurrected, and suffered at first the same kind of abominable anguish that Lazarus must have felt after he rose from the grave. Nothing that had occupied me earlier seemed important any more. How had I been able to breathe in the stifling atmosphere of the salons and coteries, where all their vain agitation . . . stirred up a dusty smell of death. This state of "estrangement" (which I suffered from particularly when I was with my own family) might very possibly have led me to suicide, were it not for the relief I found in describing it ironically in *Marshlands.*[4]

"Estrangement" in the literary salons, but even more at home. . . . Gide-Lazarus was never again to feel in harmony with that milieu outside which his cousin Madeleine Rondeaux was never to venture. The curtain had now gone up on the intimate conflict which *Et nunc manet in te (Madeleine)* eventually disclosed, hence the gravity of the crisis and the temptation of suicide. *Marshlands* reduces these feelings to a kind of absurdity.

What Gide attacked in *Marshlands* was the suffocating atmosphere of the literary coterie, the disintegration of "days into little elusive hours," [5] the sense of stagnation and his own feelings of bewilderment.

I had new things to say, yet it was impossible now to speak to them [his former friends]. I wished I could persuade them and give them my message, but none of them stopped to listen. They went on living; they kept on going, and the things that satisfied them seemed to me so paltry that I could have cried out in despair at not having been able to persuade them.[6]

Holding his new message in reserve for *Fruits of the Earth,* Gide made an all-out attack on literary life in Paris through the thinly disguised figure of a not very Vergilian Tityrus in *Marshlands.*

At the center of his tale is an unnamed author involved in the writing of a book, *Paludes (Marshlands),* whose message he tries vainly to communicate in an ever-rising hubbub of inane comment and argument. Gide tells us that three factors merged to give him the idea for his story: his own mood, one of Goya's sketches, and a few lines in Vergil's first eclogue. Goya's sketch portrayed a harassed intellectual, head in hands, surrounded by a tormenting circle of hostile people. Vergil's Tityrus, in words familiar to all schoolboys who studied Latin, claimed that, although he possessed only a small stretch of marsh, it was his and he was content with it. Gide's writer is quite clearly in the position of Goya's intellectual; as for Tityrus, he symbolizes everything that irritated Gide in Paris. In addition, *Marshlands* is a semifacetious, semibitter parody and satire of Gide's own previous literary endeavors. Gide's hero, or rather antihero, is a narrator-writer who keeps an agenda, writes notes with his novel in view, and writes a novel concerning a hero who keeps an agenda—the height of complexity. He works with Gide's former landscape of mud, moors, swamp and stagnant waters, but now it characterizes not Gide himself but the "woeful soul" of the writer's hero, Tityrus. Even the paradisiac and crystalline forms of which the *Narcissus* speaks are parodied in a fable about salt mines, peopled with slaves. Gide later remarked:

I had the greatest difficulty in getting a new foothold on reality and in relinquishing the theories of that school (I mean the

one formed by Mallarmé's followers) which tended to present reality as an accidental contingency and wanted the work of art to
escape from its grip.[7]

"Urien's Voyage made it possible for me to laugh in *Marshlands,"* he wrote. Parodying himself, Gide attacks by indirection, pushing the literary processes of the symbolists to their
most absurd consequences: in his marshes Tityrus angles for
nothing, swallows earthworms with relish; the would-be author loads his text with rare words and elaborate epithets,
he takes trips to the botanical gardens—all to give a concrete
content to a most dismal inner landscape. Having finished
Marshlands, Gide's author begins *Polders.* Pretty openly Gide
is accusing his symbolist friends of going around in circles
in their own little worlds. In fact, everything in *Marshlands*
goes in circles: events, characters, objects. Everything is
"small"; the "little pondweeds" in the Aquarium; the "little Aquarium"; the "little ventilator" in the "little salon" of
Angela, the writer's patient friend, who runs a small literary
salon; the "little journey" he and Angela undertake: "Toward evening I felt a little tired and, after dinner I went over
to sleep at Angela's. . . . She was alone. As I entered she
was playing a Mozart sonatina with precision on a newly
tuned piano. . . . She had lit all the candles in candlesticks
and put on a dress with a small check pattern." [8]

Marshlands is the story of a writer disgusted with the petty
monotony of his life who, to express his disgust, hits upon
the symbol of Tityrus in his marsh. During a short, incomplete week running from Tuesday evening to Sunday evening
we see the man struggling with his projected book and, because of it, waging a hopeless antistagnation campaign with
everyone around him. The fight culminates at Angela's dinner party where the narrator finds himself in the position of
Goya's figure. All eyes are upon him, jarring voices pick up
the word "Marshlands," throwing it at him like a sort of ac-

cusation: *"Marshlands,* what is *Marshlands?"* "You should put that into *Marshlands."*

Gide gives his story a rapid circular movement, introducing an amazingly mechanical device of repetition, a framework from which he draws his more obvious comical effects:

Tuesday: At six o'clock in came my great friend Hubert; he was on his way from riding school.

He said: "I say! Are you working?"

I replied: "I am writing *Marshlands."*

Thursday: At six o'clock in came my great friend Hubert; he was on his way back from a business committee meeting . . .

. . . At this moment someone came up the stairs; it was Martin. He said: "I say! Are you working?"

At this moment someone came up the stairs; it was Alexander, the philosopher. He said: "I say! Are you working?"

Sunday: At six o'clock in came my great friend Gaspard. He was on his way from fencing school. He said: "I say! Are you working?"

I replied: "I am writing *Polders."* [9]

The same small mechanical patterns with the same slight variations characterize the narrator's life as he solemnly records it in his agenda:

In my agenda there are two parts: on one page I write what I am going to do, and on the opposite page I write every evening what I have done. Then I compare. I subtract and what I have not done, or the deficit, becomes what I ought to have done. [10]

This, he notes, introduces the "unexpected" into his life. Thus Wednesday's page reads:

Try to get up at six o'clock. . . .

Write to Gustave and Leo.

Feel astonished at not having received a letter from Jules. Call on Gontran.[11]

And here comes the announced play of the unexpected:

Wednesday: I opened my agenda to the coming Saturday, and on the page for that day I read: "Try to get up at six"—I crossed it out.

Friday: On the agenda, as soon as I got up, I read "Try to get up at six." It was eight o'clock; I took up my pen; I crossed it out.[12]

Since even in a short week the unexpected is monotonously repeated, the hero revolts against the insignificant round of habits that circumscribes his life, a small revolt but an anguished one. His protest rises like a monotonous leitmotif throughout the tale, becoming increasingly violent:

Our lives, Angela, I assure you, are a good deal duller and more mediocre [than Tityrus'].

Really, we must try to put a little variety into our lives.

We ought to try to stir up our lives a little.

Angela . . . we ought to try to put a little variety into our lives.[13]

When the narrator describes the lives of his friends, Richard and Hubert, summarizing them in a few lines, he reduces them to a Tityrus-like marsh: Hubert's exciting panther hunt becomes an anecdotal demonstration of Hubert's inane activity. The touching story of the nightwork secretly undertaken by Richard and his wife is an anecdotal form of Richard's inane virtue. The narrator's own account of his duck-hunting expedition and his little journey with Angela are only other examples of their symbolically aquariumlike existence. By repeating his parody in this manner on various levels and through diverse techniques Gide produced in *Marshlands* a kind of literary version of the "mobile," an infinitely

amusing abstract and airy structure, which showed considerable technical mastery and a new flexibility.

Marshlands, the book the hero is writing, is as strange an
object as the cuttlefish egg in *The Amorous Attempt*, and
far more elusive as it develops and begins to impose itself.
To the questions: What is *Marshlands?* and Who is Tityrus?
the narrator at first gives a simple answer. *Marshlands? . . .*
a book. Or again, "It is primarily the story of those who are
not able to travel." Or, "It is the story of a bachelor who
lives in a tower, entirely surrounded by marshes." At first
Tityrus is mostly the narrator's friend Richard, happy in his
mediocrity. The subject of *Marshlands?* "What I wanted to
express is *the* emotion my life has given me: the boredom,
the emptiness, the monotony." But once the book is on its
way it retroacts and something unforeseen occurs. Tityrus
comes alive and begins to change. Like his creator, he starts
to think about his marsh. "I am Tityrus!" the writer ex-
claims, forgetting that Tityrus is supposed to be odious, and
he writes: "Tityrus smiles." From that point on, fascinated
by his symbol, the narrator sees everything in its light; Tityrus shows up all the marshlike sides of life. Tityrus gathers
strength and substance: now he is Hubert, Angela, everyone.
He becomes an exemplary figure, man, in one of his fundamental attitudes toward life. He is man "recubans," lying
down. From symbol he has become myth—a burlesque myth
around which everything revolves.

The narrator's relation with his hero also changes. As soon
as Tityrus becomes more complex than a mere symbol he
escapes from his creator. At Angela's dinner party all speak
of Tityrus in various ways: psychological, ethical, metaphysical. He raises all the problems of man's fate. And suddenly,
harassed and perspiring, the narrator has a kind of illumina-
tion, an *idea*, which turns on the word "retrospection." Up
to now, as his agenda showed, he has lived backwards. Each
day his agenda marked what he did not do and this becomes

his program of action for the next day. He is always in deficit with regard to the past. Hence his boredom and his unchanging marshland. In contrast, now, he hits upon the idea of the "free act," the spontaneous act, the act not written down in advance, the act "to come." In the heat of the ensuing discussion the obsessive theme of stagnation is pushed into the background. The arguments revolve around the concept of the free act. Is it possible? Is it ethical? Here Tityrus stalls and the narrator's book halts with him. But, breaking the round of routine, the theme of travel asserts itself: the hero and Angela go on their unsuccessful little journey, as Hubert and Roland leave for North Africa. At least the narrator has transmitted his feelings for a short while, if only to Angela. As for the rest, as he has said throughout the book, "I don't mind it myself, because I am writing *Marshlands*." [14] But he comes back and as he sits down to write *Polders* one of his "great friends" drops in and the merry-go-round begins again.

Complex, full of fun and humor, economical in its devices, Gide's *Marshlands* is a little masterpiece; it stirs up a world of ideas. It is a kind of manifesto too, and an act of independence which was not greatly appreciated at the time. Gide's little satire—or sotie, as he called it, using a medieval term—has its serious side. It describes the genesis of a work of art as Gide conceived it at the time. Tityrus is to the fictional author of *Marshlands* what Urien had been to Gide. Both are symbols of a mood. Tityrus and all his activities offer a consistent image of stagnation. But a mood is a shifting thing. As Gide's writer struggles along with his narrative, notes, agenda, discussions, he becomes detached from his initial symbol. Now he uses it as one might use a pair of glasses to examine a heterogeneous number of unrelated aspects of his everyday existence. And so the mood, which had produced the image, now moves from image to idea as the writer begins to interpret in its light both the inner and outer implications with which he is grappling. Tityrus now begins to grow, to embody all that stagnates; now it is about Tityrus, his attitude in life and his significance that everyone argues. The image of stagnation has moved away from its limited, subjective origin. The fictional *Marshlands* will now express the writer's temporary point of view, but with a detachment which allows him to raise any number of general questions concerning human living. But, since Tityrus is a character, living in his own world, however simplified, the interpretations he elicits will forever be a matter for argument. Tityrus raises questions; Gide does not resolve them.

By a dynamic dialectical process the character Gide imagined can retroact upon the writer and produce within the work complementary new ideas which in the beginning it did not contain. The idea of stagnation in itself excludes the idea of adventure. But in *Marshlands* both the desire for adventure and its need arise from the anguish with which the narrator envisages stagnation. The two contradictory ideas are there, though indirectly, pulling at his little tale, inciting the restlessness which is the source of his writing.

Gide's *Marshlands* contains a theory of creativity. Instead of being a "denial of the reality of appearances," the work of art is the temporary unification and interpretation of appearances, organized through an interplay of image and idea. As it had been for poets since Baudelaire, the image is the core of this work. It is still pre-eminently literary in its origin, emanating from the classics Gide knew well, and so lends itself to a certain intellectualization, suggesting, rather than other images, an idea. The idea suggests certain limits within which to work and, in turn, becomes a factor of expansion. A work of art in this sense is a proposition, as Gide said, which by a kind of autogeneration suggests its antithesis. The narrator in *Marshlands* may sit down again to write *Polders*. Gide, for his part, has finished with his marshlands. Menalcas, the man of free acts and adventure, follows Tityrus. *Fruits of the Earth* is in the offing.

The Gidian dialogue is now in operation as a creative process. Each of Gide's literary works answers the preceding one, illuminating what the other left in shadow. In the sense that each is "critical," as Gide said, and voluntarily organized to disclose in depth one chosen aspect of life, it is also, by indirection, ironical. Momentarily proportions are distorted, life is stylized, until finally the forces waiting in the dark rise once more to the surface and Gide, having carried us along in his adventure, returns us to a reality newly grasped. Without returning to the realism he detested, Gide had moved away from the dead end of symbolism. Finally, *Marshlands* formulates the two closely related ideas—the free act and the open future—which apply to all Gide's future novels.

Chapter VI

The Veil of the Maya

*Il est un temps de rire—et il est
un temps d'avoir ri.*

There is a time for laughter—and
a time for having done with laughter.

~~~~~~

"But, Nathanael," says the narrator in *Fruits of the Earth*
to his silent adolescent interlocutor, "here I will speak to you
only of things, not of an

INVISIBLE REALITY." [1]

Things as such are not really present in the book. Gide suggests their brilliance and profusion, gathering them in groups,
in the plural: gardens, doors, springs, fruits, ships, caravans.
Like an impetuous Bacchus he now invades the world around
him, mainly, in order to plunder it. In *Fruits of the Earth*
all things seem to exist only so that he can take possession
of them. He is alone, at the very center of the earth, with
his thirsts, his anticipations, his sleeps and awakenings, and
the whole range of his sensuous desires. All the rest exists

only for his immediate enjoyment: sand for the joy of sinking his bare feet in it, water to plunge into, fruit subtly to alleviate his thirst, faces gently to be caressed, and springs to drink from.

In *Fruits of the Earth* there is nothing analogous to Proust's long contemplative ecstasy before such natural splendors as a hawthorn hedge or a row of apple trees in bloom. The Proustian effort to reconstruct the individuality of things through thoroughly meticulous descriptions is foreign to Gide. Nor does Gide see any frightening antihuman forces secretly at work in the cosmos. In *Fruits of the Earth*, things pass in swift and dazzling succession, disappearing to make room for others. There will always be other fruits, other gardens, other cities. Certainly there is no reticence in the lyricism with which the young man asserts his presence in the natural world: "I love . . ." "I saw . . ." "I know . . ." "I found . . ." Life's richly fluid diversity is drunk like a heady wine. Gide's exultation is different from the more cautious feeling of writers like Saint-Exupéry, for example, who really came to grips with natural forces. Nature is present only passively, to be enjoyed. But at least it is no longer merely the indirect supplier of symbolic images.

For the first time Gide speaks in his own name, creating his own new world rather than describing our common earth. If the earth becomes a Garden of Eden without prohibitions, where all is joy, it is largely because Gide is far less concerned with real "fruits of the earth" than with the "fruits *which nourished us* on the earth," [2] spiritual fruits, derived from his new appetite for life, his mood of "availability." The world responds spontaneously ". . . for the country comes into existence only as our approach gives it form and the landscape about us gradually falls into shape as we advance." Gide's fervor does not come from a sense of fusion with nature. It is his hymn to a happiness surging because of the release of inner forces previously dormant within him. What interests

Gide is not really the veil of the Maya, but rather the freedom which makes all desirable things accessible in a sunlit, innocent world. Africa provides the setting for his joy.

The themes developed have two origins: the great voluptuous exaltation which accompanied the first erotic experiences Gide described in *If it die . . .* and his contemplative serenity as a well-cared for convalescent, surrounded only by what was beneficial. The dominant sensations are those of the convalescent: thirst and the quenching of thirst, the feel of sun or of water on the skin, light and a sense of the beauty of all things. But the note of immediate and personal urgency is related to the theme of eroticism. Menalcas appears and also Amyntas, about whom Gide was later to write a book, introducing the loves celebrated in Vergil's *Eclogues.*

> Life for us had a
> SAVAGE AND SUDDEN FLAVOR.[3]

The only slightly savage element in *Fruits of the Earth* is the tempo of the writing, due less to the violence of the desires than to the haste with which they are satisfied; life's sudden flavor disappears with satiety. Gide's exaltation seems real enough, but his contact with the world is purely emotional and he still draws heavily on literature. The moon is

> Soft, soft, soft—as for the welcoming of Helen in the Second Faust.[4]

Lynceus ascends to his watch-tower, while Menalcas and his friends converse in a Boccaccio-like setting. Bathsheba, Saul, Theseus and the Shulamite play their parts. Goethe and Nietzsche hover in the background. Gide's fruits of the earth are, in the main, fruits of literature. Far from having heeded his own advice to "throw away all books," Gide, like Urien's Ellis, travels with a suitcase full of them. The *Arabian Nights* of his childhood, the Song of Songs, and other Oriental tales and poems are the springs from which he drinks. Opening the eighth door of a solid Norman farmhouse, he finds, rather surprisingly, not just a carriage house but

Chariots! We can fly where we will; sledges, frozen lands, I harness my desires to you.

Nathanael, we will go out toward things: we will reach every one in turn. I have gold in my holsters; and in my coffers are furs that would almost make one love the cold.[5]

The passage of the doors is of course an adaptation whose origin Gide elsewhere inadvertently revealed:

Almost all Persian literature seems to me like that golden palace in the tale of one of the three Saalouks, in which forty doors open; the first on an orchard full of fruit, the second on a garden of flowers, the third on an aviary, the fourth on heaped up jewels . . .[6]

Yet, literary though they often are, Gide's vivid, fleeting impressions and lyrical enumerations have a freshness and sensuous charm of their own.

There are springs that gush forth from rocks;
There are some that we can see welling up;
There are some so blue that they look deeper than they are.[7]

As these accumulate they point to an underlying theme, reminiscent of the Psalms of David:

More springs gush from the earth than we have thirsts to drink them.[8]

From sensuous delight we move surreptitiously to the theme of limits, the limits of a man's desire, an ethical theme. Even the exquisite oasis of Blida, so lovingly recalled, serves to point an allegory of rebirth. "Blida! Blida! flower of the Sahel! little rose!" is fragrant with the scent of its orange and tangerine trees:

From the tallest of their topmost branches, the eucalyptus trees, freed again, shed their old bark; it hung, a worn-out covering, like a garment made useless by the sun, like my old ethics which were valid only for winter.[9]

For Gide, the fascination with the veil of the Maya coincides with the rejuvenation of his being, an oasis in his own life, a spiritual rebirth from which he drew a gospel no sooner formulated than abandoned.

Surprisingly, Gide once described his title—"Les Nourritures terrestres," literally "Foods of the Earth"—as brutal, an adjective understandable only within the frame of his puritanical faith or the ethereal atmosphere of his fin de siècle coterie. For what then should we say of Baudelaire's *Flowers of Evil* or Rimbaud's *Season in Hell?* At this stage Gide had many points of contact with Rimbaud: the break with the past, adventure and return; the hungers and thirsts; the refusals; the nuptials with the earth; the spiritual crisis; the journey; metamorphosis and the story of a past now left behind. Gide could have said, as had Rimbaud: "Mine, this one among my follies!" But real as it and its expression are, Gide's African adventure is manipulated, exploited, and all possible literary modulations are drawn from it. Rimbaud would probably have loathed Gide's careful blending of the spontaneous and the studied, of the unrestrained and the controlled, as well as the lyrics abundantly strewn throughout the book, deliberately composed to give an impression of free improvisation.

The book is fundamentally a spiritual autobiography organized in a loose eight-chapter cycle. A prelude strikes the opening chords, proposing the keynote words: joy, love and fervor, with their complements wisdom and merit. Rejecting the past in favor of the magical present, Gide briefly recalls the stages he has left behind: the dismal period of waiting, symbolized by the accompanying image of the window.

How long, O waiting, will you last?

Ah! let a great bay of light be opened at last!

Then comes the decisive event:

I fell ill; I traveled; I met Menalcas and my marvelous convalescence was a palingenesis.[10]

This theme of a new birth, of a spiritual metamorphosis is accompanied by an outburst of lyricism, a song of expectations fulfilled, an ambiguous song, a "round" "to worship what I have burned." [11] A Sartrean hero before Sartre, with his present actions Gide gives his past a new meaning. Once the expectations have been fulfilled, the books burned, and the past rejected, they become symbols of freedom and are glorious. The new gospel immediately follows.

The smallest amount of life is stronger than death. . . . I have no use for knowledge that has not been preceded by a sensation.[12]

The first phase in the young man's metamorphosis is a veritable invasion of his being by outer things. To the volubility of books succeeds the volubility of phenomena. Unlike Sartre's hero in *Nausea*, however, the young adventurer now goes through a period of Rimbaldian intoxication:

From that day onward, every instant of my life acquired for me the fresh flavor of an absolutely ineffable gift, so that I lived in an almost perpetual state of passionate stupefaction. I achieved intoxication very quickly and liked to go about in a kind of daze.[12]

The second phase is an inner preparation for the satisfaction of all desires, the cultivation of an inner freedom or availability, through which the young man meets life, at each moment, without any kind of preoccupation. Desires become imperious:

Foods!
I expect you, foods!
My hunger will stay at no halfway house . . .[13]

Inner restraints yield: "Nathanael, I no longer believe in sin."
Time becomes a series of disconnected instants, for an "I"
living a succession of separate moments of delight.

I became accustomed to *separating* each moment of my life to
seize the total sum of its joy, isolated . . . so that I could no
longer recognize myself even in the most recent of memories.[14]

Delivered from time, the "I" reaches a quasi-divine state
of beatitude and a sense of the strangeness of the most simple things.

I remember days when simply to repeat that two and two still
made four was enough to fill me with positive beatitude—and the
mere sight of *my* fist on the table . . .[15]

Then comes the intense and fleeting voluptuousness of desire
realized that is LIGHT. It brings a change of mood and orientation and the prelude of a contrapuntal theme, the desire
for peace and the stability of a shore.

Will the quiet haven come, after all these discouraging drift-
ings, these wanderings to and fro? When my soul, at rest at last
on a solid pier beside a flashing lighthouse, will look out at the
sea? [16]

Throughout the first three books Gide eloquently addresses
an urgent set of precepts to Nathanael, the imaginary adolescent, drinking in his words. Nathanael must benefit from
the experience of his older friend who transmits in evangelical formulae the precepts he himself received from Menalcas
and to which he owes his freedom: freedom, availability, re-
ceptivity; the break with the closed family circle; fervor in a
life open to adventure, free from the fear of consequences
and the restraints of formal ethics; inner vitality and confidence in the goodness of life.

And so, Nathanael, you will be like a man who follows as his
guide the light he holds in his own hand. . . . Let the *importance* be in your look, not in the thing you look at.[17]

This ethic is an individual way of life, not a set of rules. God, being everywhere, offers to man's love all the manifold aspects of life. His will is that all the possibilities in every being be realized. The lesser conventions and formal prohibitions of men must be broken to achieve a more spacious form of happiness.

Gide's gospel obviously applied to his own new experience. When he insists on the infinite variety of forms created by his Nature-God with no obligation other than to live in harmony with their needs, in which there are no norms nor therefore exceptions, and which was to be seen in the larger perspectives of a universal order, natural and divine, his homosexuality is freed from the stigma of sin.

In the fourth book of *Fruits of the Earth*, however, the carefree amorality and lyrical affirmations make way for a more sober critical appraisal. Menalcas, the instigator of the whole adventure, appears. On a terrace in Florence Menalcas tells his friends the story of his life. He picks up all the lyric themes and ethical precepts of the first books: the cultivation of availability, expectation and desire; the ethic of instantaneity and the refusal of continuity. The voices of his companions rise around him, each in turn offering a song in comment: "The Round of the Pomegranate"; "The Round of Fruit," which is a round of unquenched thirst; "The Ballad of Famous Lovers," those who, like Theseus, were unfaithful; "The Song of Real Property."

The scene as a whole is alluring, yet Menalcas himself appears increasingly fatuous, sterile and egoistical. Irony takes the place of enthusiasm and a countertheme is orchestrated:

"All forms of voluptuousness are good," said
Eliphas, "and need to be tasted."

"But not all by all," said Tibullus; "one must choose." [18]

The stage is set for the song of weariness sung by Hylas and for the theme of the dispossessed self which Gide was to use in a later play, *Saul:*

Desires! Beautiful desires, I will bring you the crushed grapes; I will fill anew your huge cups; but let me in again to my own house—so that when you fall into the sleep of drunkenness I may once more crown myself with purple and ivy.[19]

Finally, disenchantment is the keynote in Cleodalisa's song: "Between desire and boredom we hesitate uneasily." Menalcas has lost his hold: ". . . at daybreak I went on my way." The cycle closes on the theme of a return, sung in a minor key.

The next three parts are set in Gide's homeland of Normandy:

> Rainy land of Normandy
> domesticated countryside . . .

where a civilizing order reigns and all is carefully husbanded. Fervor gives way to thought:

All the joys of our senses have proved as imperfect as falsehoods.

There is a time for laughter—and a time for having done with laughter.
There is a time for laughter, yes—and then for the memory of laughter.[20]

To the dangers of self-indulgence and disintegration Gide now opposes the Christian virtues of self-denial and austerity:

Souls never stripped so bare as to leave enough room for love —love, expectation, and hope, our only real possessions.[21]

The adventure is at an end, the image of Menalcas exorcised as Lynceus, the watchman in the tower, borrowed by Gide from Goethe, takes his place. As in the case of all Gide's previous works, a new dawn is about to break, bringing its new gospel:

Until the end of night I clung to the hope of a new light. I cannot see yet, but I hope; I know in what direction to look for the dawn about to break. . . . I see a generation going down. I see a vast generation coming up, coming up fully armed, fully armed with joy toward life.[22]

The eighth book is little more than a travelogue, loosely connected to the whole, closer perhaps to *Amyntas* than to *Fruits of the Earth*. The "Return to Africa" is the false return of a now-married Gide. If the desert is mentioned, it hardly counterbalances Gide's nostalgic desire for oases. The spiritual adventure ends in a kind of uncertainty. The theme of serenity appears, but only sporadically:

I believe that the path I follow is *my* path, and that I follow it as I must. I have acquired a vast confidence which would be called faith if it had subscribed to any vows.[23]

Fruits of the Earth ends on a far more sober note than it begins. God is no longer mentioned. Regret seems to prevail, the regret for a lost youth: "Yes, it is true—my youth was spent in darkness"; the regret for a still more recent, lost happiness: "The time has gone hopelessly by." Hence the silent presence of Nathanael, the adolescent Gide never was, the adolescent who could enjoy what Gide was not fully able to achieve.

Gide's adventure seems more literary than real. He had not burned his books; he had not renounced the family or the "closed home." His marriage in October, 1895, to his cousin had consecrated, rather, his fidelity. He was not able, perhaps, nor willing to pay the price for a real life of irresponsibility, availability and freedom. *Fruits of the Earth* raises the problem of his sincerity. Gide's incapacity ever to choose between the solicitations of adventure and the disciplines of an orderly life allowed him only literary solutions. In October, 1899, he wrote the first act of an unfinished comic opera entitled *The Return*. But *Marshlands* is the tale of someone who cannot travel and *Fruits of the Earth* is less the story of one who has traveled than of one who stopped along the way, like another of Gide's future heroes, Philoctetes. *Fruits of the Earth* is not really, as Gide sometimes called it, a poem. It is closer in some ways to his récits, despite its form. Gide isolated certain of his own impulses, dominant for a time in his life, and pushing them to their limits drew from them a kind of parable centering around the figure of Menalcas, behind whom, perhaps, lurks Oscar Wilde.

Nothing more typically Gidian, therefore, than the end of the book: "And now, Nathanael, throw away my book . . . say to yourself that it is only one of a thousand postures in life." There is nothing dogmatic or definitive about the creed proposed. A posture need not be prolonged, and Gide, always suspicious of orthodoxy, was to take interest only in successive postures. Hence the "Protean" Gide so often alluded to. In *Fruits of the Earth* it pleased Gide temporarily to take the alluring form of an earthly demigod, but he is already at work preparing other transformations. He has thrown aside the temptation to be a Menalcas. But around Menalcas many other voices arose. To which might Gide next choose to lend his attention? Gide, now, was "peopled."

"We must carry our ideas to the very end," Gide's hero had said in *Marshlands*, a Goethean principle; to the very end, Gide would say, but not in life: in literature. Art allows what life, quite reasonably, according to Gide, cannot allow. Each of the diverse voices he heard in himself, carried to the end, prepares the Gidian récit. Their coexistence prepares the Gidian drama and defines the very strangeness of Gide's own curious personality.

Menalcas and Tityrus are the first really "Gidian" characters to appear. First they incarnate some one mood or tendency, then they become instigators, or even perverters as they attempt to impose their point of view to the exclusion of others just as legitimate and indispensable. In the meantime

Gide reserves his own critical appraisal by showing the limitations of his Tityrus and Menalcas as their lives develop and evolve in time.

In *Fruits of the Earth* the initial suggestion is far more eloquent than its subsequent deflation. It is not surprising, therefore, that the post-World War I generation of young men and women who were the first belated and enthusiastic discoverers of Gide's book saw in it only the invitation to the enjoyment of life so persuasively addressed to Nathanael. They were right, in spite of Gide himself, who in his 1927 preface spoke of *Fruits of the Earth* as a hymn to renunciation. The fervent and elaborate cadences of the book; the exotic charm of an African vocabulary: mosques, caravans; the beauty of strange landscapes and names: Blida, Athman, Oumach, Droh, Zaghouan, and, not the least, Nathanael—all were calculated to cast a spell over the reader.

The supercivilized European adolescent who avidly read Gide felt called upon to discard conventions and launch confidently into adventures unlimited. Gide inspired him to try out and exhaust all his potentials in contact with an inexhaustible reality. Life could be a royal game, played in proud freedom, an adventure, whose worth echoed the worth of the adventurer. Moral dynamism, Gide taught him, is the source of creativity, releasing the possibilities latent in each individual who continuously creates himself; character is an auto-creation.

"That manual of escape, of liberation," Gide called his book in the 1927 preface, clearly meaning by escape something very different from what is usually meant by "a literature of escape." And *Fruits of the Earth* did prove to be a manual of energy for the generation of 1920. Its hatred of moral complacency and ingrained suspicion of orthodoxy, routine and conformity tallied almost exactly with the reaction of that generation to the postwar world. They were not particularly sensitive to the aestheticism which Gide had attacked in the rather effete Menalcas. Gide's own sincerity, thirty years before they discovered him, had been primarily aesthetic. With *Marshlands* and *Fruits of the Earth* he had started to draw from more personal sources than in his earlier books. His writing was beginning to serve him as a laboratory where he could explore certain impulses which, in his life, he still had to repress. Among those impulses, the most pressing was his homosexuality.

Gide's Tityrus in *Marshlands* had no ethics, no past, and no future. Menalcas, on the other hand, had a positive, though questionable, ethic and a past. In *Fruits of the Earth* Gide shows that he was on the way to establishing dynamic aesthetic principles which might sanction his break with symbolism. Starting from his own experience he was now able to invent characters who take postures and accept commitments which Gide himself questions. Just as Gide's life took on its ambiguous and definitive form with his marriage, his literary world too emerged in its originality. "And so, Nathanael, you must be like him who follows as his guide the light he carries in his own hand." The frail image of Nathanael, lighting his own path in a world without transcendental laws, is closely linked to a whole "Promethean" trend in twentieth-century literature. God is dead and there are no "essences." Existence is all, and it is freedom. Nathanael, far more surely than Gide himself, to be sure, stands free on this earth. But in *Fruits of the Earth* the divorce between man and the cosmos—on which existential themes are based—does not exist. Nathanael is at home in a glorious world. But his freedom raises a number of ethical problems which Gide was to elaborate in his later work.

The very substance of Gide's work, therefore, originated in his African adventure and in the ambiguity of a life which his marriage to his cousin emphasized without resolving. He was perpetually confronted with the enigma of his own life and, in consequence, thought of all human life as plunged in mystery. The veil of the Maya had diverted him for only a short instant. The fundamental dynamic ideas of the "free," or gratuitous, act of palingenesis and metamorphosis came out of the new freedom he had experienced.

Marshlands and *Fruits of the Earth,* unnoticed though they were by Gide's contemporaries, marked Gide's new orientation and independence. He broke with the tempting semi-poetic forms of the neosymbolists, yet maintained the intimately individual atmosphere which set him apart among his contemporaries.

The maturity Gide had attained was reflected in the controversy which opposed him to Barrès. In his article entitled "Concerning *The Uprooted*" (1897), to Barrès's thesis that the intellectual uprooting of an individual is dangerous, Gide, with caustic courtesy, gave a firm, well-documented answer in which his fondness for botany and his practical experience as a landowner gave him considerable advantage: the fact that in order to take root and flourish seedlings have to be transplanted not once, but several times, supported his arguments in favor of freedom in intellectual debate and the interchange of ideas. Almost in spite of himself, he had set out on a long career as a liberal exponent of common sense and freedom for all. He had escaped from the esoterism which threatened him: "Saul, in the desert, looking for your asses —you shall not find your asses—but rather the kingdom for which you were not looking." He would now follow *his* path.

Puritanical as he still was, having surreptitiously tasted of his freedom, at first Gide was confronted primarily with the problem of impunity and, more essentially, with the question of the limits of individual freedom.[24] This is what led him to treat the great Greek theme of human limitation, moderation and excess. From the very first, instinctively cautious as he was and really concerned with truth, he rejected all excess in action and willingly deprived his world of the outer dimensions of tragic grandeur. To the ancient *fatum*, which required man to accept the role devolving upon him and play it to the very end, he substituted the play of human intelligence, whereby man escapes from the excessive passions of the gods. What began to interest him above all was not so much freedom itself as the art of limiting it and adapting it to life.

Chapter VII

Prophets and Eagles

*Rien ne m'intéresse dans un livre
que la révélation d'une attitude nouvelle devant la vie.*

Nothing interests me in a book
except the revelation of a new attitude toward life.

~~~~~~

"All things have always existed in man, sometimes seen,
more or less, and sometimes hidden and what a new age uncovers in him is newly disclosed to sight but had been dormant from the beginning." [1] Henceforth, what interests Gide
almost exclusively is this emergence—eclosion, as he called it
—of some of these latent possibilities in individuals and the
disturbances they cause.

All the books he planned and wrote during the lively and
many-faceted years that precede *The Immoralist* (1902) grew
out of *Marshlands* and *Fruits of the Earth*. Though the plays
King Candaules and *Saul* were not published until 1901 and
1903, respectively, Gide had written at least the greater part
of *Saul* by 1897 and *Candaules* first appeared in the small review *l'Ermitage* in 1899, a crucial year in his early produc-

tive period. In his thirtieth year Gide published, besides *Candaules*, a play called *Philoctetes*; a satire, *Prometheus Misbound*; and a tale, *El Hadj*.

El Hadj and *Philoctetes* are still, at first, described as treatises: *El Hadj, Treatise of the False Prophet; Philoctetes*, originally subtitled *Treatise of the Foul Wound*, became *Treatise of the Three Ethics*. But in form as well as content the two new treatises depart markedly from the old.

Gide is feeling his way toward a new impersonality and sobriety, toward new forms reflecting the bold shift in his own ethical and even metaphysical position. *El Hadj* is, in fact, the first Gidian tale, developing the form suggested by the brief "Story of Menalcas" in *Fruits of the Earth; Philoctetes, Saul* and *Candaules* are plays; *Prometheus Misbound*, which Gide first called a novel, was, like *Marshlands*, reclassified as a sotie in 1914, which shows the close connection between satire and novel in Gide's own mind. Among these works, *El Hadj* and *Prometheus Misbound*, slight though they may seem, have a place apart and, though entirely different in form, share a common theme. If Lynceus, leaving his tower, came down among men, what kind of human beings would he meet? Although "all things exist" in each individual, all things cannot flourish simultaneously. Each eclosion presupposes other limitations. With *El Hadj* and *Prometheus* Gide turns to this new area of exploration, questioning and conflict, to the spectacle of human transformation, growth and equilibrium which long enthralled his imagination and was to provide so fruitful a harvest of vigorous and original writing. The two works provide a point of departure for those that followed and throw light on certain crucial areas of Gide's thought, his religious thought in particular.[2]

El Hadj is a minor, transitional work, halfway between the symbolic "treatises" and the future "tales." As its setting Gide uses a vague desert, glimpsed no doubt in North Africa: vast stretches of sand broken only by deceptive salt lakes over which mirages play. The desert traditionally harbors prophets and, periodically, creates them. Gide's false prophet seems to come straight out of the Bible.

The prophet El Hadj tells the tale of an episode now over, chanting it, as might an Arabian storyteller in the market place, in long monotonous rhythmical phrases moving at times into sudden outbursts of lyricism, recalling now the Psalms, now the lamentations of the prophets, now Gide's own lyric endeavors:

Sometimes more for our own people than for these strangers who understood me ill, than for the little children who, when our camp was not too distant from their city, followed us there and stayed into the night, silent or whispering about the brushfires, but whom our travel gear and the richly embroidered stuff hanging at the dromedaries' throats seemed to astonish only enough to ascertain their reality with a touch of the fingertips—I sang and continued my chanting in the night until sleep came:

> The city we have left
> It was rich, great and beautiful.
> Had we not left it
> We would never have named it
> Because we knew no others! [3]

"Here," L. Martin-Chauffier points out, "André Gide tried out a rather paradoxical extension of the sentence, obtained neither by an imposing sequence of clauses such as Bossuet used nor through the overlapping and multiplication of incidental clauses but rather by a kind of perpetual starting over and rebound when the sentence seems to be coming to its end." [4] For the first time Gide created a particular style expressly suited to a given character, the Prophet who tells his own story. Still rather mannered and too obviously a feat of technical virtuosity, it might not successfully have sustained a more substantial work. It is eminently suited to El Hadj, a prophet untroubled by the complexities of thought.

El Hadj tells the story of the migration of a people, the

vague shadow of the theme the poet St. John Perse later developed in his *Anabasis*. The prophet describes a population
moving from its southern cities across the desert toward fa-
bled lands in the north, what lands no one knew. Like the
pillars of smoke and fire before the people of Israel moved
the curtained litter of an invisible Prince. At night the singer,
El Hadj, sang near the Prince's closed tent. The Prince called
to him one night and El Hadj became the intermediary between the uncommunicative Prince and his people. To the
Prince each night he described the goal of their long march:
the legendary northern country, with its clear running water
and green arbors where the fabulous bride of the Prince
awaits their nuptials. And each day he fed the faith of the
people in the Prince whom they were blindly following. The
singer became a prophet in the eyes of both Prince and people to whose aspirations he gave form, by the "reversed exoticism" of which Gide speaks, dreaming of water and trees
in the middle of the desert. The farther they advanced the
more arid the land became. As he drew closer to the Prince,
however, the prophet's faith waned in proportion as his love
increased.

At last before Prince, prophet and people there surged a
sea, beyond which all saw silhouetted the fabulous promised
land which the prophet had described. Prince and prophet
were filled with anguish. The march was halted. Alone at
night, El Hadj went down toward the water to find only a
mudflat covered by a thin layer of salt. The prince died with
the mirage. El Hadj was now the leader. Concealing their
defeat and the death of the Prince from the people, he then
invented a myth, an interdiction, a collective sin, a punishment. Access to the water was forbidden. Solitary, harsh with
the people, and demanding, he led them back to their starting point.

The prophet's tale now is ended but he is already tormented by the desire for a new adventure, foreshadowed in
his last words: "Here, here inside the palace of the City, I

know that a younger brother of the Prince is growing up.
. . . Is he waiting for my voice to guide him? and am I to
start again with him and a new people, a fresh story, which
I shall recognize step by step?" [5]

The symbolism of *Urien's Voyage* was complicated rather
than obscure; *El Hadj's* is enigmatic, and the prophet himself is an ambiguous figure whose tale is doubly difficult to
interpret. How true is it? How and to what extent has it more
or less unconsciously been manipulated by the prophet, much
in the same way as Freud suggests our dreams are fictional-
ized versions of a truth they both disguise and reveal. With
El Hadj Gide no longer proposes an interpretation for his
central character. He emphasizes the mysterious connection
between the prophet and his tale and leaves it to the reader
to furnish his own interpretation.

The march through the desert of a people led by a prince
who advances without knowing where he is heading is a fairly
transparent and almost conventional symbol of the human
lot. Gide's veiled prince seems to symbolize the fundamental
and noble human need, or will, to transcend all limitations
in a drive toward an ideal, an absolute. But in Gide's fable
the drive is purely human, uncorroborated by the certain existence of a God. When the march has reached a limit, all
the prophet can do is return and perhaps start off again for
the same adventure. El Hadj is a Sisyphus, ever ready to set
out once more on an adventure that has neither objective
nor purpose. Gide uses simple biblical themes: the myth of
the promised land, divine interdiction, collective guilt, the
forbidden entry into Paradise, in order to define his own point
of view. All metaphysics, he suggests, are man-made.[6] One
cannot transcend human limitations; beyond a certain point
all attempts to push farther are fatal, leading only to sterility,
frustration and death.

In *El Hadj*, without revolt or despair, Gide lays aside the
metaphysical problems that had haunted his adolescence.

Some years later in *Strait Is the Gate* his heroine Alissa will take up the theme of a princely soul who dies in anguish, haunted by a sense of the futility of the whole endeavor. But when still later Gide turned to the Scriptures, in *Numquid et tu . . .* , he was in search not of a metaphysical vision of life but of an ethic.

Gide in no way denies the drive toward transcendence in the heart of man. El Hadj's shadowy promised land is nonetheless an attempt at evading the stern facts of reality. In this sense *El Hadj* is anti-Nietzschean and might better have been subtitled *Treatise on the Necessary Surrender to Reality* than *Treatise of the False Prophet*.

But the expedition is not a fruitless "eternal journey," to use Claudel's words, "that goes from nowhere to anywhere." The starting point is real enough, and so are the march through the desert and the return to a reality newly felt: a fundamental Gidian cycle.

But what of the false prophet, who stands with Tityrus and Menalcas as the first in a long procession of Gidian "counterfeiters"? As Menalcas had done before him, El Hadj reveals to others their own hidden dreams. He tells them the truth concerning their hopes, a lie concerning their real situation. Facing the salt lake, he becomes a false prophet in his own eyes. But is he really so? Preferring a living illusion to a desperate truth, he forges the myth which allows him to bring his companions back to the city they had left. And the spell of the fabulous north is not broken. He is ready to start again. The human adventure has no end; princes die but prophets remain. Enthusiastic, idealistic, ready for high adventure; cautious and lucid in the face of reality; a liar when confronted with the evidence of his defeat; a perspicacious inventor of useful myths; the creator, servant and burier of princes—El Hadj is a kind of prototype of all artists.

Gide's *Prometheus Misbound* also deals with the human lot, but in a more amusing and devious way. In its blending of disparate tones *Prometheus* recalls *Marshlands*. To the reader's surprise it starts with the matter-of-factness of a police report, in spite of the ominous background suggested by the title:

In the month of May, 189–, at two o'clock in the afternoon, the following incident was seen which might have appeared odd.

On the boulevard which leads from the Madeleine to the Opera, a stout middle-aged gentleman, whose unusual corpulence alone distinguished him, was accosted by a thin gentlemen, who smilingly, and, in our opinion, without ill intention, handed to the first a handkerchief which he had just let fall. The stout gentleman thanked him briefly and was about to continue his way, when, changing his mind, he leaned toward the thin person, and must have asked him for some information . . .[7]

A banal anecdote whose sequel is still "odder." For the stout gentleman hands an envelope to the thin one who writes an address, then:

The thin gentleman . . . had not had time to smile a good-bye, when the stout gentleman, to express his thanks, slapped his hand abruptly on the other's cheek . . . and disappeared. . . .[8]

In spite of the prosaic, factual tone, a dozen questions are raised by this curious anecdote: Why the slap? To whom is the envelope addressed and what is its content? What happened next? A slight shock is in store for the reader, with the casual remark concerning the stout man: "I learned afterwards that it was Zeus, the banker." A little later Prometheus walks into a café on the same boulevard. Zeus and Prometheus, on a Paris boulevard? What connection can there be between the incongruous behavior of the banker and the grandeur of those Aeschylian adversaries?

In the circumscribed setting of the café[9] at the intersection of the two Paris boulevards, Gide introduces a strange set of people. There it is whispered that Zeus, the banker or "Miglionaire," the giver of the slap, is God Almighty:

—Do you know what people say? the waiter asked the banker.
—What do they say?
—That you are God Himself.
—Let them say it, he answered.[10]

The mythical hero Prometheus soon drops in, singularly transformed:

When, on the top of the Caucasus, Prometheus had fully realized that his chains, fetters, strait jackets, parapets and other scruples were all in all making him feel very stiff, in order to change position he rose on his left side, stretched out his right arm, and, between four and five o'clock in autumn, walked down the boulevard which leads from the Madeleine to the Opera.[11]

Out of another realm come two characters familiar to all schoolboys who struggled with Latin: the one-eyed Cocles, defender of his country, and Damocles, the courtier seated for all eternity at a banquet with a sword held by a hair dangling over his head. Fresh out of Gide's own *Marshlands* appear Angela and Tityrus, joined soon after by another character, Meliboeus,[12] the flute-player taken, like Tityrus, from Vergil's *Eclogues:* a curiously anachronistic group with whom the waiter in the café enjoys chatting. By its very absurdity so burlesque a situation destroys any preconceived notion the reader may have had of Gide's purpose, and whets his curiosity.

After the initial anecdote, Gide's *Prometheus* proceeds by leaps and bounds through dialogues and speeches, each more startling than the one before. Ideas spark in all directions: What is a gratuitous act? An idiosyncrasy? Are eagles to be cherished? The brilliant profusion and baffling incongruity of realistic details, the rapid tempo of the action, the disparities and contrasts in style, and the nonchalant tempo of the whole are the complex ingredients which Gide uses in order thoroughly to mystify his reader.

As each character in turn moves to the front of the stage,

caught as if by a moving spotlight, it may seem at first as if Gide is focusing his attention entirely on the events and the dialogue. At this point the satire seems droll, somewhat frivolous, and rather superficial. The narrator entitles the first part of his tale "A chronicle of Private Morality": "I shall say nothing about public morality," he warns, "because there's no such thing." He exploits the rather facile comic effects that arise from the unexpected transformation of a serious myth into prosaic modern reality. Prometheus, asked to state his profession, declares himself to be a manufacturer of matches. Sometimes Gide indulges in sheer impertinence: since Prometheus can give no satisfactory account of his occupations, the waiter classifies him as a man of letters. Sometimes he plays with the legend allowing Prometheus to set aside his self-imposed chains or reversing the laws of perspective for the descent of Prometheus's eagle among the café habitués:

A bird, which seemed enormous from a distance, was seen at close quarters to be not so large after all.

And there are many witty exchanges in the dialogue in the best tradition of the boulevards. The most comical and at the same time disruptive element in the satire is the precariously ambivalent seriousness with which each of the motley crew of characters insists on playing the role assigned him, however incongruous it may seem in relation to the situation as a whole.

Is there any other purpose to Gide's novel-sotie? All Gide ever said about it when he re-edited it much later was that he had hardly had to change a word. Should it be read as an arbitrary and somewhat haphazard improvisation? Everything suggests, rather, that the complex and funny superstructure of the work is built on very solid foundations, that it has unity and makes sense.

Three seemingly unrelated stories are told in the course of

the tale, from various points of view: the story of Cocles and Damocles; the story of Prometheus and his eagle, and, related by Prometheus himself, the story of Tityrus, Angela and Meliboeus. The first part of the sotie focuses mainly on Cocles and Damocles; the second on Prometheus; the third on Tityrus. Each part concludes with a marked change in the relationship of Prometheus with his eagle. At the end of the first part the eagle, descending upon the Parisian café, smashes its glass front and accidentally puts out one of Cocles's eyes. "Prometheus took leave of the waiter and of Cocles, and as he slowly made his way back to the Caucasus he pondered: 'Shall I sell it?—wring its neck? . . . or tame it, perhaps?' " [13]

At the end of the second part the eagle triumphs: "Gentlemen," Prometheus proclaims, "you must love my eagle." [14] As the *sotie* ends, with total disregard for his legend, Prometheus has killed his eagle and is eating it for dinner with his friends. The eagle, clearly, has a leading part in the whole. But exactly how is it connected with the story of Tityrus? And what did Gide mean by his title describing Prometheus as neither bound nor unbound, but illbound or misbound? The facts in the case are the following:

Zeus drops a handkerchief. He asks Cocles, who picks it up by chance, to give him an address, any address. Zeus carries an envelope containing 500 francs—a meager sum today but quite considerable at the time—which he sends to the address chosen at random by Cocles, whom he then slaps. Zeus' activity amounts to just this; it is quite trivial. Cocles and Damocles meet by chance in a café near the Madeleine, ruled over by a bustling and officious waiter. Prometheus chances to come by. The waiter quite gratuitously brings the three characters together:

The restaurant here is very well arranged; with tables for three. . . . Tables for three, yes, I've found very convenient. Three gentlemen arrive; we introduce them . . . Then they sit down . . . they talk. . . . I set relationships going; I listen, I scrutinize, I direct the conversation. When dinner is over I know three inner beings, three personalities! But they don't. As for me, you understand, I listen, I relate; they undergo the relationship.[15]

This is all the waiter ever does. His role, like that of Zeus', is strictly limited.

In contrast Cocles and Damocles have a story to tell for which Zeus is, in part, responsible. "I have led a perfectly ordinary life," says Damocles, "and made a duty of this formula: to resemble the commonest of men." [16] The mystery of the 500 francs, coming out of the blue, makes him unique among men. Consumed with anxiety, Damocles first looks in vain for his benefactor and then dies, worried to death by his unresolved problem. Cocles, an average, moderately good, nondescript man was strolling down the boulevard in search of some opportunity to distinguish himself from other men. Kindly, he picks up the handkerchief. The blow he receives undeservedly revolts him by its injustice so that when, accidentally, the eagle later puts out his eye, he is transformed into a man with a grievance, hence a cause.

Zeus moves and acts in the most irresponsible way, and admits it:

I am rich, richer than anyone can imagine. You belong to me; he belongs to me; everything belongs to me. . . . My influence on Paris is hidden, but it isn't any the less important. It is hidden because I don't follow through. Yes, above all I have a spirit of initiative. I launch. Then, when some affair is launched, I leave it; I don't touch it again.

The Waiter: Isn't it true that your actions are gratuitous?

The Miglionaire: I alone, he alone whose wealth is infinite, can act with absolute disinterestedness; man, no. Thence my love of gambling; not of gain, understand, of gambling. . . . I gamble by lending to men. . . . I play but I hide my cards. I experiment

. . . what I lend to Man, what I plant in him, it amuses me to see that it grows; it amuses me to see it growing.[17]

Amoral and absurd, he plants anxiety or revolt, gives eagles, plays with man, all to no purpose. The waiter, on his level, despite what Zeus says, is equally irresponsible.

But neither Cocles nor Damocles can accept Zeus' irresponsibility and the random nature of the circumstances that have affected them. Moral and rational themselves, they insist upon introducing moral evaluations and logic everywhere. Damocles, having received an unexplained gift, feels indebted to the giver—an idea quite foreign to Zeus. Damocles must find a reason for what occurred: "I pondered a great deal, in accordance with the best methods of inquiry: *Cur, unde, quo, qua?*—whence, wherefore, how, why?"

Whereas Damocles searches for a cause, Cocles concentrates on consequences: reparation for the injustice done him. Damocles dies and Cocles prospers in line with his own, more aggressive temperament.

Gentlemen, declares Prometheus, whatever we do, we shall never escape from begging the question. What does it mean, to beg the question? Gentlemen, if I may venture to say so, begging the question is always an assertion of temperament; for where principles are lacking, assertion of temperament steps in.[18]

There is no way out of the *petitio principii*, the logical fallacy here described by Prometheus, which consists in disguising in a premise the proposition to be proved. Why does Prometheus propose that every man have an eagle? Because he himself has an eagle. Why does Zeus perform gratuitous acts? Because it is in his nature so to do. Why do Cocles and Damocles react so violently to Zeus' gratuitous act? Because it is in their natures to establish rational links of cause and effect. They and we are all exactly in the position of the Parisians in Prometheus's final tale: having seen the nude flute player, Meliboeus, walk down the boulevard with Angela, they grabbed the evening papers "and suddenly everyone learned that the woman was Angela, and this Meliboeus was someone without any clothes on who was going to Italy."

Gide brought together his heterogeneous group of characters in a kind of fable to suggest to his readers, or perhaps even more to explain to himself, the new world view which he now held and of which they are the "givens." "I would like to be able to consider the works of an artist as a complete microcosm," Gide wrote at that time, "entirely *strange* but including the whole complexity of life." [19] *Prometheus* is just such a microcosm. In Gide's world neither Zeus nor Prometheus has supernatural powers. They did not create Cocles and Damocles nor do they control them. All the characters exist on the same level of equality. Zeus may drop his handkerchief, but he obliges no one to pick it up. Prometheus proposes that men should adopt eagles; he cannot order them to do so. There is a very clearheaded and reasonable point of view behind Gide's allegory. Zeus symbolizes the elements of a determinism which man can neither understand nor explain because it *is* his very existence. Zeus creates the random situation, which in itself has no sense and need have no further consequence. Cocles and Damocles are drawn into his game only by chance. He has no hidden fate specifically in store for them.

But Zeus does, unwittingly, challenge something basic in the two men: their need to make sense. Since this is impossible, the very existence of Zeus will be felt by them as absurd, as a sickness. Zeus' role is discussed from five points of view, within the framework of the sotie, and never yields anything further. Like the existentialists, Gide had come to accept the notion of the incomprehensibility, in human terms, of man's position in the natural world. Zeus has lost his power on the human level, and the questions man asks have no value other than human; Zeus has no use for them.

The waiter's café is the place where, already troubled by

Zeus, Cocles and Damocles meet, on the initiative of the waiter. Here social connections are established and idiosyncrasies revealed, but nothing more happens until Prometheus, who after all is the hero of the tale, enters the game.

Prometheus is a very disruptive character. Even his voice, in spite of himself, is disturbing: "his voice, after that of the others, immediately seemed so deep that everyone realized that until then he had been silent." [20] He alone is not limited to the drab, small world of the café. He has had a long and varied past history and, in the course of the story, goes back and forth from the Caucasian Mountains to the boulevard; he is at one moment confined in a prison that "was isolated from the rest of the world and from which nothing could be seen but the sky," where he enjoyed an ecstatic solitude. Like the waiter, he speaks with Zeus; he is the only character to sympathize with Damocles's misfortune; he gives lectures and makes speeches. His eagle smashes windows, puts out eyes, and the pair cause considerable trouble wherever they appear.

Although he doesn't realize it, Prometheus is a stranger among men, a Gulliver in a world of Lilliputians. What is more, unlike the other characters, he freely and constantly changes. First, by his own choosing, he was tied to the Caucasus; tired of this posture, he decided to take a look at Paris. He calls forth his eagle more or less at will and when he decides to do so he kills it. His convictions change as much as he does: he first says he loves men; then that he loves only what devours them; he did not always have an eagle. With pathetic eagerness, before he kills his own, he insists that all men must have an eagle. Then he makes obscure and facetious remarks, quite varied in tone. He spends his time freeing himself—from his chains, from his prison, from his eagle. The Gidian Prometheus, with the inner depth of his voice, seems to embody man's inner drive to transcend his fate.

For Gide, all human possibilities, adventures and tragedies

seem to originate from the ever-present and eruptive power of Prometheus, restricted though it be by the flat and rigid limitations of human existence. In the satire Prometheus acts out some of these adventures: the chains, the eagle, finally the carefree irresponsibility suggested by Meliboeus.

Like Zeus and the waiter, Prometheus is amoral and irresponsible. But, each time, he is himself involved in his own game, undergoing an inner metamorphosis. What is more, he feels he must draw all men into the game. From his own relations with his eagle he draws a gospel which he preaches most pathetically: all men must have eagles. He offers them a highly schematic form of the Nietzschean *amor fati:* Cocles must cherish his wound, in fact deepen it; Damocles must delve deeper into his anguish. But a short while before, feeling a sense of "great expectation," he had preached with equal conviction a doctrine of progress, and later he produces Meliboeus, the carefree nude flute player on his way to Rome.

Prometheus is a dangerous character, persuading Damocles, for example, to cultivate an inner anguish for which Damocles pays with his life. He is the great deceiver, the only deceiver in fact in the microcosm in which he moves, disregarding the limits imposed on human beings by the chance circumstance of the human lot. The Prometheus in us, Gide suggests, is always "misbound," and ready to teach us how to play with fire. It is he, not Zeus, who cultivates chains and eagles. At the instigation of Prometheus, nondescript human beings start out along dangerous paths, and in so doing test out their possibilities. But somewhere along the way they must, they will, encounter Zeus.

So, the freedom of human beings can of necessity be maintained only by a precarious equilibrium. For Gide, man's ethical freedom is analogous to the artist's: he must create a harmonious whole out of separate, incongruous "givens," of which one at least will always be unique, his own idiosyncrasy.

In his subsequent work Gide takes up his characters at the point where Prometheus abandons them. Had Zeus been a writer, he would no doubt have written a naturalistic novel; the waiter would have composed a drama of psychological analysis and Prometheus would have created a problem novel. Gide with his flexible point of view will write the story of men who attempt to live coherently in an incoherent world, who commit themselves to absolutes in a universe of shifting variables and relativity. "Man serves one or several gods in himself," wrote Gide, "before he projects his faith into the skies." [21]

Brilliant and significant in Gide's development as this sotie is, it is too stylized, too complicated perhaps to attain any great intrinsic value of its own. Gide, incidentally, was quite willing more or less transparently to make fun of himself in his own sotie. Prometheus, shackled by his own scruples to his Caucasian rock, a melancholy preacher to whom no one listens; Damocles, on whom Zeus bestows a sum of money; Cocles, who devotes himself to good works—in a mock-heroic vein, all seem aspects of Gide himself. The story of Tityrus, with which the book ends, is a kind of allegorical summation of young Gide's own life. Tityrus, in his marshland, plants a seed; it turns into a tree which calls for a garden, gardeners, a whole organized city, until at last, devoured by the ensuing responsibilities, Tityrus gives up the tree, as Prometheus gave up his eagle.

Gide was no longer a man to allow eagles, trees, books or prophets to devour him; he intended to follow his own path and keep his freedom. But Prometheus also touches lightly upon another matter of great importance to Gide: the strenuous effort he was making, along with others in his generation, to solve to his own satisfaction such literary problems as those of vision and form, the adaptation of traditional forms to changing intellectual perspectives. The writer is a kind of Prometheus too, but a Prometheus whose own work commits him as Prometheus can never be committed. Gide suggests that the very writing of the work and its completion gives limits to the idea that fashioned it—"informed" it, as Gide would say—those very limits that Prometheus cannot be bound by.

Chapter VIII

Interlude: The Gidian Drama

> *On est sûr de ne jamais faire que
> ce que l'on ne pourra jamais com-
> prendre.*
>
> One is sure to do only that which
> one will never be able to under-
> stand.

~~~~~~

While writing *Prometheus* Gide had already turned to the theater. *Philoctetes, Saul* and *Candaules* raise the problems of freedom and balance in a uniquely human perspective. In each of these dramas a hidden subconscious Prometheus suggests to the hero a "new attitude" which is "disclosed to sight" through the action. More or less definitively Gide was leaving behind the theories and preoccupations of his early works.

Gide's three plays, *Philoctetes, Saul* and *King Candaules* differ as markedly as Claudel's from the plays that were being performed in Paris at the end of the nineteenth century. Alongside the traditional theater which aimed exclusively at providing entertainment, both the naturalists and the sym-

bolists had attempted to renew the drama. Ibsen, Strindberg
and Hauptmann were being played as well as Maeterlinck,
but only sporadically. The renaissance of the drama was to
gather momentum around 1910, fully flowering only after
World War I. In the 1890's the harvest was meager. With
some reason, Gide's plays never fared well with critics or
audiences for they lack a certain dramatic forcefulness. Nonetheless, they open up new paths to experimentation in dramatic form, departing radically from the naturalist drama in
situation, ideas, psychology and action. Although Gide relied
in part on suggestion and symbolical indirection, he handled
his stage and characters in a very different way from the symbolists. In spite of the legendary disguises he chose for his
characters, he was inspired neither by antiquity nor by the
French classics. Arresting and original, the Gidian drama pre-
sages new forms of drama which were to mature with Sartre
and Camus.

It is not really surprising that at this stage in his career
Gide felt drawn to the theater. After a short intellectual flirtation with certain simplified Nietzschean concepts—regener-
ation through the casting off of the debilitating aspects of
Christian ethics—he seems to have felt the need to examine,
weigh and project outside himself the diverse and often conflicting impulses in his own thought and life. He had now
taken the fateful step of marriage, and was still in conflict,
inwardly at least, with all that his wife represented and which
he never disowned. The drama could provide a corrective to
the overly subjective and esoteric character of his work and
yet allow him to treat the problems which most deeply concerned him at the time. Although he had no practical contact with the theater and never showed much interest in the
technical problems of the stage, Gide was a reader of Greek
tragedies, of Shakespeare—whom he was later to translate
with distinction—and of Goethe. He was well aware of the
deficiencies of the drama which his countrymen had compla-

cently enjoyed for half a century. He had his own ideas about the theater which he casually introduced in his *Letters to Angela* and developed briefly in 1904 in a short lecture on "The Evolution of the Theater."

In the theater an *idea* should be a character, a situation; the pseudo ideas that one puts into the mouths of characters are never anything but opinion and should be subordinated to the characters; it is not *principally* through these opinions that they express themselves; these should only be the conscious content of their acts. . . . The unconscious support—more interesting, more important, and stronger—is the character himself.[1]

What Gide attempted to do in his three dramas was to isolate the "unconscious support of a character," the emotional drive originating in subconscious levels of the personality, which deviously yet inexorably drives the character to act as he himself had not foreseen. On stage, and within a limiting situation, the central character "commits himself" as Sartre was later to say, to an inner hidden desire which breaks through to the surface in an irremediable act.

Among the many heroes of legend and history, the three Gide chose have certain common features: all, for example, at one moment in their lives freely made a decisive act. Philoctetes,[2] the Sophoclean hero, we are told, had volunteered to land on the island of Chrysea where he was to suffer his terrible wound. Saul[3] himself, the Bible tells us, had advanced the hour when he was to learn his fate in divine consultation. King Candaules,[4] in spite of Gyges and all warnings to the contrary, had decided to reveal the beauty of his queen to his friend. All three thus appeared to Gide as impatient heroes, Nietzschean in the sense that they seemed eager to challenge their own fate. From the sources he used, Gide took only those incidents which seemed to reveal the inner, unconscious drive of the character behind the impatience. Among the Greek heroes, Philoctetes was the only man who had dared set fire to the funeral pyre of Hercules, who had dared go ashore alone on Chrysea; he seemed to have a Nietzschean passion for "surpassing" himself. In Saul, as he is described in the Bible, always probing the future, accompanied by prophets, witches and soothsayers, Gide saw a man driven by a morbid anxiety with regard to his undisclosed future. From the story of Candaules, Gide isolated the King's overwhelming and rash generosity which led him to offer to Gyges what was not really his—the beauty of the Queen.

Gide handles characters and episodes with considerable freedom, even in the case of *Philoctetes,* which at first sight seems to stay fairly close to Sophocles's play. In so doing he introduces into all three plays certain thoroughly Gidian themes which the classical or biblical sources may vaguely suggest but certainly do not emphasize. All three heroes—Philoctetes, Saul and Candaules—are men who welcome and protect a stranger who then despoils them. Philoctetes is charmed by young Neoptolemus whom Ulysses has brought with him and who steals the famous bow needed to win the war against Troy. Saul welcomes David, who will take his throne from him. Candaules greets Gyges—whom Gide has transformed from a companion into a stranger—who takes his wife.

The stranger in all three plays is a pure, grave and beautiful adolescent. There is no feminine part in *Philoctetes.* Saul's queen is murdered in the first act as is Gyges's mute wife, and Candaules's queen, Nyssia, never comes to life. In these plays Gide attempted more or less consciously to deal indirectly with the question of homosexuality, a central problem of his own. The young man in all three, reminiscent of Nathanael, strips his benefactor of the attributes of virility: bow, crown, wife, and the despoiled himself participates in the act with a curiously voluptuous sense of delight. Perhaps this bond of attraction between plunderer and plundered escaped Gide's control; it is stubbornly recurrent. Neoptolemus loves Philoctetes and steals the bow; Gyges loves Candaules, steals his wife and kills him; David loves Saul: the beloved victim and the admired despoiler and sacrificer form a curiously revealing couple. At the time Gide seems to have felt his homosexuality both as a fascinating source of vulnerability and as a wound, like Philoctetes's "foul wound," a wound inflicted by an irresponsible Zeus, and which grievously isolated him. Thanks to Wilde, young Gide had experienced the sudden surge of passions he had harbored unknowingly and which, after a slow germination fostered by circumstance, had come into the open. He made of this experience a dramatic motif in all three plays, hence, in part, their originality. But hence also their great and almost insuperable weakness.

In form and structure the three plays differ considerably. Each is an independent experimental venture. Philoctetes is spare and stark, played out between three characters in a single stylized setting, a symbolic glacial island where nothing lives. We could hardly be farther from the Greek Lemnos. The emphasis is clearly an ethical one, the island, an inner island in harmony with the hero's mood: ". . . for I learned," he says, "that everything around me is sick . . . and that the cold is not normal." At the end of the play the setting changes with his mood: ". . . around him flowers are showing through the snow, and birds from heaven come down to feed him," a rather evangelical and obvious form of symbolism.

Gide's play begins like Sophocles's, as Ulysses and Achilles' son, Neoptolemus, arrive at Lemnos—where the wounded hero Philoctetes has lived alone since the Greeks abandoned him. In the Greek play Ulysses and Neoptolemus are sent to bring back Philoctetes with his bow and arrows to the Greeks. In Gide's play there is a vital change. Philoctetes's bow and arrow, his only means of subsistence, are to be taken away and he is again to be left defenseless on his island. Gide makes no pretense at following the myth. The Philoctetes his

Ulysses and Neoptolemus discover has nothing in common with the Greek hero, nor has the outcome of Gide's play, where Philoctetes voluntarily surrenders his bow to Neoptolemus.

Saul, on the other hand, is grim and spectacular, filled with murders, battles and scenes of madness reminiscent of Shakespeare's *Hamlet, Macbeth,* and *King Lear,* and in it Gide seems to have attempted a dramatic tempo altogether lacking in *Philoctetes.* It progresses by means of a series of tableau-like scenes that shift with increasing speed: from royal palace to desert, to mountain cave, armed camp, and so forth. Around Saul are grouped nine secondary characters, David most prominent among them, but many other characters throng the stage as participants or commentators: demons, servants, guards, common people, soldiers.

Gide took great liberties in his treatment of the biblical story. His Saul's personality and downfall are more obscure and complex. The episodes leading to the final catastrophe come about in an equivocal, uneasy atmosphere where murder and madness are hard to distinguish from masquerade, and tragedy from burlesque. Everything in the play disintegrates with the subtle, weak and sullen King himself.

King Candaules is permeated with the glow of twilight and the sound of music, the festive atmosphere of a banquet in the legendary gardens of a sumptuous palace. Gide took nothing from Herodotus—for whom Candaules's story was a minor episode in the struggle between Greeks and barbarians— except the curious outline of his play. Gide was not unaware of Herodotus's thought, to which he gave his own, modern interpretation:

This play derives, perhaps, simply from a reading of Herodotus; yet somewhat, perhaps, also from the reading of an article in which an author of talent, pleading "for moral freedom," came to the point of blaming the custodians of art, beauty, wealth— in short, the "ruling classes"—for not having the sense to attempt

to educate the people by setting up for them exhibitions of certain kinds of beauty. The author did not say—in fact, he was careful not to say—whether the people would have the right to touch
. . . Hence my *Candaules* was born. And then, before long, the
newborn drama grew up and ran away.[5]

It was, on the whole, fortunate that *Candaules,* almost entirely of Gide's own invention, ran away with itself, for it is
certainly the most successful of his three plays.

Although *Philoctetes* and *Saul* are constructed as five-act
prose plays, while *Candaules* has three acts and is written in
verse, all three plays progress through a sometimes outwardly
alogical sequence of tableaux, whose unity and significance
can be understood only in terms of the development of the
central character. Though Gide dutifully divides his plays
into acts and scenes, the use he makes of these is certainly
not classical. "Silence" accounts for one scene in *Philoctetes,*
and in another instance a single sentence fills one act. Gide
is quite unconcerned too about the surface credibility of his
action. Philoctetes, whose wound gives out a horrible stench,
can nonetheless hide and, undetected, overhear a conversation between Ulysses and Neoptolemus. Even though he has
murdered the soothsayer and the Queen, King Saul can twice
slip out from his palace alone. And no one is in the slightest
bit disturbed by the murder of King Candaules. In fact, in
the last two plays murder has no consequences, emphasizing
the symbolic character of the act. Saul's crown is a strange
one, dependent as it is upon two adolescents and a child. As
for Candaules, what kind of king is he, with his inexhaustible wealth, his kingdom without limits? His sole occupation
is entertaining the lords of his kingdom at sumptuous feasts
which bore them.

Gide's plays thus sometimes move uneasily between dream
and reality. In order to impose themselves on the audience
they would demand a firm command of the poetic mood and
language, which only *Candaules* manages to maintain all the

way through. In all three plays Gide exploits such well-worn theatrical devices as enigmas, warnings and prophecies, necessarily ambiguous, hidden magic rings, conversations overheard—all of which emphasize the essentially figurative, poetic quality of the action.

The language is sharply differentiated in the three plays and attuned to the mood Gide wished to create. It is stark and austere to the point of abruptness in *Philoctetes,* sensual and ornate in *Candaules,* tormented and ranging from satire to pathos in *Saul.* Within the general tonality of the plays each individual character brings his own modulations, the whole conveying the sense of a dramatic composition rather than a play. "Voices" oppose, complement or reinforce each other, the plays developing less as conflicts than as blendings of complementary themes.

Of the three dramas *Philoctetes* is the simplest. The action develops in three stages: the meeting of Philoctetes, Ulysses and Neoptolemus; Philoctetes's discovery of the plot to despoil him; his sacrifice as he allows Neoptolemus to rob him. Sacrifice is the central subject of the play.

"My mind too is made up," are the first words of Neoptolemus, "it is ready for sacrifice. Speak now, Ulysses, and tell me; all is ready." [6] Since Ulysses has kept silent concerning the purpose of their journey, Neoptolemus has concluded that, like Iphigenia, he is to be sacrificed. "What we have to do here, Neoptolemus," answers Ulysses, "is not so easy as dying," thereby preparing Neoptolemus for the strangely modern conflict he has to face. In the name of the gods Ulysses asks him to perform a dastardly act, to seize by stealth the weapon of a sick and unfortunate warrior, his father's friend.

Neoptolemus: Philoctetes will not want to give it to us.
Ulysses: So we shall take it by trickery.
Neoptolemus: Ulysses, you are abominable. My father taught
              me never to use trickery. [7]

For the first time in his life Neoptolemus sees that duty may be ambiguous and equivocal, incompatible with a personal ideal of virtue.

Ulysses: Tell me, Neoptolemus, what is virtue?

Neoptolemus: Teach me, wise son of Laertes.

Ulysses: To calm one's passions: putting duty above every-thing. . . .

Neoptolemus: But what is duty, Ulysses?

Ulysses: The voice of the gods, the order of the city, giving ourselves to Greece. . . . Don't you think, Neoptolemus, that what is most important of all is that the gods' orders be carried out? Even if it must be done without everybody's consent?

Neoptolemus: All you said before, I approve; but now I no longer know what to say, and it even seems to me . . .[8]

At this point appears Philoctetes, the man who is to be robbed by trickery for the greater good of the Greeks. In spite of being solitary and racked by pain, he is singing, until, at the sight of a Greek helmet and weapons, he falls into deep silence.

Philoctetes's first speech reveals the inner trend of his thought, that "unconscious support" of which Gide spoke, which prepares the way for his future and as yet unforeseeable act of renunciation:

"I tell you, Ulysses, only since I have lived apart from men do I understand what they call virtue. The man who lives among others is incapable, believe me, incapable of a pure and really disinterested action."[9]

To Ulysses' definition of duty, fairly reminiscent of Maurice Barrès's nationalism, Gide prefers his own—Goethean—idea of a virtue inherent in each person that transcends the confines of any one nation: "On this island, you know, I have become every day less Greek, every day more a man."[10] Pure virtue in Philoctetes's eyes is a sense of detachment and mastery, a self-possession from which all feeling has been excluded:

I walk securely over things, over frozen fluids. I never dream any more; I only think. I can no longer taste hope, and for that reason I am never elated. . . . And my acts, Ulysses, and my words, as if they were frozen forever, surround me like rocks arranged in a circle. And because I find them there every day, all my passion is quieted, and I feel the Truth always firmer—and I should wish my actions also always sounder and more beautiful, beautiful, Ulysses, as those crystals of clear frost through which the sun, if the sun appeared, could be seen whole. . . . I should like to achieve the greatest transparency, the suppression of all my opacity; and I should like you, watching me act, to feel the light yourself.[11]

Philoctetes's last words reveal that in the glacial zones in which he lives passion once again has appeared with other human beings: he must persuade Ulysses, he must answer Neoptolemus's appeal: "Philoctetes, teach me virtue." For Philoctetes the real test starts when he discovers Ulysses' plot. Something is stirring deep within him. "Child!" he murmurs. "Ah! if I could only *show* you virtue." He is ready when Neoptolemus comes to him and denounces Ulysses' deceit. His own subconscious desire to *show* Neoptolemus what virtue can be carries him beyond his own conscious will and self-interest. Voluntarily he takes the vial and drinks the drug which will put him to sleep.

All the preceding scenes lead to this one decision and act which, performed, commit Philoctetes to an unforeseeable new existence that terrifies him. Thus Neoptolemus's confession makes Philoctetes the arbiter of his own fate, not a victim. For a few seconds, before taking the vial, he is free. He acts and then experiences a moment of sheer panic. But, in the eyes of Neoptolemus, the sleeping Philoctetes has vanquished Ulysses:

"Philoctetes! . . . Can't you hear me, Philoctetes? . . . I wanted to tell you—you have convinced me, Philoctetes. I see virtue now; it is so beautiful that in your presence I no longer dare to act." [12]

The play ends in rather naïve fashion with an unconsciously comic beatification of Philoctetes, whose voice becomes "extraordinarily mellow and beautiful"; the snow around him melts and, like some saint from the golden legend, he is fed by the birds from heaven. His foul-smelling wound seems to have disappeared and there is not a trace left of the Sophoclean hero who shrieks with pain and hatred and whom nothing can persuade to go with Ulysses until the gods themselves intervene.

In Gide's hands Philoctetes seems to turn into one of those creators of values of which Nietzsche speaks. Ulysses only smiled when Philoctetes tried to explain to him a newly emerging idea of virtue he found difficult to formulate clearly. Witnessing Philoctetes's act, however, Ulysses grasps its greatness. Having expressed what he had struggled to say, and having been understood, Philoctetes has accomplished his own particular destiny, which is to propose to his fellow men, represented by Ulysses and Neoptolemus, a new form of ethics. His act frees him from his glacial solitude.

"A Treatise Concerning Three Ethics," Gide called this play. Ulysses prescribes an ethic which is not without grandeur: the subjection of an individual's will and judgment to the interests of his community. It has its dubious sides, which Gide, as one would expect, emphasized too: justification of the means by the end and the willingness to sacrifice others, complacently, in the name of the greater good of all. The opposing ethic that Philoctetes vaguely senses and then exemplifies is based on the free aspiration and judgment of each man, an ethic of freely assumed sacrifice but one which must be reinvented for each act, an almost Sartrean ethic were it not for the positive role played in its genesis by Philoctetes's wish to appear noble in the eyes of others.

Neoptolemus is the confused witness to a discussion between two men who have little left in them of their original Greek counterparts. The island where the action takes place is as abstract as Sartre's hell in *No Exit* or the room in which Paul Valéry's M. Teste lives. Ulysses sacrifices part of his integrity to his ethic with a heavy soul but a clear conscience. But Philoctetes troubles him, and the contempt he fears Philoctetes feels is only a projection of Ulysses' own sense of the dubious nature of his point of view. His is a hollow triumph.

So long as he lives in isolation, however, Philoctetes's virtue is fruitless. "When I was thinking out my *Philoctetes*, Robinsonism tormented me," Gide said,[13] alluding to Robinson Crusoe's isolation. In order to have meaning Philoctetes's virtue must benefit others. By renouncing his bow, he becomes more human. A new Philoctetes is born, without wound or weapon. Ulysses and Philoctetes's ethics thus complement each other.

As for the third ethic, is it perhaps Neoptolemus's? With his passion for acquiring wisdom, Neoptolemus personifies an ethic of anguished sincerity somewhat like Gide's own. But Neoptolemus seems instead to show up the limitations of both points of view. "All you told me has taken root in my heart," he says to Philoctetes, but he ends up by doing what Ulysses tells him to do.

The third ethic and the meaning of the play seem to emerge from the ending and explain the changes Gide made in the Greek story. Without expecting any reward, Philoctetes gives up his only weapon, his bow. The decision is difficult but his act is free and gratuitous. Happiness comes as an extra dividend, a quite Christian point of view. But might not the bow renounced express something else? For some years young Gide had felt increasingly isolated in an icy world. The bow renounced might well stand for the abandonment of the austere ethical discipline within which he had sought to live. Philoctetes achieves happiness when he achieves "availability." Yet in this first play theme and action are not developed well enough to sustain the strength of the character Gide had conceived.

In *Saul* Gide has all the elements of an original and exciting play, which fails to come off largely because he was unable to handle the theme of sexual inversion. Centered as it is on the complementary and opposed figures of Saul and David the play might have achieved an almost mythical grandeur. Gide was keenly aware of the dramatic value of two poetic and tragic themes inherent in the biblical story: the fall of one dynasty in order that another may rise, and the struggle between the destructive nocturnal powers about Saul and the brilliant solar light of God's grace upon David.

Gide conceives of Saul as a being both disturbed and disturbing, plunged in darkness, forever brooding over the enigma of an ominous future which for him contains only disaster, sinking ever further into murder and madness. A shadowy figure, he is surrounded and spied upon by a set of sinister masklike characters: the Queen, the High Priest, a facetious barber. Outside the city walls, the Philistines insultingly promenade their giant, Goliath: a monstrous, bizarre situation, unresolved. Two young boys stand by the King: Jonathan, his son, a sickly youth who cannot bear the weight of his inheritance, and Saki, the King's cupbearer, a frail and innocent child.

Into this court comes David, bringing all that the King lacks: force, innocence, self-assurance and light. Everything in the palace calls out to him, welcomes him, loves him, needs him. The King alone remains aloof from the youth who is dedicated to the salvation of his kingdom.

In the first act Gide contrasts the twilight of King Saul, once God's elect, with the dawn of the newly chosen David, unaware of his own election. With the second act, all, except the palace dwellers and David himself, know that David is now God's anointed. The next three acts show Saul's gradual disintegration as the fate he fears inexorably comes to pass.

Unfortunately, Gide also extracted a situation smacking of vaudeville from his biblical source. The Bible relates that David found grace in the eyes of Saul and was bound in friendship to Jonathan. But it does *not* suggest that Saul desired David physically nor that David's ties with Jonathan were erotic. That an entire royal family, doomed to destruction, should be irresistibly attracted to someone who will later destroy them is a legitimate psychological situation with real dramatic and tragic potentialities. David radiates what Saul's dynasty has lost: divine grace and light. The Queen is drawn to David just as Saul and Jonathan are. But to reduce this attraction to an erotic impulse is to weaken its dramatic impact. When Gide permits a kind of flirtatious rivalry among all three members of the royal household concerning David's name, the situation becomes positively comical. Who in the royal family may call David "Daoud"? David reserves this right not to the King or the Queen but to Jonathan. The debate on this vital question calls forth a set of dialogues worthy of Gide's Vergilian idyls involving Arab lads like Mopsus and Amyntas. The very name "Daoud" is borrowed from Gide's young Algerian companion and servant, Athman. By the third time the endearment "delightful Daoud" is used to determine a crucial development in the action, Gide's play comes close to turning into a bedroom farce. The sensation caused in Saul's palace by the seventeen-year-old "little singer" is a bit too reminiscent of the emotion Gide felt before Donatello's statue of David. Gide's admiration was most certainly not aesthetic; it was the same emotion he was always to feel with regard to adolescents. At times Gide's play almost implies that Saul goes mad because the adolescent he desires prefers his son. Yet Gide might have made a subtler and less offensive use of his theme. The name "David" might

come to Saul's lips every time he ponders the riddle of his
future, until at last he, and the audience, might grasp the
dual nature of the attraction impelling him to seek out David.

There are three distinct dramatic situations in *Saul* which
are never satisfactorily fused. The first concerns Saul's state
of mind and is introduced in the opening scene. Saul is alone
and, invisible to him, demons play around him more and
more impertinently until they seize the insignia of his roy-
alty.

First Demon:	You, over there, say: what do you choose? . . .
Sixth Demon:	His cup. My name is anger, madness: when he seeks intoxication, he will find me.
First Demon:	Good. Now you?
Fifth Demon:	For me, his bed—I'm called lust. I'll be there when he tries to sleep.
First Demon (to another):	And you?
Fourth Demon:	Fear—I'll sit on his throne . . .
First Demon:	And you?
Third Demon:	I'll take his scepter. . . . My name will be domination.
Another Demon:	I choose his purple, my name is Vanity . . .
First Demon:	I take his crown and my name is Legion . . .

Saul is a man "possessed" in the biblical sense; "dispossessed" in the Gidian vocabulary of *Fruits of the Earth*, that
is, dominated by his passions and reduced to a state of moral
anarchy.

At the end of Act II, with the further degeneration of
Saul, the demons, no longer invisible, play their tricks under
the very eyes of the King, who greets them with a kind of
weary tenderness. In Act III, as Saul makes a last attempt to
control his passions, the demons disappear. With Act IV, a
demon is ever present at his side, and in the last act the demons play inside the tent of the pitiable King, tormenting
him at will.

Besides the theme of moral disintegration, a second theme develops—separately, it seems. In Act I, alone on a terrace at night, devoured by anguish and worn out by twenty sleepless nights, Saul broods over the future, trying to comprehend the darkness God has left him in:

And yet I am King Saul—but there is always a point beyond which I can no longer know. There was a time when God answered me; but then, it's true, I asked Him very little. Every morning the priest told me what I was to do: that was the future; and I knew the future. It was I who made it. Then the Philistines came; I was uneasy; I tried to put questions to God myself; and from then on God fell silent. How did He expect me to act? To act rightly, one must know the future. I began to discover it in the stars; for twenty nights now I've looked, patiently. I saw nothing concerning the Philistines. No matter now! But I did discover something, which made an old man of me: Jonathan, my son Jonathan, is not the one who will succeed me on the throne, and my line will end with him. But who will take my place, that is what I cannot find out.[14]

That very night the King's secret knowledge about the succession to the throne prompts his order to have all the soothsayers of Israel killed. "And when I am the only one who knows the future, I think I shall be able to change it." Saul's mad wish to change what he knows cannot be changed—the future partially revealed of which he knows one facet only and over which he broods—and his alienation from the real and dangerous situation of his kingdom contribute to the somber and eerie atmosphere of the palace.

But something has stirred in Saul, a new need. Although he has consciously decided no longer to admit strangers to his presence in case one might be the usurper, all his senses are awake and yearning to welcome some gentle and insinuating call from outside:

The nights are too short in summer; it is so hot that nothing around me can sleep; no one but my tired cupbearer; I need the sleep of others; I am always being distracted. The slightest noise, the slightest fragrance, calls to me; my senses are turned outward and no sweetness passes me unperceived.[15]

Though the King has resolved to outwit fate by refusing to admit any stranger, his subconscious desires already drive him in another direction, hence the unpredictability of his reactions. He is, in fact, mentally and physically unbalanced.

Temporarily, with David's victory over Goliath and his arrival in the palace, order seems restored, but the movement is reversed when Saul kills the Queen who—like Polonius in *Hamlet*—was spying upon him: "You are wrong, madame," he murmurs. "The secret you would find is another." By Act III, Saul knows that David is the answer to his riddle: Who will succeed to the throne? The truth comes out in several powerful scenes inspired by the Bible. Saul consults the phantom of Samuel, called back to earth by the Witch of Endor. Three times David is clearly designated during the scene: by Samuel, by the witch, whom Saul assassinates; and finally by Saul himself. The name "David" is pronounced by Samuel only when Saul lies unconscious at his feet; the witch warns him only indirectly: "O King, too deplorably inclined to open your heart, close your gates. . . . Close your gates! Shut your eyes! Stop your ears—and may love's fragrance never again find the way to your heart." [16] David again is the name that first comes to Saul's lips when he recovers consciousness: witches, prophets and stars can tell him nothing but what lies hidden in his own heart. But Saul becomes fully conscious that he has the answer to his question only when, a little later on, David plays the harp before him. Disarmed by the music, Saul speaks aloud his hidden thought:

Horror! Horror! Horror! They want to know my secret and I don't know it myself! It is slowly taking shape in my heart. . . . But music stirs it. . . . Like a bird beating against the bars of its cage it has risen to my very teeth; it leaps toward my lips,

leaps and seeks to rush out. . . . David, my soul is tormented
beyond all bearing! Whose name do you hold, my lips? Be tight,
O lips of Saul! Draw your royal mantle about you, Saul! You are
besieged by everything! Stop your ears! All that comes to me is
hostile. Delight! Delight! Why am I not with him, beside the
stream . . . a goatherd? I would burn in the heat of the air! I
would feel less the burning in my soul—my soul that songs move
—and which leaping from my lips—goes out toward you—Daoud
—my delight.[17]

Of the three main themes Gide develops in his play, the
theme of moral disintegration, an inner theme, is treated almost allegorically. The various insignia stolen by the demons
readily symbolize an inner dignity and command. The pro-
liferation, in anarchy, of sensual desires is projected through
the demons who toss the hapless King back and forth and
leave him powerless to act. They prepare the appearance of
the most compelling of all his desires: his desire for David.

The theme of Saul's obsessive preoccupation with a fate
partly disclosed, partly hidden, is clearly stated through the
episode of the witches. Saul attempts to silence forewarnings
that fill him with dread. His love for David in this context
is a form of the Nietzschean espousal of one's destiny.

The two themes of fate and moral disintegration could
have combined to create a unique dramatic situation. Saul,
in his relation with David, would then have discovered his
repressed homosexual desire as a doubly dangerous trap
placed along his path. But what meaning, then, could we
attribute to the love of David and Jonathan? One can hardly
consider Saul's desire as a sign of moral disintegration if
Jonathan and David's is not reprehensible. In this light Saul's
torment becomes nothing more than the jealousy of an elderly man. As a consequence with Act III the play loses momentum. The King sinks into madness, while around him
three adolescent knights—David, Jonathan and Saki—tussle
with his demons. Nowhere is the weakness of the dramatic

handling of a remarkably suggestive idea more clearly apparent than in the scene in which Jonathan playfully crowns
David. Weary of his crown, Saul had placed it on Jonathan's
frail head. Jonathan in turn crowns David as, hidden, Saul
watches the scene. "Oh, David," he cries, "why, could it be
you . . . ?" At this quite dramatic point Gide develops a
naïve exchange of sentimental, exalted dialogue between David and Jonathan which arouses Saul's fury. That Saul's erotic
impulses could blind him to the menace David represents in
spite of himself is psychologically sound. But in the father-
son rivalry for David's charms there is something potentially
burlesque that a great playwright would have avoided. Because of his own involvement, perhaps, Gide did not avoid
that danger.

Yet *Saul* is not a negligible play. The slow advance of Saul's
mind toward the realization of a fact he has repressed and
is combating is a genuinely modern, dramatic situation with
tragic possibilities. In the case of Gide's *Saul*, the King's
tragic dignity is preserved to the very end by the pathetic
shame with which he witnesses and lucidly judges his own
downfall, a moral downfall involved in the disintegration of
his will.

Ah, what am I waiting for now? Why do I not get up and act?
My will! My will! I call to it now like a shipwrecked sailor hail-
ing a ship he sees disappearing in the distance—going—going.[18]

Saul is a man who has a secret, or at least a semisecret,
which, obsessively, he wants entirely disclosed. Candaules is
a man without secrets. Saul hides what he knows or fears;
Candaules reveals everything, removing even the veil from
the face of his queen. Saul welcomes what comes from outside; Candaules gives away and dissipates all he owns. In both
plays, however, the future is involved in some outer thing the
King could not foresee or control, which only the action dis-

closes. In the case of Candaules, it is the ring hidden in a fish served during one of the King's banquets.

Candaules, as he informs Gyges, the fisherman, is a king as wealthy as Zeus in Gide's *Prometheus:*

King Candaules:	Do you believe that I am rich?
Gyges:	Yes.
King Candaules:	Very rich?
Gyges:	Very rich, yes.
King Candaules:	But tell me—how rich?
Gyges:	I know that as far as my sight can reach, your kingdom reaches out toward the horizon.
King Candaules:	O Gyges! It goes far beyond the horizon.[19]

Not only is he rich, he is happy, almost passionately happy:

> "Oh the fullness of my happiness!" he exclaims,
> "How could my senses alone ever drain it?" [20]

Outside the court lives Gyges, a poor and austere fisherman. Gyges's pride and independence make him Candaules' only equal, limiting the King's power:

> "And I am out fishing at dawn," says Gyges,
> "With my net on one arm and my strength in the other;
> Because in the sea, where everything is born,
> The fish are new and belong to no one
> As long as they have not been caught." [21]

The sea where everything is born does not belong to the King. From the sea, with Gyges's fish, comes the ring, the instrument of the King's fate, but not through the machination of any of his courtiers. The fish caught by Gyges is being prepared for the feast as the action starts. Though no one as yet suspects the existence of the ring, hidden inside the fish, Gyges's first words are exactly those inscribed on the hidden ring:

> Whoever possesses happiness, let him hide!
> Or else hide his happiness from others.[22]

Candaules' own bent is to do just the opposite. At the banquet, where wine flows freely, he insists that Nyssia, his queen, should appear without veils so that all may enjoy her beauty:

> Indeed, I suffered too much because I alone knew her.
> The greater my admiration of her,
> The more I felt how much I deprived you all.
> I felt like a greedy monopolizer
> Wrongfully withholding light.[23]

He is intoxicated by his own generosity. As with Philoctetes and Saul, what Candaules "hides within himself" comes out in moments of a kind of spiritual intoxication, a form of what the Greeks called hubris.

King Candaules: Gentlemen, I have resolved to test you all.
Nicomedes: Test us, Candaules? How?
King Candaules: Through intoxication.
Phaedrus: I am a sorry drinker, drunkenness frightens me.
Leave me out, Candaules, I beg you.
King Candaules: Well, Phaedrus! what do you fear?
Drunkenness can only discover in us what we have within ourselves.
Why should a man be afraid
Who has only noble things to show?
Drunkenness does not deform, it exaggerates.[24]

At that precise moment one of Candaules' courtiers finds the ring with its enigmatic inscription "I hide happiness." "The fish gave it to me," he announces, "I give it to the King." For the first time the King has received instead of giving, and the gift with its tantalizing inscription troubles his serenity:

Pharnaces: To Candaules, the happiest man on earth!
King Candaules (striking the table violently with his fist): Come now! What do you know of my happiness indeed? [25]

Pressed by his new uncertainty, almost in spite of himself, Candaules now expresses a new idea emerging from the subconscious depths of his personality as Gyges's fish had come out of the ocean:

> After all, what do I care about happiness?
> Don't you think it is right only for the poor
> To be concerned about being happy? . . .
>
> Every new thing that one possesses
> Brings with it a new desire to test it out—
> For me, to possess is to experiment . . .
>
> To risk! That is the other form of happiness;
>   the rich man's happiness.
> And it is mine.
> I am rich, Phaedrus, and so intensely alive.[26]

Gyges now comes before Candaules. Gyges, the poor man who has just lost, in an accident, two of the four things he owns: his cabin and his nets. The third, his wife Trydo, Gyges kills under Candaules' eyes when he is taunted by the courtiers for her infidelities. His last possession, poverty, Candaules now takes away from him. The "new gift" the King is going to test is his friendship for the fisherman, Gyges.

Act II shows a thoroughly bored Gyges, weighted down with presents, seated sadly at table with his royal benefactor. Unable to admit that his gifts might not endow the recipient with a share of his own happiness, Candaules is gripped by a new, an audacious idea:

> (Candaules, vexed, rises; disturbed, he strides up and down at
>   the back of the hall; then in an undertone)
> What is this you propose, my unquiet thought? . . .
>
> Louder, speak louder, my youngest thought!
> Where do you mean to lead me? Ah, admirable Candaules! [27]

By now Candaules knows that the ring has the magic power to make its wearer invisible. He knows Nyssia is about to ap-

pear. He slips the ring on Gyges's finger. Terrified, Gyges
wants to flee. For a few seconds Candaules holds his destiny
in his hands. He can arrest the future. Like Philoctetes, he
goes through a brief moment of terrible anguish: "It's mad,
the thing I am about to do!" But he persists and Gyges remains alone with Nyssia. "And now," says Candaules as he
withdraws, "let all things around me be happy." [28]

The last act moves at a rapid tempo. Invisible, Gyges wan-
ders about the palace spreading panic around him. He too
is gripped by a slowly emerging though as yet unformulated
idea: the murder of the King.

> My ring. My ring!
> Hide my thoughts from me! . . .
> You frighten them all, invisible Gyges.
> Ring! If you could only hide me from myself!
> Gyges is afraid of Gyges.[29]

Candaules, equally troubled, is looking for him. He encounters Nyssia, who tells him: "Ah, of all our nights, this was
the most beautiful night of love!" The invisible Gyges who,
unknown to her, shared with her that one ecstatic night,
overhears her words. Tearing off the ring, he throws himself
at the Queen's feet. Her horror at the betrayal Candaules
has forced upon her coincides with Gyges's as yet unformulated impulse. Protected by the ring Gyges will kill the King.
"What! It's you, my own Gyges?" Candaules says when Gyges strikes him:

> Why did you strike me?
> I felt nothing in me but kindness. Nyssia!
> Gyges, I gave you the knife too.
> Take off your ring—I want to see you again.
>
> Gyges (terrified and grieved): Candaules, my friend! . . .[30]

Succeeding to the throne, Gyges's first act as king is brutally to cover the face of Nyssia. "I hide my happiness," the

ring said. What the ring has hidden all through Act III is
Gyges. Like David in relation to Saul, Gyges is the answer
to Candaules' hidden desire. What Candaules and the courtiers lacked was a master. Gyges comes out of the sea, where
everything is born, the sea, symbol of that great reservoir of
secret forces in which the human subconscious is immersed.
Candaules, the immensely wealthy king, surrounded by his
bored courtiers, yearns for something else. He gambles with
Nyssia and loses her, but, dying, hears the words of Gyges,
"Candaules, my friend." He has won the friendship of Gyges by the very folly of his act.

Gyges succeeds Candaules, as David succeeded Saul, illus-
trating the dialectical movement discernible in all Gide's previous work: each mood, once established, grows, reaches limits, and then creates the need for an opposed and complementary mood which replaces it.

Gide's three plays concern inner, not outer kingdoms, suggesting the ebb and flow of a complex psychological life, the
inner play of forces out of which definitive choices and acts
arise. Extremely modern in their limited way, they were oriented away from the patterns of naturalistic or psychological
drama whereby characters reach to outer circumstances according to preordained motivations; they concentrate rather
on complex inner patterns of feeling and thought from which
emerge the unexpected turns that fashion the characters' destinies and create their highly distinctive personalities.

Saul and Candaules are especially striking and original because of the highly dramatic psychology of the subconscious
conceived by Gide to motivate them. Before he ever heard
of Freud, Gide had understood the dramatic possibilities of
a character who discovers within himself "another" hidden
self, all the stronger for having been long repressed, and
whom the impulse of a moment may bring to light. "What
is the most unknown of all futures?" asks one of Saul's demons. "One that never comes," answers another.

In contrast with the concept of a linear predetermined development moving irrevocably from past to future, Gide created situations in which the future might always have been otherwise, one of many futures that, because of a decision made, "never come." For each of his characters there are in theory many possible futures. Gide conceived his plays as tracing the emergence of one particular future to the exclusion of the others. In each play there is a moment when the future hangs in the balance: just before Philoctetes drinks the potion; just before Saul refuses to follow Jonathan; just before Candaules decides to leave Gyges with Nyssia. There is, therefore, a Sartrean moment of decision before the final instant when an irrevocable act "manifests," as Gide would say, the hidden inner direction beneath an apparently coherent and stable personality. But the Gidian character is far more emotionally complex than the Sartrean and far more symbolical. Philoctetes's transformation is an interior one, even though it is revealed by a change in the décor of the play. In the palingenesis of Saul and Candaules, the undisclosed self appears in the symbolic guise of "another." Saul's guilty obsession with the future is really the regret for a past self, when young and handsome like David, he was beloved of God.[31] Candaules' generosity becomes the desire to risk all his possessions, leading him eventually to yearn for an austerity equal to that of Gyges.

Gide was unable to sustain his central theme and characters. His secondary characters tend to be weak and the action too slight to support such legendary figures as Saul and Philoctetes. Yet his first plays suggest many levels of interpretation and have the distinction of bringing to the theater new ideas, forms and psychological themes. "I meant, quite simply, to create a work of art," Gide wrote in 1904 in the preface to *Le Roi Candaule*. "But since, today, art no longer exists, and since, anyway, there is no longer anyone who understands it, I am obliged to bring to the fore the part played by ideas, precisely the part that in my eyes is not the most important, the one that must remain, I believe, in the service of beauty, but can serve beauty only if it is itself, first of all, perfectly solid and right." [32] More literary, certainly, than dramatic, and more involved with Gide's own development than with a real concern for the stage, Gide's three plays never really reached a public. *Candaules* alone was produced —unsuccessfully—at the time it was written, *Philoctetes* and *Saul* only many years later.[33] Gide's plays never influenced the French theater. Aside from their intrinsic interest, however, they prepared the way for the récit, or tale, the next form with which Gide was to experiment. Although Gide played with various forms of dramatic composition all his life, he was to write only one more major play, his *Oedipus*, published in 1931.

Chapter IX

Sorcerer's Apprentice:
The Immoralist

*Numquam hodie effugies; veniam
quocumque vocaris.*

You will never escape; wherever
you call me, I shall meet you.
—*Menalcas,* Vergil, *Eclogue* III
1-49

∿∿∿∿∿∿∿∿∿∿∿∿∿∿∿∿∿∿∿∿∿∿∿∿∿

The Immoralist, published in 1902, is a long short story.
According to Gide, he had had the book in mind as early as
1895, and had worked on it for at least two years, developing and transforming the form of the récit he had first experimented with in *Fruits of the Earth* in Menalcas' brief
story of his life, and at greater length in *El Hadj.* In theme
The Immoralist is very close to Gide's three plays. It traces
the emergence from a subconscious level of existence of a
new demanding personality which slowly circumvents, destroys and replaces the old.

This is Gide's first novel, if we discount his adolescent

124

André Walter. It takes the form of a letter and seems at first to rely on the conventional and rather awkward narrative device by which the story purports to be told by a witness—in this case a friend of the central figure. As a way of setting his story in motion, Gide uses another well-worn device, the adolescent pact:

> You know the schoolboy friendship that bound Michel, Denis, Daniel, and myself togther—a friendship strong even then but which every year grew stronger. Between the four of us a kind of pact was concluded: the slightest call from any one of us would be answered by the other three. So when I received that mysterious cry of alarm from Michel, I immediately informed Daniel and Denis, and all three of us, dropping everything else, set out.[1]

Four friends, we thus learn, are seated on a terrace in an isolated village in Kabylia. At nightfall Michel, the one who has called them together, tells the story his friend's letter supposedly reproduces word for word. The group plays no further role in the story. At this stage Gide's inexperience as novelist is obvious. He found it difficult to create a suitable background for Michel's long oral confession; the parallel with Job and his friends is fairly artificial. Yet, artificial though it is, some such introduction had to be found for Gide's story. From the very beginning he wanted the narrative to be read in a perspective other than Michel's own; the dismay the opening lines of the letter register suggests that the interest of Michel's story reaches beyond the narration of the events themselves and has implications which escape Michel himself. What, Michel's friend asks in the opening pages, can be done for Michel, and is there time to save him from disaster? "Michel is still capable of devotion. Yes, he still is. But soon he will be devoted only to himself."[2] The problem so enigmatically but insistently posed concerns Michel's present personality and future, rather than his past. Of this Michel himself is aware. The tale is a means and not an end, a desperate attempt at elucidation by which Michel hopes to reach an understanding of himself. He is really interrogating himself as well as his friends, and, through them, all the readers of the book:

The only help I ask is this—to talk to you. For I have reached a point in my life beyond which I cannot go. Not out of weariness though. But I can no longer understand. I need . . . I need to talk, I tell you. To know how to free oneself is nothing; the arduous thing is to know how to be free.[3]

Michel is, as it were, a Philoctetes, a Saul or a Candaules who has continued to live in inner incoherence and indecision bearing the weight of that "other" self within him. He has arrived at a dead end, as the circular movement of his narrative shows; the end goes right back to the beginning:

Take me away from here and give me some reason for being. I can find none. I have freed myself, quite possibly. But what does it matter? This useless freedom is a burden to me. It is not, believe me, that I am weary of my crime—if that is what you choose to call it—but I must prove to myself that I did not overstep my rights.[4]

Michel's "rights" to his "crime" pose a paradoxical moral question of judgment which each reader must answer for himself. With *The Immoralist* Gide calls upon the reader to give the novel its moral extensions. Far from being a novel of psychological analysis, as critics have often said, *The Immoralist* breaks abruptly with the techniques of psychological analysis. Michel describes facts and moods; he does not, he cannot explain them, hence the anguish he feels and his friends' dismay.

His story reveals a state of mind which is itself as thoroughly enigmatic as the tone he assumes throughout:

He finished his story without a quaver in his voice, without an inflection or a gesture to show that he was at all moved, either because he took a cynical pride in not showing his emotions, or because a kind of reserve made him unwilling to arouse our emotions by his tears, or again he may not in fact have been moved. Even now I cannot guess in what proportions pride, strength, reserve, and want of feeling were combined in him.[5]

The "strange feeling of uneasiness" into which Michel plunges his friends is accentuated when, at the end of his tragic story, Michel, the man without a purpose—who in his distress spends his time cooling his hands with pebbles soaking in water—suddenly speaks with heightened excitement of that young "rascal" Ali, his boyservant. A rather disturbing future seems to be opening up before him.

Once again, as with King Saul, Gide's own personal preoccupation with sexual inversion in those early years tends to limit and to mask the originality and force of his conception. All seems to lead merely to Ali, a disappointing end. Yet, until that end, Gide had succeeded in giving his subject much broader implications. Michel's real drama is not caused by his latent homosexuality, as Gide himself rightly pointed out:

If certain distinguished minds have wished to see in this drama nothing but the exposition of a curious case, and in its hero only a sick man; if they have failed to see that a few ideas of very urgent import and very general interest may nonetheless inhabit it—the fault lies neither in those ideas nor in that drama, but in the author—I mean in his lack of skill.[6]

Homosexuality is in fact only one among a number of Michel's hidden "demons." Michel is not the "immoralist" because he is a potential homosexual; but that potentiality is the hidden and dynamic force through which his immoralism is revealed. Each episode in Michel's evolution revolves around the figure of an adolescent: Bachir, Moktir, Charles, Heurtevent, Ali. Each of the boys corresponds to one of Michel's inner impulses that Michel does not immediately discern. Bachir represents health and joy; Moktir, freedom from the restraints of ethics; Charles, the pleasure of the orderly exploitation of one's resources; Heurtevent, the return to barbarism; Ali, pure sensuality. With a remarkable foreknowledge of the discoveries Freud was to make, Gide deliberately exploited in *The Immoralist* the ambiguities of his character's subconscious life and its equivocal power. The dynamic principle in Michel's evolution is latent and subconscious so that his life is rather like a game of chess played against a baffling, elusive partner, informed beforehand of all his moves and countermoves.

Michel's story covers about three years of his life, from the time of his marriage with Marceline in autumn to her death in the spring, three months before that month of July when his friends had come to join him. Three months of solitude have preceded his confession. "It all happened barely three months ago. Three months which stretch like three years between then and now." Michel's point of view is therefore more detached and more lucid than it would have been at the time of his wife's death. But the three months of solitude raise other questions. His story reveals that during the three years he lived with Marceline all his actions were controlled by forces of which he was unaware. What secret motivations may even now be shaping Michel's tale, unknown to himself and despite his apparent sincerity? Is the story itself merely another form of an inner psychological strategy, secretly aimed at justifying Michel's future in the making?

Michel's story begins with his marriage, at twenty-five, to a twenty-year-old childhood friend. Unfortunately, both Marceline and Michel seem old rather than young. For Michel, this is justified and an important factor in the story. Molded by the grave Huguenot teaching of a mother who died when he was fifteen, brought up by a learned father immersed in the study of the past, himself a historian, Michel had lived a hothouse existence: "And so I reached the age of twenty-five, having looked at nothing except books and ruins and knowing nothing of life." [7]

His marriage is a purely conventional affair. He is not in love with Marceline but marries her to keep a deathbed promise made to his father. There is, however, nothing in the novel itself to explain why twenty-year-old Marceline seems so wearily old, nothing except, as we shall see, certain connections between Michel's story and Gide's own experience.

Michel's tale moves through three stages corresponding to the three parts of the novel: the young couple leave for their honeymoon in Africa, where Michel almost dies of tuberculosis but recovers, and they return via Italy to their native Normandy. Michel apparently has moved from his initial indifference to his wife and life in general to a state of happy equilibrium. He and his wife love each other with deep tenderness. They look with confidence to the future. Michel holds a professorship at the Collège de France, a high academic honor. His wife is expecting a child. On their estate of La Morinière, Michel prepares his lectures and cultivates his lands. On the surface his life is the image of serenity, strength and productivity.

The second stage begins in the peaceful summer days at La Morinière and ends, about a year later with the complete destruction of all their hopes. Marceline loses her child and falls sick of tuberculosis; Michel resigns his chair at the Collège de France; La Morinière is put up for sale. "Everything in my life is falling to pieces!" Michel cries. In a desperate effort to recover their past happiness, Michel and Marceline start off toward the south.

The third part ends in disaster. With ever-increasing velocity Michel and Marceline journey back along the same paths they had taken for their honeymoon. But there will be no return. Marceline's illness serves Michel as pretext to drag her from Switzerland, to Italy, to Africa, ever farther south into the Sahara to the oasis of Touggourt where, completely worn out, Marceline dies and the violent impetus driving Michel turns into the dull distress and apathy described as the novel begins. Of the two main characters, Marceline is described only through Michel's eyes and she is dead before the novel starts. Yet *The Immoralist* is a novel of married life. With marriage, Michel became responsible for another life. Hence the question raised as to his "right" to his "liberation." How ill-prepared he was for his new responsibility is obvious. Although married, he had never really looked at his young wife:

> She was sitting in the bow; I approached, and for the first time really looked at her. . . . Up to then I had lived for myself alone, or at any rate in my own fashion. . . . And now at last I had just realized that the soliloquy had come to an end. . . . So she to whom I had attached my life had a real and individual life of her own! [8]

"I had lived for myself alone." Whatever the changes Michel undergoes, this is, in fact, the "unconscious support" of his personality. But he does not recognize his own monstrous egoism when it appears in the guise of sunny days, horseback rides or nocturnal poaching. Had Marceline's life not been involved in his, his blindness would have no visible consequences. But Marceline's death is a fact nothing can alter and one with which he must come to terms. Gide has given Michel the difficult task of unintentionally drawing his own moral profile and revealing flaws of which he himself is unaware yet which cause his disaster.

Michel's story really begins with his newly awakened interest in Marceline. For the first time his curiosity goes out toward someone else's life, toward life itself. His education, singularly Gidian, had inhibited his senses and his sexual experience; for many months his marriage had remained platonic. Impotence in Michel's case is only one of the consequences of the young intellectual's incuriosity for anything beyond his books. Suddenly, with his new freedom from scholarly pursuits, his senses begin to awaken; he is available to outside impressions. "Tunis surprised me greatly. At the touch of new sensations, certain portions of me awoke, sleeping faculties, which, never yet having been used, had kept all their mysterious youth." [9] Brutally, tuberculosis puts a stop to this first awakening. Michel is engulfed in sickness. Able for many days to discern only Marceline's face bent over him, he clings to her as to life itself: "I lost all knowledge of who or where I was. All I can see is Marceline, my wife, my life, bending over me." [10]

A little later Michel moves through the various stages of his convalescence with ever-intensified passion. Increasingly indifferent to his wife, he concentrates all his attention on the invisible healing forces at work inside him, and on the impressions, even the most tenuous, which his body is now beginning to register. To whet his interest in life and amuse him, Marceline brings home young Arab children, one of whom, Bachir, sets off the second stage in Michel's convalescence. No longer passive, Michel develops a violent hatred of disease, the inverted form of his now powerful desire to live: "I put myself in a fervent state of hostility." Systematically he fights his illness. The old Michel, formed by a grave Huguenot teaching, takes things in hand. He transforms his instinctive reaction into an ethic, a provisional ethic to be sure: "Evening was falling; I planned my strategy. For some time to come, my recovery was to be my only concern; my duty was my health; I must think good, I must call *right* everything that was salutary to me, forget everything that did not help to cure me." [11]

The immoralist has taken root in Michel. Associated with his illness, Marceline is hereby condemned, she who later so inconsiderately falls sick herself. Michel now tells of the devious ways by which his provisional ethic directs his life, long after it should have been discarded. He has committed himself intellectually and ethically to an experiment which carries him a good deal further than he ever thought possible.

From this point on, with a deliberate egotism, in his eyes justifiable, Michel encourages all the experiences which seem to increase his hold on life. Pleasure he experiences as beneficial, and sensuous pleasure is what he exclusively seeks: "I did not have enough strength to keep up a twofold life. . . . It seemed to me that up until now I had felt so little and thought so much that I was astonished by this fact: my sensations were becoming as strong as my thoughts." [12]

The convalescent begins to discover that in the past, unknown to himself, his senses although repressed had really led a latent and devious life. Here Gide's perspicacious point of view and Michel's separate. Because Michel discovers that the joys of the senses are legitimate and healing, and simultaneously that in his case they were latent and devious, he concludes that all latent and devious forces are as legitimate as they. He eagerly and secretly encourages the new ambiguous impulses he feels. In particular, when he sees Moktir stealing his wife's scissors, he feels elated. A latent and devious ethical revolt against all that Marceline represents is gathering strength inside him. A new Michel is in the making, one who, for a time, will transfer his new energies to his wife as the African spring surges in the oasis: "This African land, with whose expectations I was unfamiliar and which had lain submerged for many long days, was now awakening from winter, drunk with water, bursting with fresh sap; it was now laughing in the wild spring which found an echo in me, a double, as it were. . . . I turned the elation of my mind and senses toward Marceline." [13] Suddenly, on his last night in Africa, Michel is seized by a feeling of anguish, which, before Unamuno, he calls "a tragic sense of life." Never again will he rest as before in tranquil security. "Here, nothing seemed asleep; everything seemed dead. The calm appalled me; and suddenly there rose in me anew the tragic sense of my life; it came as though to protest, to assert itself, to be-wail itself in the silence, so violent, so agonizing almost, so impetuous, that if I could have I should have cried aloud like an animal." [14] Michel is fast becoming a new person. The ethic spelled out by the convalescent has now achieved its purpose, but Michel yields excitedly to its urgent suggestions.

Physically changed, he is also becoming a new man intel-lectually. Erudition, history and research first lose their mean-ing, then take on another. He rejects his own past self: "From then on I despised the secondary personality, the superficial, acquired, learned personality." Beneath it he begins to dis-cern another, which he considers authentic. He scrutinizes its every appearance as if it were some old palimpset or occult text. The sunbaths and physical exercises, a body "not yet robust but capable of becoming so—harmonious, sensuous, almost beautiful," are now no longer ends in themselves, but a means to an end as yet unknown but eagerly anticipated; like Saul, Michel shaves off his beard—a symbolic gesture:

When I felt my beard fall beneath his scissors, it was as though I had taken off a mask. No matter! When later I saw myself, the emotion that filled me, and which I repressed as best I could, was not pleasure, but fear. . . . I thought myself quite good-looking . . . no, the reason for my fear was that it seemed to me that my naked thoughts could now be seen, and they suddenly appeared to me redoubtable.[15]

Two men now live side by side in him. The first, the gentle intellectual Michel, held in contempt by the second, is the only one Marceline knows. To protect himself, Michel starts to dissemble: "So I showed her only an image of myself which, although it remained constant and faithful to the past, became falser and falser each day." Yet it seems for a while that the two selves may complement each other. One day when Michel sees his wife carried off in a runaway cab, he stops the horses and saves her life; at last, that same night, their marriage is consummated.

Normandy, where they next settle down, suggests to Michel a state of perfect equilibrium and complete harmony:

> From its ordered abundance, its joyous acceptance of service imposed, its smiling cultivated fields, a harmony emanated, dictated not by chance but by intention, a rhythm, a beauty, at once human and natural, in which one no longer knew what was more admirable, so perfectly combined were the teeming fecundity of nature and the wise effort of man to regulate it. . . . I imagined a code of ethics which became a science for the perfect utilization of one's self by one's controlling intelligence.[16]

Michel's new self, however, still continues restlessly to grow, now taking place in his mind more than in his acts, subconsciously shaping his new preference for the Goths rather than the Romans he had formerly admired. The destructive barbarity of the Goths now appears to him synonymous with a fresh unspoiled vitality, and their fifteen-year-old king Athalaric becomes a symbol of Michel's smoldering revolt: "surreptitiously excited by the Goths . . . balking at his Latin education, rejecting culture and . . . for several years enjoying a violent, voluptuous, and unrestrained life with rugged favorites of his own age."

In the second part of the novel Michel's new self comes more and more brutally into the open. He incarnates all that the former Michel had repressed, and with gleeful ferocity he now destroys everything that recalls Michel's old self: Michel's weakness, but also his scruples and humanity. "You like what is inhuman," is one of the last things Marceline says to her husband.

The period of incubation comes to a head with the help of a new character, Menalcas. Before he met Menalcas, Michel had, if we are to believe him, no real awareness of his new orientation: "What did I know of all that was growing up inside me, of all I am now telling you about? The future seemed to me assured and I had never thought myself more master of it." [17] In spite of the physical portrait Michel draws of him, Menalcas is the only truly enigmatic character in the book. An explorer, living alone, sophisticated yet austere in his tastes, he appears one day at one of Michel's lectures in Paris. It is he who disrupts the tenuous state of equilibrium in which Michel had been living. At first he appears to Michel in the guise of a tempter, then of a revealer. In his Normandy domains Michel had begun to give his "authentic self" full sway. He had become the accomplice of all the nocturnal, destructive, anarchistic forces around him, gleefully helping the poacher Heurtevent to poach on his own land. As Menalcas' influence grows, Marceline begins to waste away; she loses her child and falls sick, abandoned while her husband and Menalcas drink Cyprean wine and talk: "Disease had entered Marceline, and henceforth inhabited her, marked her, stained her. She was a thing that had been spoiled." [18] The authentic self now in command of Michel must destroy the "thing that had been spoiled," dragging Marceline relentlessly to her death. As she had before the night she lost her child, Marceline spends her last night of agony alone while her husband roams restlessly through the small alleys and cafés of Touggourt.

With the appearance of Menalcas, Michel's story raises a number of new questions. One of the most pressing, of course, is the relation of the novel to Gide's own experience. Gide himself admitted that *The Immoralist* was the last of the books into which he had introduced large segments of his life. It was also the first in which many of the recognizably autobiographical elements Gide had used in *Fruits of the Earth* are used objectively: his trips to Africa; his sickness and convalescence; the physical, intellectual and ethical palingenesis he experienced; his return, with his marriage, to the domesticated way of life; and even La Morinière, which

is very like La Roque Baignard, the country estate Gide himself inherited and which he later sold. In addition, Michel's
education, his marriage and honeymoon, and his occupations
as a landowner all recall Gide's own; just as the meeting with
Menalcas recalls Gide's acquaintance with Oscar Wilde.

But there are also marked differences between the fictional
Michel and his creator. Michel had never been a fervent
Christian like young Gide; unlike Gide, he had not been in
love for many years with Marceline; and tuberculosis never
played in Gide's life the determining role it played in Michel's. Gide sold La Roque Baignard simply because he and
his wife preferred to keep Cuverville, the Norman estate his
wife Madeleine had inherited and where she eventually spent
the greater part of her time. And Marceline, of course, can
hardly be considered as anything but the palest reflection of
Gide's wife. For Menalcas, Gide borrowed from Wilde the
"shameful lawsuit that had caused a scandal," along with certain of Wilde's sayings. But under the hardness of his mask,
the explorer Menalcas is a courageous and dedicated man
whom the government singles out for dangerous missions. In
this respect he has little in common with Wilde or with the
hedonistic Menalcas of *Fruits of the Earth.* The voluntary
self-destruction and weakness Gide had discerned in Wilde
is approximated much more closely in Michel. To consider
Menalcas merely as a symbol is impossible, for in some ways
he too recalls certain aspects of Gide, for example, the "in-
famous" habit of masturbation he had as a child.

Clearly, in spite of many changes, autobiography and fiction closely parallel each other in *The Immoralist.* The introduction Gide added some years later emphasizes his involvement in the book: "I present this book for what it is
worth. It is a fruit filled with bitter ashes; it is like those
colocynths of the desert that grow in a parched and burning
soil, and offer to your thirst only a still fiercer burn, but ly-

ing on the golden sand they are not without beauty." [19] "The author," he continues, "put into this book all his passion, all his tears and all his care." Certainly the book reveals Gide's very real concern about his own strange situation and his lucid appraisal of the subterfuges to which it led him. But Gide's emotion is shot through with literature and his real purpose is unequivocally expressed: "For the rest, I did not attempt to prove anything but only to paint my picture well and to set it in good light." [20]

However personal his materials, the only responsibility Gide acknowledges is his responsibility as an artist. The significance of the story is stated indirectly and ironically in the verse of the psalm Gide used as an epigraph: "I will praise thee; for I am fearfully and wonderfully made." Michel makes just such a discovery but in a bitterly ironic way. He is the sorcerer's apprentice who cannot control the creature he discovers and unleashes, and finds himself enslaved. A biblical verse, twice repeated, succinctly describes Michel's state as he speaks: "When thou wast young, thou girdedst thyself, and walkedst whither thou wouldest: but when thou shalt be old, thou shalt stretch forth thy hands . . ." Michel is stretching forth his hands.

The Immoralist focuses our attention on the illusions which, disguised as new and beneficial ideas, can raise havoc in certain lives. That no ethic is applicable to everyone, that every ethic requires self-discipline, is what Menalcas tries to convey to Michel, and not, as has been suggested, that he should engage in homosexual practices. The Socratic "know thyself" becomes imperative if Michel is to deal at all with the ruthless, devious forces of the subconscious. Menalcas sees the flaw in Michel's ethic of availability: "One must choose," he murmured. "The chief thing is to know what one wants. . . . Of the thousand forms of life, each of us can know but one." [21] For his part Menalcas has chosen one of these forms, accepting its limitations: "I will not say I like danger, but I like life to be hazardous, and I want it to require at every moment the whole of my courage, my happiness, my health." [22] Menalcas—Gide? Perhaps the man Gide would have liked to be. A true pre-Sartrean hero, Menalcas consciously assumes a mode of life that corresponds to his exigencies. A courageous outcast and adventurer, he warns Michel rather than perverts him. It is by contrast with him that Michel seems a mere sorcerer's apprentice. Michel does not choose, he is led.

That the most innocuous human being harbors disturbing forces within him is a pretty commonplace literary theme. But Gide handles it in a new way, with great originality, an originality long overlooked because of the ease with which simple Freudian interpretations were soon widely to be used in literature. By means of the first-person narrative Gide exposes to the reader not only the most commonplace, restricted and orderly surface of Michel's life, but he also delves into the strange and yet familiar depths it hides. Michel's fault, since fault there is, cannot be tied to any one of his acts or thoughts. His intentions, as he knew them, were good. Yet he is tricked by himself alone, the outcome of the story shows, ironically emphasizing as it does the discrepancy between the future he had projected and the future as it materialized.

Michel is an immoralist not because, indirectly, he has caused Marceline's death but because he has been too weak intellectually to comprehend the forces with which he was playing, too weak morally to make a choice. He never lucidly perceives the difference between what he wants to accomplish and what he actually is accomplishing: the destruction of his married life, his wife, his moral integrity. For three years he sought to free his life of disease, death, and restrictions. "Sometimes," he says at the end of his story, "I am afraid that what I have suppressed will take vengeance on me." [23] What he suppressed has already taken vengeance. All the things he thought he had conquered are heaped upon him with his sudden awakening after his wife's death.

The question raised in *The Immoralist* is, in fact, the existentialist question of responsibility and freedom. Over the three years, considered at any one point and arrested there, Michel's story could have had other overtones, taken other directions. Michel's own inner will, his Nietzschean identification with what he considers his authentic self, is the *fatum* that leads him to disaster. The question his friends raise is not the Christian question of remorse or atonement, but that of a new choice freely made. Can Michel rectify the course of his life by an act of will? Or has he definitely accepted being that other self?

A Gidian ethic is clearly delineated. Michel is an anti-Nietzschean, antiheroic character. Far from proposing a doctrine of availability, what Gide is now proposing is an attitude of careful scrutiny and self-awareness. Michel's blindness is his most dangerous characteristic. But Gide's point of view appears only indirectly through the carefully controlled development of his apparently objective story. *The Immoralist* is neither merely another psychological novel nor a simple fictional transposition of Gide's personal experience. It is constructed of a complex network of correspondences, all of which contribute to making the story of the colorless little professor something more than simply a special, supposedly real, case history. Michel leaves his native Normandy for Africa, a new, unknown land, just as he ventures to the borders of death when he is ill. He returns home, meets Menalcas and goes back to Africa, but this time far beyond Biskra to Touggourt, where the desert is king.

Marceline's strength waxes or wanes in harmony with the fluctuations of Michel's voyage. She is with him as a vague figure when he takes off for the unknown; she becomes a real person and a part of his own life as they make their way back; she blossoms in the fertile, happy, ordered peace of Normandy; she falls sick when Menalcas appears; and dies at last in the inhuman aridity of the desert, a symbolic destiny if ever there was one.

And what about Menalcas, who brings Michel the scissors stolen in Biskra, appearing unannounced exactly in the middle of the novel, soon disappearing just as completely? Michel, Marceline, Menalcas—a strange, divided trio. Only the power of Marceline's devotion or Menalcas' lucidity might have freed Michel from the monstrous egotism that was taking possession of him.

In retrospect, the small, separate incidents related by Michel, which hardly ruffle the outer surface of his life, also acquire symbolic value: the scissors stolen, the beard shaved. The second part of the novel opens with an apparently incidental description of ordinary events on a farm: the breaking in of a horse by Charles, the farmer's son. Brutally handled by rough and frightened peasants, the horse becomes increasingly dangerous. Gently and firmly guided by Charles, the horse is soon disciplined and Michel rides him when he goes out to survey his land. The symbolism is clear: the danger is not in the strength of the horse, but in the treatment it receives. In much the same way Michel cannot measure or govern certain forces in himself because they have been repressed rather than disciplined.

Given this underlying symbolism, the time factor itself is deftly introduced as one of the more baffling facets of Michel's experience: how can it happen that days successively lived, each with its own burden of happiness, illness, work and thought, finally add up to the vacant boredom of Michel? Time is the true artist in the book, slowly sculpting the figure of the immoralist. Gide uses time not merely as duration but to create an aesthetic dimension within which Michel's inner drive can be contained, fully revealing its creative and destructive powers. Gide's imagination works with this time dimension, molding an imaginary figure and an imaginary fate from the data he culls from life. Michel becomes a mythical character.

Detached from any specific period in time, the tale moves with rhythmical smoothness through three quasi-musical movements. The first and third are symmetrical: the themes introduced in the first reappear and are resolved with a marked change of tone in the third. Between them, the second movement intellectualizes the themes. As a whole, the novel slowly ascends, levels off, then rapidly descends again as the themes taper off. Later Gide, speaking of *The Counterfeiters*, mentioned his attempt at creating a kind of literary counterpart to the fugue. There is only one voice in *The Immoralist*, but the themes are developed on several levels—physical, intellectual, ethical, sentimental—and combined in intricate variations.

The term "new realism" [24] seems inadequate to describe Gide's novel. In "The Importance of the Audience" and "The Evolution of the Theater," two lectures almost contemporary with *The Immoralist*, Gide states his opinions on realism. All art, he said, has its roots in reality. But the label "realism" covers only what he would call "episodism," from which he would like to free both novel and theater. Style, he continues, conferring its generalizing force on a particular, concrete representation, is what can save art from episodism. The free play of art, if it is to recover its power of conviction and truth, must separate reality from fiction. The artist, whether playwright or novelist, must be willing to put out to sea. "I am reminded of the 'deep sea' of which Nietzsche speaks, of those unexplored regions of man, full of new dangers and surprises for the heroic navigator." [25] Pygmalion or Prometheus, the artist must fashion new and as yet unforeseen images of man. "Every turn of the wheel of history brings to light what before had lain invisible in the darkness. 'Time in its illimitable course,' says the Ajax of Sophocles, 'brings all hidden things to light and buries all that is manifest; and there is nothing which may not happen.' " [26] This power of the wheel of time to reveal what is hidden is what Gide attempted to make perceptible in *The Immoralist*, a masterly work.

In the récit Gide had found a definitive form from which to draw many a variation, modeling many "new," autonomous characters who, like Michel, "hold out their hands" to us. But Michel's story, with its contained sensuality, its rich notation of fleeting impressions, its luminosity and studied beauty, is still very close to Gide. In order to allow his characters their full independence, Gide would later studiously find for each his own range of expression, sacrificing thereby many of the stylistic effects which make *The Immoralist* so persuasive.

Gide was over thirty when he published *The Immoralist*. For ten years he had been experimenting, trying out various idioms. Now he had come into his own.

Chapter X

Of God and Man

*Je ne cherche à prouver la vic-
toire sur moi d'aucun dieu.*

I have not sought to prove the
victory of any god over myself.

~~~~~~

The Immoralist was finished in October, 1901. During the
next six years, until the fortnight in 1907 during which he
composed *The Return of the Prodigal Son,* Gide went
through one of what he called his periods of apathy. This
rather long-drawn-out depression is noted in the *Journal,* as
are his efforts to break away from it. Yet despite his restlessness and constant moving about, including a return visit to
North Africa in 1903, Gide managed to write a number of
things. *Amyntas,* which included a later essay on "Renouncing Travel," was published in 1906. Gide was simultaneously
describing his clandestine love for the dark-skinned Arab lad,
of whom he speaks under the Vergilian shepherd's name, and
indicating that he had now renounced his own vagabondage.
He wrote *Bathsheba,* worked on *Strait Is the Gate,* planned
a *Proserpine,* and, vaguely, a *Scylla* and began to toy with

ideas for his future character Lafcadio. His careful reading
of Dostoevsky and his critical articles prepare for the period
of heightened activity which opens with *The Return of the
Prodigal Son.*

Bathsheba,[1] a rather melancholy and quietly charming dramatic poem in three scenes, written in free verse and inspired
by the biblical story, recounts David's crime against Uriah,
a crime which brings him disgrace in the eyes of God. Here
Gide lyrically transposes the story of *The Immoralist:* David
seeks happiness, enjoys an illusory fulfillment, and then suffers the anguish caused by the realization of his crime against
Uriah. Like Saul, Gide's David is discovered in prayer before
the God who has abandoned him. A golden dove flutters
down, a sign, David thinks, from God, and he follows the
dove to "a little secret terrace that [he] didn't know," a
thinly veiled symbol. From the terrace the King's glance falls
upon a lovely woman bathing among the rushes. When he
goes a little later to reward Uriah the Hittite for his military
prowess, David discovers that the woman he saw bathing is
Bathsheba, Uriah's wife. As in the Bible, David commits the
crime of sending Uriah to certain death. But in Gide's version, David's is a purposeless crime for he never desired Bathsheba, a typically Gidian situation. So David remains with
his guilt, before his absent God. There are some eloquent,
moving lines in the play:

> But desire, Joab, desire enters the soul
> Like a hungry stranger.
> But now I ask God, Joab, what can man do
> If behind every one of his desires God is hidden?[2]

The play reveals a good deal of indecision in its treatment.
Why does David commit his crime? Because he follows the
dove? Because he envies Uriah's happiness? Because he has
strayed from God? The reader never really knows and Gide
himself seems uncertain. *Bathsheba,* however, anticipates the

form Gide was so successfully to use later for *The Return of
the Prodigal Son.*

Infinitely more interesting in theme and form is the unfinished sketch for *Proserpine.*³ Here again Gide anticipates,
this time certain techniques which Cocteau was later to use
in some of his early plays. Dance and mime become the essential elements of the production, considerably reducing the
text. And in the Gidian Elysian fields, whose inhabitants are
tortured by their imperfect acts and unfulfilled desires, there
is more than a touch of Sartre's *No Exit* hell. "The inhabitants of these subterranean places begin over again unceasingly
the imperfect actions of their lives. They know no torment
other than the vain pursuit . . . than the endless beginning
over again of desire."⁴

A projected *Ajax,*⁵ begun in 1904, also remained unfinished.
The Immoralist would seem to have temporarily exhausted
Gide's creative energy.

His life seemed to be settling down into the routines he
abominated; his work, with the exception of his critical essays, had attracted almost no attention. It would seem that,
having renounced travel, and outwardly normalized his own
life, Gide felt as if life were now eluding him. "It is most
often because of the absence of opposition that one doubts
the value of what one affirms. How can I firmly take my position without an adversary?"⁶ he wrote to Raymond Bonheur in 1901. The conversion to Catholicism of his friends
Francis Jammes, Paul Claudel, and others in his literary circle was soon to furnish Gide with the adversaries he needed.
A dramatic poem, *The Return of the Prodigal Son*; a récit,
Strait Is the Gate; and *Lafcadio's Adventures,* a sotie, were
part of his response to their debates about the Christian faith.
Gide was exploiting literary forms he had already tried out,
giving them more breadth. By now irony had replaced lyricism as the dominating feature of his work. Gide's adversary
was no longer within himself.

It has sometimes been suggested that Gide's relative sterility during this period was linked to a religious and moral
crisis, that he was attracted by the Catholic Church in spite
of himself. The two works he published in 1907 and 1909,
The Return of the Prodigal Son and *Strait Is the Gate*, the
first of Gide's works to reach more than a very limited public, both dealt with religious issues. And from 1905 on, when
it moved beyond the question of literature, Gide's correspondence with Claudel also touched principally on the question of conversion.

Yet during these years the *Journal* contains hardly a trace
of religious or moral anxiety. Much more striking is the caustic irony of Gide's comments on his two recently converted
Catholic friends, Claudel and Jammes. "In art there is nothing more disastrous than the notion of utility; one tends, imperceptibly, to put ideas to use and the free movement of
the mind is compromised," was his comment on their doctrinaire approach to literature.[7] "Religious certainty," he wrote
of Claudel, "gives his robust mind a deplorable fatuous-
ness."[8] And in answer to Jammes's claim that he felt in
Gide a divinely inspired anxiety, Gide wrote: "Perhaps I am
about to enter Paradise, but not through the door he thinks.
. . . I'm anxious whenever I can't work as much as I should
like."[9]

In reading Gide's correspondence with his friends one must
remember his need to find understanding, a need which sometimes led him temporarily to an intellectual mimicry of his
interlocutors. Nor should one forget the great pleasure Gide
found in following "the free movement of the mind," a joy
which, when it was a question of Christianity, depended a
lot on his exceptional familiarity with the biblical texts he
loved to quote. During these years he was also reading Pascal,
less for himself than with a view to enriching *Strait Is the
Gate* and the psychology of its heroine, Alissa. Gide notes
his admiration for Pascal's mind with a matter-of-factness

that in no way impedes his ability to reproduce in his novel the emotional and lyrical pathos of Pascal's style.

Gide's *Journal*, meanwhile, reflects his interest in the dubious adventures of a young friend named Gérard and in the genesis of his future picaro hero Lafcadio, far more than any concern with religious issues. Gide sometimes makes thinly veiled allusion to his clandestine adventures, with their complement of joy, satisfaction, fatigue or remorse; but his sexual life does not seem to torment him. His depression, physiological though it no doubt was, seems closely connected to his career as a writer. His *Journal* and the loose notes that accompany it are filled with literary projects he never carried through.

Gide seems to have experienced a new assault of the mental dispersion and void caused once before by his African voyage and which his *Saul* and *Michel* both experience. "I must struggle by every means against the breaking up and scattering of my thought," he wrote in his *Journal*, noting also "the disorder" [10] of his mind.

Recalcitrant from the very start, *Strait Is the Gate* caused him endless trouble. He continually had to make "an enormous effort to roll that mass a bit further forward," [11] and felt that his subject was "anachronistic amid everything we think, feel, and want today." [12] His anguish seems to derive from the apparent failure of his works. "There are days when I live as in the nightmare of a man walled up alive in his tomb," [13] he wrote of the silence surrounding them. Everything seemed to favor the abandonment of the work schedule he was always trying to set up: his health, his failure, the emptiness of his mind, his sense of the passing of time: "How late it is already! in the day and in my life." [14]

Up to *The Immoralist*, Gide had progressed in great leaps and bounds toward clearing the way for what he wanted to achieve as a writer. Enriched by his unflagging habit of reading, often aloud, and appraising what he read, he had developed his own stylistic principles. With the help of the classics he had gradually discarded the nebulous imagery and languid rhythms of neosymbolism. The classics taught him to think of language as an instrument and not as an end in itself. Henceforth his use of language was to be severely restrained, not through any lack of imagination but as the result of his conscious effort to create the exact effect he sought with the strictest minimum of expression. To use the gardening terms he liked so well, Gide felt an almost inhibitory need to prune and weed his language. Already at work in *The Immoralist*, this self-imposed discipline became a distressing obstacle to the writing of *Strait Is the Gate*.

The artist's task, according to Gide, consisted primarily in sifting and winnowing from the formless substance of life materials to be shaped into a harmonious form, reflecting a unique point of view. It was by carefully establishing the point of view, Gide felt, that the novelist could produce in his work a desirable and "powerful erosion of contours," a Nietzschean expression he often used. Gide's goal was to eliminate from the novel everything that was not implicitly needed to "inform" this organizing idea.

In his earlier works Gide had drawn from Greek or biblical legends to give substance to his thought. With the exception of André Walter, Michel was the first character to belong to the contemporary world. Although Alissa had originated in Gide's mind almost contemporaneously with Michel, *The Immoralist* for a while had seemed to monopolize Gide's thought. "I should like," he wrote in his *Journal*, "to take in hand all the causes of sterility that I discern so clearly, and strangle them all. I carefully and skillfully cultivated every negation in me. Now I must struggle against them; each one taken alone is easy enough to subdue, but rich in relationships, skillfully tied to another. They form a network from which I cannot escape." [15]

In *Prometheus Illbound* Gide had staked out the new

area he was to explore: the inevitable collision between man's moral exigencies and the ferocious amorality of the natural universe, with all its human consequences—tragic, comic or heroic. For a human being to insist on maintaining, against all natural evidence, an absolute fidelity to abstract ideals now appeared to Gide as one of the major forms of Promethean dupery. Admirable as this attitude might be ideally, it was absurd practically, besides being antivital. After *Philoctetes* Gide had, therefore, created only antiheroes. In the Gidian universe the effort to make oneself available to other potentialities in oneself is both a source of growth and a potential source of disaster. Besides, as is clear with *The Immoralist*, Gide felt that only on the stage could a single act be a solution to the problem of living out one's life. *The Immoralist* had brought into play the themes of the multiplicity of the self, of the power for both good and evil of subconscious drives within the ego, of the traps lying in wait beneath the most plausible forms of rationalization. Gide now was looking for new directions for his ever-alert mind to explore.

Contrary to what has sometimes been suggested, Gide was a demanding artist, averse to imitating himself, but *The Return of the Prodigal Son* was an exception; it raised no new aesthetic problems for him. It is, in fact, a "treatise" developed with all the artistic deftness Gide had perfected since writing such earlier treatises as *Urien's Voyage*. He had known the biblical parable by heart since childhood and he easily recaptured the grace and moving gravity of a childlike faith. Gide's version of the story is handled with the smiling tenderness often reserved for childhood memories. It is charming, a trifle self-conscious, and borders on sentimentality. After this last prose poem he was never again to draw on the Bible for a subject, and he returned to Greek myths only much later, in 1930, with his *Oedipus*. The parable of the prodigal son really concludes a literary period.

"I am composing a *Prodigal Son*," he wrote, "in which I am trying to make a dialogue of my spiritual reticences and impulses." [16] But the literary, rather than the religious, nature of his objective comes through clearly in this next sentence: "I was afraid, if I brooded over it any longer, of seeing the subject expand and lose its form; finally, I was tired of not writing any more, and all the other subjects that I had in mind presented too many difficulties to be treated immediately." [17]

Gide's concern with the execution of his theme was clearly uppermost in his mind. To tax him with hypocrisy in regard to the content of *The Prodigal Son* or to read into it a confession of anguish is to confuse the work and the workman, a thoroughly romantic misconception when applied to Gide, except in his very early works. The very tone of the writing is deliberately keyed to the biblical parable; its rhythm is consciously controlled so that the cadences of the language, the pauses, the slightly archaic simplicity of the vocabulary all suggest the same emotional, gravely religious mood. The opening sentence sets the mood, the tonality of the whole: "I have painted here, for my own secret joy, as was done in ancient triptychs—the parable told to us by our Lord Jesus Christ." [18] By analogy with the medieval triptych, the author appears "kneeling, a companion piece to the prodigal son, like him, smiling and with a tearstained face." Gide suggests that he himself is the donor-artist, but certainly not that he is either a damned and tormented soul or the prodigal son himself, yearning to be admitted once more into the Father's House. Reverential as Gide's literary pose may be, his point of view is not in the least evangelical.

The story is conceived as a series of dramatic tableaux: the prodigal's return; his successive dialogues with his father, mother, elder brother and nonbiblical, strictly Gidian younger brother; concluding with the younger brother's departure at dawn. Rather than as a painting, however, Gide develops his story as a musical composition. The theme is introduced with the prodigal's return; then the four dialogues develop, each a variation on the theme; and finally the opposing voices disappear as the motif of departure triumphs, giving the biblical parable its Gidian overtones.

Gide first recounts the story almost exactly as the Bible tells it, but with new modulations:

> When after a long absence, weary of his passing moods and as it were tired of himself, the prodigal son, from the depths of the destitution he was seeking, thinks of his father's face, of the not narrow room where, over his bed, his mother would lean, of the garden gorged with running water and from which he always longed to escape, of the thrifty elder brother he never loved but who still holds in trust for him that part of his estate that he, the prodigal, was not able to squander—the son admits that he has not found happiness nor been able to prolong the kind of exaltation that, in lieu of happiness, he had sought.

A single sentence unfolds, introducing in its long, sensuous, circuitous development all the images connected with the underlying Gidian themes: the urge amid abundance to taste of dearth; the imprisoning security of an enclosed garden from which one seeks escape; the ecstatic joy of escape itself; the death of ecstasy and happiness; the lost heritage which beckons in the starkness of destitution; weariness, remorse and return. The successive dialogues each pick up and develop these themes from different points of view.

Certainly Gide's discussions with Claudel and Jammes are intimately connected with the genesis of his story. But in Gide's parable the Father's House does not necessarily represent the Church, whether Catholic or Protestant, any more than for Kafka the "law" necessarily designates Jewish orthodoxy. "I have not sought," Gide said in his preface, "to prove the victory of any god over myself." The small "g" is telling in relation to the capital "H" of House. The House suggests all the institutionalized forms of belief, whatever they may be, in which men enclose themselves so as to live in security without once looking beyond at the unknown.

The master of the House, as Gide conceives it, is in fact the eldest son, pompous and limited, who takes interest only in the orderly administration of his heritage. The Father is an ambiguous, elusive figure; he does not deny the reality of the desert nor its challenge. To him the House is a fitting refuge for the weak. It is he who puts the ring on the finger of the prodigal, a token of esteem. The mother is all love. For her the House is the place where solitude ends and human love flourishes. It is she who brings the younger brother to the prodigal's attention. Because of her, and yet despite her, the prodigal wins out, transmitting his own desire to the young boy. While the House for the two elder sons is a refuge or inheritance, duty or love for one's elders, for the lad it is an unbearable restraint which he must eventually reject.

What Gide suggests as the parable progresses, unwinding the reticences of his thought, is that one must consent to venture forth alone. However secure the House, there will always be a prodigal son who must taste the acorns in the desert—to the Father's not too great displeasure. If the prodigal's return is a defeat, it was Gide's only temporarily. From within his own House, the Norman estate and traditions he had inherited, Gide was dreaming of caravans. Lafcadio was taking shape in his imagination and not far away was *Corydon*, the avowal and justification of his form of sexual inversion. Rest was not what Gide craved; he felt no need for a god of any kind.

"We were born for a happiness other than this" and "However blessed it might be, I cannot desire a state without progress,"[19] says Alissa, the heroine of *Strait Is the Gate*. With Alissa's adventure Gide traces one of those inner spiritual odysseys which *The Immoralist* had announced. But, whereas the adventure in *The Immoralist* primarily raises questions concerning the mutations of the self, *Strait Is the Gate* primarily poses the question of the nature of happiness, a secondary theme in the first récit. That "men die and are not happy" is a problem Gide considered long before Camus's *Caligula.* In her quest for the absolute ideal fulfillment that she desires, Alissa follows a single direction. What is important is less that her ideal is derived from a Christian, Protestant faith than its genuinely religious dimension. Alissa is a prodigal who ventures out alone toward a definite, high-minded goal, an ideal goal. She never turns back. It was perhaps her adventure, with which Gide was wrestling and which was giving him so much difficulty, that suggested to him as a kind of healthy corrective the tale of the prodigal who makes his way back. Alissa recalls the Prince in *El Hadj,* who dies of exhaustion at the edge of what he suspects and fears, perhaps even knows, is nothing but illusion. The false prophet who undertakes to lead Alissa on is Gide himself, who, unlike the prophet in *El Hadj,* knows just where she is headed.

The story of Alissa had taken shape slowly in Gide's mind. Originally it was connected with the death of Anna Shackleton, his mother's pious English governess and lifelong friend. Gide's first subtitle for it was "Essai de bien mourir"—the attempt to die well. *Strait Is the Gate*'s close thematic connection with *The Immoralist* is something Gide remarked upon. Rather irritated by the assumption that *Strait Is the Gate* indicated an evolution in his religious attitudes, he made a special point of clarifying that attitude in notes for a preface that he jotted down some years later.[20] While writing the story of Alissa and Jerome he had felt that its emphasis was anachronistic, in the sense that it was unconnected with his current state of mind, but still that he must write it.

Gide borrowed much of the material for his novel from his own life. The Protestant milieu of his and his wife's childhood, as well as her home at Cuverville, Fongueusemare in the story, and the whole, very recognizable atmosphere of Sunday sermons, Bible readings, family prayers. Quite blatantly, too, Gide made use of intimate family situations involving his own wife: her mother's untoward conduct, deeply scandalous in the pious middle-class home to which she belonged, and his own long-drawn-out courtship of Madeleine. With surprising detachment Gide reread the youthful letters he had written Madeleine, as though they were interesting documents which he could put to good literary use. Certainly he was fascinated by his own enigmatic marital situation. *Strait Is the Gate,* following *André Walter,* prepared the way for *If it die . . . ,* and finally the scrupulous yet incomplete account of *Et nunc manet in te (Madeleine).* If in the early 1900's, when Alissa was taking shape in Gide's imagination, Madeleine Gide seemed in some respects still very different from her, the fact that twenty years later she closely resembled Gide's heroine casts a rather disturbing light on Gide's awareness of the life he was imposing upon the woman who was his wife, and whom he so deeply loved.

Strait Is the Gate uses, with some modifications, the form of the récit evolved in *The Immoralist.* Ten years after Alissa's death, Jerome attempts to relate or reconstruct their story. Gide disappears entirely behind Jerome, the first-person narrator: "Some others might have made a book out of it; but the story I am about to tell required all my strength to live it, and all my virtue was spent in the living. So I shall write down my recollections very simply." [21] But to illuminate the story further Gide holds in store for the reader a rather artificial surprise. Jerome's narrative is followed by excerpts from a diary Alissa had written years before, which introduces new perspectives and raises questions of interpretation. Since Jerome presumably has had the diary in his possession for some time, why has he disregarded it in giving his own version of the story? How too, one wonders, would a young woman, even the most Gidian, dying alone in anguish still have the strength to keep a diary? Gide plays the literary game carefully, even subtly. What he wants to achieve is not so much a completely logical framework for the novel as the sense that his characters are completely autonomous and that there is no author acting as an intermediary between them and the reader. Yet, more than is the case with Michel, Jerome and Alissa seem never quite to escape from the control of their creator. They lack a certain vitality and complexity of their own.

In this novel, for the first time and with the strictest economy of literary means, Gide succeeds in portraying a particular social group—the upper middle-class French bourgeoisie. This genuine though limited world is brought into focus without any background description; Gide has no need of such lengthy developments to justify the actions of the two protagonists. Three families appear, Jerome's and his cousins', the Bucolins and the Plantiers. The clan has certain ramifications; in the Protestant area of Languedoc in southern France there is a future Bucolin son-in-law, Monsieur Tessières, who divides his time between Nîmes and Aigues-Vives; there is an inevitable famille de pasteur; and the family life at Fongueusemare where the clan gathers in summer is pretty accurately described: the outdoor games, the hours of reading, the emphasis put on worship, the moral idyllicism and austerity which Gide later was to describe ironically as Alpine.

From the very beginning one senses within this rarefied atmosphere a disturbing element in the person of the one outsider in the Bucolin clan, Lucile Bucolin, Jerome's aunt, a Creole from Martinique. Although she disappears almost immediately, indirectly Lucile continues to affect the future fate of Jerome and Alissa. In the first few pages, with almost imperceptible suggestions, Gide establishes a network of family ties and situations. Jerome is very much like his scholarly father. Alissa's sister, Juliette, who falls in love with Jerome, is the image of her aunt Plantier. Alissa is very much like Jerome's own mother and yet resembles the wanton Lucile. Jerome's predicament of being loved by both Alissa and Juliette, mirrors that of his father who once hesitated between Aunt Plantier and the woman he eventually married. At the very end one wonders if, in one form or another, the story may not be re-enacted again by a new Alissa, the heroine's niece.

Within this tight family circle the Bucolins do harbor a stranger whose indolent Creole sensuality is sharply censured. One of Jerome's earliest recollections is connected with a disturbing caress from his aunt that "turned into pure hatred the complex and uncertain feeling [he] had previously felt toward Lucile Bucolin." Almost immediately after this recollection, Jerome unwittingly remarks of Alissa: "No doubt she was very like her mother." And much later, recalling one of the climactic encounters with Alissa, he remembers her father's words to his daughter: ". . . when I came into the drawing-room and saw you lying on the sofa, I thought for a moment it was your mother." Lucile Bucolin stands between Jerome and Alissa. Her illicit love affair and her departure with her lover, followed the next Sunday by the pastor's sermon on the "strait gate," are still indelibly engraved in Jerome's mind many years later. By now the biblical image has taken on a very personal symbolism: the "wide gate" has become the open door through which he had caught sight of his aunt's lover bending over her as she lay on the sofa, the wide gate of perdition, carnal love. Jerome's childish hate for his aunt and his suspicion of all sensual desire or pleasure make him powerless truly to reach Alissa. Juliette senses this when, disturbed by the procrastinations of the young couple, she says: "It isn't Alissa that I distrust." Alissa herself writes in a flash of insight: "Poor Jerome! If only he knew that sometimes he would have only a gesture to make, a gesture for which sometimes I wait." [22] But as a child Jerome once and for all had equated the strait gate, the strait and narrow path, with the closed door of Alissa's room. Both Jerome in his narrative and Alissa in her diary seem to be obsessed by Lucile and the pain her actions have caused, to Alissa herself and to Alissa's father. "To tell you the truth," says Jerome's friend Abel at one point, "there's something I don't understand in your story." Perhaps it is simply the invisible wall of repression separating the two lovers since they witnessed Lucile's disgrace.

In this sense *Strait Is the Gate* is a story of frustrated love. In showing the origin of an unconscious inhibition in the emotional reactions of two children for whom the idea of sensual love is fraught with guilt and remorse, Gide brought something quite new to the novel. It is Jerome's consequent passiveness—his "flabbiness," as Gide called it—that eventually obliges the equally inhibited but more passionate Alissa to find some other outlet for her deep capacity to love. What she does is to find a devious path by which she can both believe in Jerome's love and accumulate plausible reasons why it cannot materialize. For a while the removal of each obstacle offers immediate goals, keeping alive in the couple the illusion that in the future they may achieve happiness. This mechanism of perpetual deferment projects Alissa in spite of herself ever farther along a dangerous and solitary path. What both Jerome and Alissa attempt to deny is that part of Alissa which she inherited from her mother, and as with Michel, it is that repressed part that takes its revenge.

Alissa's sister, Juliette, on the other hand, by marrying Tessières, a man of "a different class, a different world, a different race," finds a form of earthbound happiness, limited but real. The novel suggests that the stranger when accepted can be a source of strength. "The roots of every plant," wrote Gide in his *Journal*, "distill a poison for plants of the same species." An argument Gide used against Barrès's doctrine of "enracinement"—an ethic of absolute fidelity to one's origins —it also clarifies perhaps Gide's own position with regard to the Bucolins.

Two highly significant images, with their descriptive and symbolic variations, are woven into the very fabric of the novel: the door and the garden. The door—open, closed, partly open, locked, and finally, but too late, wide open— is always a real door at Fongueusemare with its counterpart in the garden of Cuverville, but it always suggests an ambiguous and manifold symbolism, whether Christian, Freudian, ethical or ironic. Alissa's garden with its seasonal cycles is always the backdrop for the lovers' meetings; they cannot move beyond its confines. At the end of the novel, when Jerome makes his last, almost clandestine trip to Fongueusemare, the once-familiar garden has become hostile; the dog barks at the stranger Jerome has become and the gardener is unknown to him.

Another image also has symbolic overtones: Alissa's room in its increasing bareness reflects the inner barrenness of her life, until, in the end, she dies shut away from all she loves, in the frightening sterile atmosphere of a hospital. The Fongueusemare house, once so gay and full of life, is finally empty and silent, about to be sold to strangers.

The subtle symbolic suggestions and leitmotifs Gide wove into Jerome's apparently drab and factual story give it that extra, timeless dimension Gide considered indispensable if a novel was to be a work of art and not merely an episodic case history. Yet in seeking as he did for this particular novel the greatest restraint and purity of line, he eliminated both spontaneity and richness in his characters. He worked many long hours on the first pages of *Strait Is the Gate*, which are "as full as an egg," according to the expression he used in *Marshlands*. As a result, the fiction of Jerome as an autonomous character is not entirely convincing. Gide rather obviously directs his pen. Jerome and Alissa have real charm, but the charm of two-dimensional characters in tapestries where background and human figures blend in harmonious decorative motifs. The two lovers seem timeless and ageless; like their love, their story is static, as indeed Gide meant it to be. Only Alissa, motionless, follows her own inner, apparently self-chosen fate.

At first, like most lovers, Jerome and Alissa seem to confront only normal obstacles. Jerome is younger than Alissa; Alissa's father needs her; they are cousins. But chapter two begins to throw light on the new depths of the psyches Gide is probing. Deeply impressed by the pastor's sermon, frightened of their own feelings, the two adolescents begin to sublimate their love. These "subtle feints" of love, unrecognized, lead the fervent adolescents far astray.

Jerome, quite simply, associates love and virtue: "I sought in the future not so much happiness as the infinite effort to attain it and already confused happiness with virtue." [23] To deserve Alissa becomes the object of his life: "I never sought more directly to possess her whom, as a child, I hoped only to deserve." [24]

Alissa's rationalizations are more complicated, as appears in a conversation with her father that Jerome overhears, remembers, but never bothers to probe further. She has idealized Jerome. For her, he is a man destined to "become very remarkable in the eyes of God," a man whom she must help and encourage in this task. Their love is free to develop but only in the guise of the most idealistic form of selfless devotion: ". . . what we called 'thought' was often only a pretext for some more subtle communion, only a disguise for our feelings, only a mask for love." To refuse Jerome for his own sake, for the perfection of his soul, is the form of sacrifice which Alissa unconsciously comes to associate with the highest form of love she can give him. The path of sacrifice has great appeal: she dreams of sacrificing herself for Juliette, for her father, for Jerome. But Juliette has no need of her sister's sacrifice, their father dies, and Jerome does not become "very remarkable" in anyone's eyes.

At the beginning of chapter five, exactly in the middle of the novel, the love of Jerome and Alissa seems at last to move toward fulfillment. Juliette is reasonably happily married and has left Fongueusemare; Jerome is traveling in Italy at Alissa's request, while at her father's side Alissa lives vicariously through her correspondence with Jerome, often echoing his thoughts but with a passion quite her own. Her heart is filled with inexpressible love. "Whenever I think of you my heart fills with hope," she declares, "my heart melts with joy as I read you." She writes of desiring Jerome's presence "with such violence that perhaps you felt it." [25] All her senses are alive with expectation.

"When I came in, I was excited rather than tired, intoxicated with sun and joy. How beautiful the haystacks were in the burning sun." [26] But she speaks also of "divine glory." Her love for Jerome, joy, and the road to heaven are one and the same thing for Alissa at this stage.

Having reached this center and focal point, the whole story shifts and begins to move in new and disturbing directions. For the first and only time in her life, Alissa ventures outside Fongueusemare to visit Juliette in the relaxed atmosphere and sunny sensuous climate of a Languedoc more disturbing to Alissa than even Menalcas was to Michel. For the first time she glimpses another form of happiness, one stemming from the acceptance, not the refusal of natural feeling. "Ah!" she notes, "how what people call 'happiness' seems familiar to the soul." [27] But, having staked her all on reaching a heroic, difficult goal, Alissa despises the very ease of this kind of contentment: "Because of what selfishness, conceit, lack of hunger for improvement does all development so soon come to a stop, making every creature accept definitive limitations when still so far from God?" [28] She writes troubled and pressing letters to Jerome, her health begins to fail. "I feel my past comes to an end here," she writes, "I see nothing beyond."

Beyond comes disaster. Alissa is now going to try to achieve alone that "other happiness" promised by the gospel, since, clearly, Jerome will never give her the earthbound joys for which Juliette has settled. *"Hic incipit amor Dei,"* [29] she writes. Alissa now thinks of Jerome's love as an obstacle on her road to saintliness, a new subterfuge to persuade herself of its existence. Blindly pursuing her own heroic self-destruction, baffled by all that escapes her, Alissa becomes the most moving of all Gide's creatures, perhaps in fact the only truly moving character he created.

Strait Is the Gate is not a novel about a mystical faith, nor is it even a religious novel. Jerome and Alissa are moved by physiological and psychological forces, by their feelings, thought and imagination, but certainly not by faith. "All heroism," says Jerome, "attracted and dazzled me. . . . Any path, provided it climbed upward, would lead me to her." And Alissa's attempt to reach holiness is a desperate gamble to achieve by sheer force of will the happiness that eludes her in her relationship with Jerome. Hence the ambiguous sense of her echoing words: "Holiness is not a choice; it is an *obligation*," [30] and her final, bitter defeat.

Gide denied his heroine the certainty of faith. "It is through natural nobility and not hope of reward," she says, Protestant Jansenist that she is, "that the soul that loves God steeps itself in virtue." But Alissa loves Jerome and not God, hence the speciousness of her case. What she holds fast to is the heroism which fascinates Jerome. This is why the Pascal-inspired pages of Alissa's journal (of which Gide was so proud) have no value as the record of an authentic religious experience. Gide's point of view, however veiled, is unmistakable. His aim, he said, had been to portray a Protestant exaggeration, therefore a deformation of the Christian ideal. But his novel suggests that this exaggeration is a gratuitous substitution by which even so scrupulous a person as his Alissa seeks to compensate for an incapacity to find happiness in life. It is a compensation for the lack of humanity and brings no fulfillment.

Yet Gide succeeds in leaving somewhat unresolved the final answer to Alissa's fate. The last lines of her diary picture her on her knees, alone, anguished, feeling not a trace of the joy she had sought, crying to God, who may, at last, have answered her. But on this earth the other happiness which Alissa had hoped to attain has dissolved into anguish and death. She is the victim of those destructive elements that Gide felt were inherent in all absolute Promethean idealisms.

Chapter XI

Transition 1910-1914

*J'aime aussi que chaque livre
porte en lui, mais cachée, sa propre
réfutation.*

I also like each book to carry
within itself, but concealed, its own
refutation.

~~~~~~

Isabelle (1911) [1] has little in common with Gide's two previous récits or with the poem-parable of *The Return of the
Prodigal Son.* His outlook and mood were once again changing. *Strait Is the Gate* had been a success, not only in France
but in England, where Sir Edmund Gosse had given it high
praise. Though erstwhile friends like Jammes and Claudel
now tended to attack him, Gide no longer felt isolated. He
had around him a solid group of more than ordinarily talented men who were to remain his friends to the end of his
life: Jacques Copeau, drama critic and future founder of
the Théâtre du Vieux Colombier which was to rejuvenate
the French theater, and the novelists Roger Martin du Gard
and Jean Schlumberger, among others. The successful launch-

ing of the *Nouvelle Revue Française* (N.R.F.) in 1909, after a first stormy attempt in 1908, also contributed to his new sense of achievement.

Gide was no longer feeling his way. With *The Prodigal Son* he had taken his position firmly, and extricated himself from the none too discreet attempts made by Claudel and the recently converted (1905) Jammes to bring him into the Catholic Church. His *Journal* mentions the Christian problem only sporadically and quite unemotionally. "I can still not bring myself to hurt his feelings," he says of Claudel, "but as my thought becomes more affirmative, it gives offense to his." [2] Noting "the pitiful bankruptcy of Christianity," [3] he summarizes briefly the point of view which was now definitively to be his: "My Christianity springs only from Christ." [4] He jots down the project of an essay on "Christianity against Christ," a first draft of his future *Numquid et tu . . .* , certainly the least religious of books. Articles like his "Nationalism and Literature," for example, published in the young N.R.F., reflect a quiet self-assurance, and in the years between 1909 and 1912 his *Journal* is often gay, animated by a new vitality. Temporarily at least, Gide had obviously achieved an inner equilibrium.

With his usual fervor Gide plunged into the writing of *Corydon*, an essay on homosexuality. Not that the question was troubling him deeply: "I must artificially revive a problem to which I have found (as far as I am concerned) a practical solution so that, to tell the truth, it no longer bothers me . . . (Likewise for *Strait Is the Gate . . .*)." [5] Only the shocked reactions of his friends stopped him from pressing further with his *Corydon* which, nonetheless, was printed in 1911, though in a strictly limited edition. For Gide, *Corydon* was not a confession but a testimony, an attempt to bring out into the open for frank appraisal the drastic results which can stem from the repression of certain latent, unrecognized tendencies. Such a disaster had occurred with Oscar Wilde, whose fate had deeply affected Gide as a young man. In 1907 and 1908 the question was raised again when a series of scandals and highly publicized trials in Berlin ended in disaster for such well-known figures as Prince Philip von Eulenburg, a friend of the Emperor's. Gide began his *Corydon* around 1908, at a time when the topic of homosexuality inspired a flurry of publication.

But Gide's activity during this period of transition reflects rather his often amused curiosity toward new aspects of life, his eagerness to partake in them. He made a number of journeys, visits with friends or at the abbey of Pontigny where the intelligentsia of Europe now met yearly for open discussions on varied topics. He published vigorous articles and made extensive reading notes, enjoying in particular a renewed interest in Darwin and the French entomologist Fabre. In 1912 he served as a member of the jury in the criminal trials of the Assize Court of Rouen, from which he drew his *Recollections of the Assize Court* (1914). There are, to be sure, particularly around 1912, brief "periods of lack of interest." [6] But it took the war of 1914, for which Gide, like the great majority of his fellow citizens, was totally unprepared, to plunge him once more into real anxiety. More than ever he thought of himself as a man of letters, one who, as he wrote, is concerned "only with his art (and I was about to say his craft)."

Once again, as during his early years, Gide treats mainly of literature in his *Journal*, "Propositions" and "Detached Pages." It has often been said that Gide gave the N.R.F. its orientation. It is quite clear, however, that he too benefited greatly from his contacts with the many writers the N.R.F. attracted. Left to himself, Gide might very well have remained unaware of the revolutionary trends in art rapidly developing in Paris around 1910. In his *Journal* he hardly mentions the cubists. Of the poet Apollinaire, the impresario of the avant-garde, whom he mentions only once, he merely notes: "Very much amused and attracted by the personality of Apollinaire." [7] Nor does he seem at all interested by the avant-garde experiments in music. He was no longer, as he had been in the 1890's, a member of an impatient literary avant-garde. But as he came into contact with the younger N.R.F. writers—Valery Larbaud, the future translator of Joyce, more brilliantly cosmopolitan in his tastes even than Gide; Jules Romains, the then vigorous young promoter of "unanimism"; and the charming and versatile Jean Giraudoux—Gide too felt the need for renewal. "Break with certain habits of writing," he noted, "and since this particular notebook happens to be filled, begin another in which I shall get into training, in which I shall cultivate *new relations.* Avoid living off my own terrain." [8]

As early as 1905, while working on *Strait Is the Gate*, Gide had been sensitive to the lack of volume of his writing. "The lack of volume in everything I write bothers me, but what can I do about it? My fierce hostility toward prolixity, rhetoric and eloquence explains it." [9] Around 1912 or 1913 this concern grew, as several projects for prefaces—left unpublished—show.[10] Gide now christens as récits the novels he had previously written and puts back into circulation the medieval term "sotie," not merely for his new novel *Lafcadio's Adventures* but retrospectively for *Marshlands* and *Prometheus Illbound.* Clearly he is still in search of a medium and detached enough from his work to appraise it critically in order to clarify, if only for himself, the directions in which he is moving as a novelist.

Yet he seemed to feel the need concurrently to reiterate the principles of his art as he understood them,[11] art, outside of which he notes that "I am unable to find a reason for living." [12] Attacking the Protestant spirit which requires "a meaning, a lesson, and some usefulness" in art, he insists upon the "gratuity of a work of art" which "a certain public, stumbling over the choice of subject" fails to recognize, "as if the choice of subject had ever been important." [13] He reformulates a point of view inspired by Mallarmé: "The work of an artist fully interests me only if I feel it both in direct and sincere relation with the outer world, and in intimate and secret relation with its author." [14] But, although he insistently points out that what he wants to achieve is a complete transparency in writing, and that the clarity of a work may mask its profundity just as successfully as might an apparent obscurity, Gide seems to have some misgivings as to the validity of his point of view: "Perhaps, after all, my belief in the work of art and the cult that I make of it prevent that perfect sincerity which I henceforth demand of myself. What interest have I in limpidity when it is nothing but a quality of style?" [15] Both in his *Journal* and in his projects for the prefaces to his works, he mentions certain limitations he feels and the fear that all his work heretofore has been only "ironical—or critical."

"It sometimes seems to me that I have not yet written anything serious; that I have presented my thought only in an ironic manner," [16] and again: "It seems to me that all I have written up to now has been only a curtain-raiser before the *real* show begins." [17]

Both *The Immoralist* and *Strait Is the Gate* had developed forms of the first-person narrative that raise questions of interpretation and demonstrate the relativity of point of view. The central narrative in the récit is "reflection," in the double sense of the term, the mirroring in a mind of a succession of events which take on meaning only through the awareness of the character, his manner of singling facts out and relating them to each other. Behind the character lurks Gide, whose own purpose fashions or, as he would say, informs the work. Seen from outside by a noninvolved spectator, Michel's story or Alissa's would seem singularly devoid of interest. The tragic emotional repercussions, the human content of each of the stories in its moving truth, escape analysis and are transmitted to the reader through image, tempo and rhythm. The intimate and secret relation between the narrator and the story is the real topic Gide explored. He was moving, though independently, in the wake of Henry James.

More complex in structure than *The Immoralist, Strait Is the Gate* suggests several points of view or secret relations: Jerome and Alissa's of course, but also Juliette and Aunt Plantier's, besides a few fragmentary glimpses of the reactions of minor characters. In *Strait Is the Gate* Gide introduced problems of time left untackled in *The Immoralist*: Jerome's story, in that it is, like Michel's, carefully thought out and presented retrospectively in logical sequence, is a kind of fiction when contrasted with the fragmentary snatches of Alissa's *Journal*, alive with the conflicting and fluctuating emotions of the present. Here the nature of "fiction"—the ambiguity inherent in any attempt at ordering or comprehending events—merely suggested in *The Immoralist*, is more clearly emphasized. But the basic point of view behind both works remains unchanged. Gide's characters, present-day counterparts of the shadowy Menalcas and Tityrus, experiment with ethical ideas which they apply to their own lives and carry to their extreme limits. At first this brings them an exhilarating sense of development and conquest; later they reach a kind of plateau where the ascending movement stops and the exhilaration gives way to a vague feeling of danger. The idea then begins to control them, fixing their line of conduct, shutting them away from life until it destroys them, and Gide brings the reader, puzzled and questioning, back to everyday circumstances. Neither tale ends, each is merely an episode within a complex web of relationships. As in the case of *El Hadj*, the adventure may start all over again. Michel's ethic and Alissa's are diametrically opposed but equally self-destructive.

Clearly Gide is not expressing any one thesis, but far more generally his own complex feeling that we live through ideas, but that ideas in turn can kill us and that when they tend to become all-encompassing they must be discarded. Hence the critical or ironic mood of these tales which contain their own refutation. Hence, too, the typically Gidian movement of the stories, which progress like a musical composition, through an initial allegro presenting the main themes, thence into an andante in which theme and countertheme are opposed, ending with a final movement where the initial theme disintegrates.

Fascinating though they are, Gide's tales have obvious limitations, which Gide's next work *Isabelle* (1911)—a "semiplayful interlude" between the serious *Strait Is the Gate* and *Lafcadio's Adventures*—makes fun of, just as *Marshlands* had made fun of Gide's symbolist ventures.

Isabelle is a first-person narrative, told by a young historian and would-be novelist, Gérard Lacase. Gide starts off the tale by making use of a "true story" technique, recalling the real circumstances that inspired the tale: a visit he and his friend Francis Jammes [18] had made several years before to a Norman estate, Formentin, near Gide's own home. Formentin becomes the "Quartfourche" of the story. The abandoned estate had fascinated Gide when he was an adolescent as had the story behind its ruin: family discord, a daughter who squandered family revenues, a child abandoned to servants, the estate burdened with debt, the ruin and final disintegration of a once-prosperous landed family. What the young historian Lacase makes of these facts entirely "taken from outside" is the crux of the Gidian tale.

Gide himself cannot, for once, be confused with the narrator, whom he views with an amused irony and detachment far removed from the underlying emotional involvement which sustains his two preceding récits. The tale is

written with a certain briskness, free from most of the mannerisms of style Gide was still cultivating in *Strait Is the
Gate*,[19] as he himself recognized.

In line with the oldest conventions of the mystery story,
Gide introduces himself and Jammes, along with the fictional
Lacase, in the position of listeners to a tale they beg Lacase
to tell, thus focusing the reader's attention on the true-story
atmosphere and masking the complete artificiality of the device. No man could speak a story with such finished perfection, quoting without hesitation from a letter or reproducing
verbatim whole dialogues. But this matters little, for the pro-
cedure is used with a quiet deftness and mastery.

The facts Gérard recalls are straightforward and simple.
He first came to Quartfourche to do some scholarly research.
There he fell among the strangest set of characters: the owners, M. and Mme. de Saint-Auréol; their in-laws, M. and
Mme. Floche; a housekeeper, Mlle. Verdure; an abbé; a sullen servant, Gratien; and a young boy, Casimir. Slowly he
began to uncover signs of an underlying drama: the portrait
of a beautiful girl, an unsent letter written by Isabelle de
Saint-Auréol when she was twenty-two to the lover with
whom she was to elope that night; the story of the "accidental" death, on that very night, of the young Viscount
Blaise de Gonfreville; a nocturnal visit and family scene. . . .
The mystery centers on the enigmatic Isabelle and her tragic
love affair.

Through Lacase, Gide handles his tale with the skill of a
seasoned detective-story writer. Various interpretations are
suggested as the story progresses, always on the brink of melodrama, until the very end when unexpectedly Lacase comes
face to face with the real Isabelle. In this tale, for the first
time, Gide provides a vigorous, realistic setting. The château
and its inhabitants are seen with a clarity that contrasts
sharply with the vague aura of mystery that finally envelops

his bizarre characters as they slowly take on human consistency and depth.

Lacase's arrival seems at first to animate a world of Balzacian grotesques. During the first four chapters each of the strange persons among whom he is staying is scrutinized in turn, and successive keys to the Quartfourche enigma tantalizingly suggested. Are they all mad, as gentle M. Floche suggests? Are they lifeless mechanical puppets who merely exist automatically? Are they sinister and criminal? Which are good, which are bad? Where is the Isabelle of the title? The seriousness with which Lacase tells his story, in which he is deeply involved, is a subterfuge which dissimulates the fun Gide is having with his all-too-naïve historian.

Characteristically, in chapter four, the central chapter of the seven, Gide at last introduces his heroine, but indirectly through a medallion which fascinates Lacase. She is the enigma of the château incarnate. When, in the last chapter, the mystery is dispelled by a set of hard facts, the characters seem to the reader all the more puzzling for their humanization. *Isabelle* leaves our imagination at a "Quartfourche," a crossroads, leading in many directions. Gide successively plays on all kinds of emotions: curiosity, suspense, fear, pity, indignation, moral sense, the need to find out the truth. Casimir, the poor abandoned child, is there to draw a few tears. His transformations in Lacase's eyes are typical of what happens to all the characters. Suspect at first, and morally black, they turn to gray and finally tend to appear white, with the exception of poor Isabelle, who, through a truly Dickensian reversal, moves from pure white to black.

Gide, obviously, knew how to tell a good story and *Isabelle* can be read as such. Yet, as one might expect, his intent was not so simple: "Finished my novel the night before last with too much ease," he noted in his *Journal*, "and this makes me fear that I did not put into the last pages all that it was *incumbent upon me* to put there." [20] The subtitle he had in mind for his tale, "The Pathetic Fallacy," casts light on his intentions, and on his contention that the hero of the story is Lacase rather than Isabelle.

Young Lacase, before he even sets foot at the Saint-Auré-ols', dreams of participating in the romantic rituals of "châ-teau society." The grumpy coachman and run-down carriage sent to meet his train soon warn him of his mistake. Two days with the family prove so utterly boring that, to his hosts' consternation, he plans to leave. Gide is obviously playing with a Pirandellian theme: if Lacase should leave, what would become of the Floches, Saint-Auréols and company, who have just "found an author"? There would be no novel. How would all the fragments Lacase observes and that Gide has taken as data be "related," made into a story? Isabelle is the bait that arouses Lacase's curiosity because Lacase is a sentimental young man. The minute his imagination has settled on this one center of interest, his boredom is dispelled and his curiosity awakened. Item by item he compels the hidden fragments of the puzzle to appear. Though a budding scholar, he had wanted to experience adventure and find material for a novel. Given his heightened sensitivity, a subterranean network of relationships begins to be apparent. But the covert life of Quartfourche that Lacase senses corresponds in reality to his own predilection for the romanesque. Isabelle herself, until the very end, is only seen by him at night. Lacase's secret pursuit of a truth hidden in shadow is very similar to the task Gide had set himself as a novelist.

For the first time Gide makes use of such hackneyed novelistic devices as hidden letters, secrets pried out of locked writing desks, false-bottomed cabinets—all of which reappear in *Lafcadio's Adventures* and *The Counterfeiters*. They have a double function, suggesting clandestine activities which barely ripple the apparently even surface of life, and, concurrently, marking definite stages in the story, each discovery adding one more link to the chain.

Lacase, of course, falls in love with Isabelle. Historian that he is, on the lookout for all relevant information, he nonetheless singles out only those facts which support his hypothesis and thus fabricates the most ethereal and victimized Isabelle and the most romanesque of love stories. He can make sense of the facts only as they satisfy his own conventional sentimentality.

Later he finds himself face to face with the true Isabelle. The park is now devastated; the owners have died, the child Casimir has been abandoned to the gruff and sullen care of Gratien, the servant. A hard-boiled and discontented Isabelle stares out at Gérard, neither the mechanical doll of one of his dreams nor the sweet and inconsistent Isabelle of his imagination, but a real, impenetrable woman. The pathetic fallacy which had "informed" Lacase's interpretation of the Quartfourche mystery becomes apparent. Lacase immediately loses interest in the real Isabelle. But the reader does not. What is Isabelle really like? Is she really a murderer? A nymphomaniac? A woman who in true Gidian style has ruined her chance for happiness and brought about her lover's death because she feared to live? Isabelle's face, at any rate, as she at last looks out at the reader, is the hard and disconcerting face of reality. Until this point each of the other characters —Lacase, the abbé, Gratien, the Floches, Mlle. Verdure, Mme. de Saint-Auréol—has quite simply interpreted Isabelle according to his or her own idea of what motivates human beings, thereby introducing into the story a human content not inherent in the bare facts and which expresses only their own inner sensitivity. The theme of pathetic fallacy is repeated at all levels, giving Gide's story—as distinguished from Lacase's—its meaning without requiring either explanation or symbol.

On the surface *Isabelle* may seem to illustrate only the

very commonplace idea that dreams lose their poetry when confronted with reality. In fact, what the tale conveys is that no dream is equal to a reality it can only impoverish or disguise, but never grasp. Lacase's story illustrates the elusive, Protean aspect a set of events assume as soon as one tries to find rational explanations for them from the outside.

The path that Lacase follows as apprentice-novelist is Gide's own. Life, Gide suggests, yields to the novelist's attention only fragmentary, unrelated data. Only when some avid, inner feeling orients the novelist-observer's attention does he begin to relate the facts observed, to grasp their hidden relationships. The "figure in the carpet," as it emerges for Gide, derives its substance from reality but its organization and meaning from the subjective inner impetus that guides the writer's search.

Isabelle emphasizes the twofold relation between the facts objectively observed and the young novelist's subjective mood. A fictional world emerges when the outer and inner worlds are momentarily in equilibrium, a temporary state in a doubly dynamic process which can never be halted. The novelist's work, like Lacase's story, will thus perpetually evolve. As he probes more deeply into the hidden dynamics of human destiny and motivation, the modalities they assume change in his eyes and so will the tale he tells and the perspectives he establishes. Each tale will assume its own form, a form which cannot be repeated. The story told, the writer is free to start again. Lacase is no novelist in Gide's eyes. Like the would-be writer of *Marshlands*, he will only write other stories which mirror his own inner sensitivity.

Isabelle greatly clarifies the place in Gide's work of the two more ample and far more impressive tales, *The Immoralist* and *Strait Is the Gate*. In a way both Michel and Alissa resemble Lacase, pursuing, as he does, an elusive and shadowy face—their own. But the harsh reality Michel and Alissa discover hurts them far more irremediably than the discovery of the real Isabelle could ever hurt Lacase. At least, all three went beyond the insignificant and boring surface that life offers the unthinking. What each perceives is one point of view only, but a point of view that opens on a vast and turbulent Protean reality. The writer, by maintaining unchanged throughout the story the particular nature of the characters' relation to the world about them, their pathetic fallacy, rounds out and completes what in real life can only be tentative, temporary, incomplete. Gide seems to hint that the perfect organization and tonal unity of his own récits derive from a form of pathetic fallacy, literary rather than sentimental. He was now impatient with the limitations imposed upon the récit by the tonal unity it required and the tremendous effort it demanded of the writer. To write as Jerome might, in a rather dull, pedestrian way, had proved one of the major difficulties he encountered when working on *Strait Is the Gate*. In *Isabelle*, with Lacase's descriptions of the novel's rather burlesque set of characters, Gide was experimenting with certain deliberate breaks in tonality, juxtaposing satire and pathos.

Chapter XII

The Elusive Reign of Proteus

Le mauvais, ce n'est pas la doctrine, c'est . . . de s'y reposer.

What is harmful is not the doctrine but . . . to rest upon it.

~~~~~~

When *Lafcadio's Adventures* [1]—entitled in French *The Vatican Cellars*—appeared in the summer of 1914, the sotie came as a surprise to most of Gide's friends. The reviews were almost unanimously and huffishly censorious and the book inspired the first really fierce attacks on Gide from the literary clique on the Catholic right. Of all Gide's works, however, this was to be the one that for a short time endeared him to the iconoclastic Dadaists at the opposite pole of the literary spectrum. Jacques Vaché, who was so deeply to impress young André Breton, carried *Lafcadio's Adventures* with him to the trenches during World War I, starting Lafcadio on a career Gide had certainly not foreseen, as precursor to the surrealists.

The book was first published in a pseudo-anonymous fashion with the subtitle "sotie [2] by the author of *Marshlands*."

Since very few people remembered the brilliant little satire Gide had published some twenty years before, a portrait of Gide dissipated any chance of an error in attribution.

Gide went to some pains to situate *Lafcadio's Adventures* in the development of his work. Far more than *Isabelle*, which he had written without much trouble as a diversion, it reflects a new mood and new preoccupations incorporated into a daring new narrative structural pattern. By adopting the designation "sotie" for all three works, Gide retrospectively referred the work back to his amusing but puzzling *Marshlands* and *Prometheus*.

The fantastic and provocative imbroglio, in which Lafcadio is only one among many other equally improbable participants, began to take shape in Gide's mind around 1893, when he first spoke of it, in Biskra, to his companion, Paul Laurens. From then on Gide occasionally referred to it in his *Journal*. He had apparently been greatly amused by the imaginative audacity of a gang of swindlers, who had achieved a brief notoriety in 1892. Exploiting the political situation of the 1890's and the position taken by Pope Leo XIII in favor of the French Republic, they had launched the rumor that the Pope had been imprisoned in the Vatican cellars by the Freemasons, with the help of a group of cardinals, and that a false pope now occupied the Holy See. On this pretext they collected funds from the gullible among the faithful to whom, in great secrecy, they disclosed this horrible situation and their own counterplot to free the captive. Gide apparently read of this colossal confidence racket and was immediately struck by its piquancy. He dated his own story as of 1896 and borrowed the outline of his plot from newspaper accounts, enlarging upon only those implications of the swindle which particularly diverted him.[3]

Gide insisted several times that *Lafcadio's Adventures*, *The Immoralist*, and *Strait Is the Gate* should be viewed as companion pieces, each qualifying the other, and that they by no means reflect an evolution in his philosophical position. He emphasized that all three books were conceived as a whole and published successively only because of the necessary lag between the conception of a work of art and its execution. This is probably quite true in so far as his ethical point of view is concerned. All the familiar Gidian themes appear in this sotie, including the theme of homosexuality which so deeply shocked Claudel. But between 1901, when Gide wrote *The Immoralist*, and 1912-1913, when he really started work on *Lafcadio's Adventures*, Gide's ideas concerning the novel had changed. Themes and characters were now to be subordinated to an over-all structure which had very little in common with Gide's earlier work.

In spite of occasional discouraging moments of boredom or even "horror," particularly in 1912, on the whole Gide seems to have derived a great deal of amusement from the writing of this story. He worked hard, stubbornly stripping down his text so as to give the narrative a quasi-Voltairian tempo and incisiveness. The spontaneity and directness he sought and brilliantly achieved was designed to keep in check the interplay of nonsense, fantasy and satire in which he indulged with bland and consummate skill. That is perhaps why *Lafcadio's Adventures* gave rise to the strangest misunderstandings, not the least of which was the surprising assumption that Gide approved such improbable acts as Lafcadio's tossing a fellow traveler out of a train window to his death. The "absurd," another facet of the pathetic fallacy in the Gidian world, is everywhere implicit, though not explicit. It cannot be separated from the characters, their adventures and discussions. When Claudel called the book "sinister," it can only be that, unable to detect the humor at work beneath the surface, he mistook the mask for the face.

It was hardly surprising that Gide's contemporaries were baffled. As he had already done in *Prometheus*, Gide had deliberately discarded the conventional processes of narration.

Lafcadio's Adventures is very carefully organized, and the structure of the story a function of the idea from which it sprang. In cubist fashion, Gide borrows certain heterogeneous elements from reality and reorganizes them according to an abstract design, creating the "new relationships" from which each apparently unconnected part derives its significance. The real originality of his sotie lies in the over-all organization which, if overlooked, can leave the reader with only vague impressions. The book may seem simply to yield a few amusing dialogues; a rather outdated satire on typical nineteenth-century attitudes toward science and religion, a mild take-off on literary academicism, and a new version of the picaresque hero, Lafcadio. The latter was so dear to Gide's heart that in 1924 he extracted from the novel the set of episodes which concern this young man for separate publication. But *Lafcadio's Adventures* is worth closer attention, even if the going seems overcomplicated at times.

As with *Prometheus*, the work is divided into several "books" of parallel but apparently unconnected stories, so that superficially the whole appears rather desultory. The first three books are subtitled for important characters each of whom is setting out on a separate adventure. In the fourth book, "The Centipede," the separate lines of action appear accidentally to converge. The tempo accelerates, until finally in the fifth a cascade of unlikely circumstances brings everyone to Rome to appear at the funeral of one of the main characters. The plot never develops in a logical way. It moves erratically, bouncing unexpectedly from one chance encounter to another, apparently leading nowhere.

Yet "all paths lead to Rome," and from rebound to rebound it is in Rome that Gide's set of masques all come together, though some of them never come face to face. They form two groups: the swindlers, or "Centipedes," and the righteous, who though they don't always realize it, belong to the same family and become enmeshed in the machinations of Protos, the leader of the Centipede. Little by little Gide establishes a network of connections between his characters, connections the reader can grasp but not the characters, who remain unaware of the repercussions their smallest gesture is likely to have.

At first it might seem that Gide set out to write the mock-heroic tale of a fight between the "good" characters and the evil Centipede. But one soon perceives the many invisible threads connecting one camp with the other. It is through direct action rather than by description that Gide sets up that unique milieu, or circumstance, where each character is a "crossroads." Each is situated in relation to all the others, although each thinks of himself as an independent unit, the center of his own closed universe.

In the first three books of the sotie Gide sets his characters in motion, winding them up, as it were, one after the other, like mechanical toys. Each one starts out on an adventure, and certainly this is a "novel of adventure," adventures avoided or carried through, adventures physical and intellectual, including a very romanesque love affair. Though each character is totally absorbed in his own affairs and unaware of his relation to the others, all partake unwittingly in a vaster collective adventure to which their individual adventures are related, and around which they all revolve. This raises the problem of the nature of the characters and the significance of their chance meetings, curious conversations and activities.

The characters in *Lafcadio's Adventures* are schematic, distinguished by a few comical, easily recognizable physical traits. Gide gives their background with bland gravity, meticulously exaggerating and magnifying certain outstanding characteristics. While he was working on this book he complained that his characters tended to escape from the absurd, caricaturelike pattern in which he wanted to enclose them. Nonetheless, they remain consistently true to type from start to finish. Only one of them tends to become a little more complex toward the end. To give his absurd heroes full scope, Gide relied mainly on dialogue, using a semidramatic form [4] which allowed him to reduce the narrative to a strict minimum. "I must draw the nude under the clothing as did David," [5] he noted.

The first character to appear is Anthime Armand-Dubois, complete with a wen and sciatica, a freethinker, Freemason and scientist, whose thinking follows the simplest logical patterns. He lives in Rome, where he carries out experiments on the conditioned reflexes of rats. From these experiments he deduces laws governing the behavior of living organisms, which he reduces to various forms of "tropism," [6] the response to external stimuli. He is famous and crippled. His wife, Veronica, as well as his in-laws, the Baragliouls, are Catholics, complacent and self-righteously orthodox in all their opinions. Anthime's views shock them and theirs irritate him. During one of their stormy visits, however, the naïve piety of Anthime's small niece moves the scientist more than he likes to admit. Annoyed with himself, in a moment of sacrilegious fury, Anthime hurls his crutch at the statue of the Virgin at whose feet, most aggravating of all, candles are burning expressly for him. He succeeds only in breaking the Virgin's arm. That same night the maimed Virgin appears before him and cures him of his crippling sciatica. Converted, Anthime abandons science, fame and Freemasonry, plunging into a devout and ecstatic saintliness, which contributes to his rapid impoverishment, the promises of the Church notwithstanding.

Julius de Baraglioul, author of mediocre, conventional novels and a candidate for the French Academy, has just published an edifying biography of his father entitled *On the Heights*. His book has been greeted unenthusiastically by the critics and mercilessly jeered at by the old Count himself, who informs his son and biographer that, inconsistent though it be with his son's impression, he has produced an illegitimate son, Lafcadio Wluiki. Julius seeks out Lafcadio, finds him, and as a result conceives a new type of novel based on a different conception of character. He dreams of discarding the novel of psychological analysis in favor of the description of nonlogical patterns of behavior manifested in gratuitous acts which escape analysis.

Lafcadio is a young man of some sixteen years, an adolescent, who lives freely outside society with his mistress, Carola, a prostitute for whom he has no particular affection. Only as a result of Julius's visits does he discover he is the illegitimate son of Count de Baraglioul. Having been brought up in great luxury thanks to a series of "uncles"—his mother's rich lovers—he has an aristocratic contempt for all social conventions. Proud and handsome, possessed of a fine athletic body and an independent mind fashioned by the unorthodox education prescribed in turn by each of his uncles, he is a young barbarian who recognizes only one imperative: to remain intact, inaccessible to others. To punish himself whenever he feels he has yielded on this essential point, he jabs a penknife into his thigh. Apart from this self-discipline, Lafcadio follows only the rules of his own fantasy and purely disinterested fondness for sport. He admits to no duties or attachments or needs beyond the most basic. He goes to see his father, inherits a comfortable income, and starts off in search of adventure. In an Italian train he finds himself sitting opposite a repulsive elderly man. An impulse comes over him to throw the man out. And this he does as the train is crossing a bridge.

Protos, the leader of the Centipede, appears in Pau disguised as a priest. In a highly dramatic interview with Julius's sister, the Countess de Saint-Prix, under the seal of secrecy he discloses the Pope's imprisonment and extorts from the terrified Countess a very large sum of money to aid in a crusade to deliver the Pope. Inspired by his sister-in-law the

Countess, Julius's chaste provincial brother-in-law, Fleurissoire, makes a heroic departure for Rome, his first venture
outside the precincts of his native Pau. The poor fellow becomes the bewildered victim of Protos's mystifications, until
he finds himself riding opposite a delightful young man in
a train. Lafcadio's act precipitates his death and finally the
denouement, since by an unexpected ricochet it eventually
rids the world of Protos, creator of the False Pope. Although
many critics have assumed that Lafcadio is the hero of Gide's
story, Fleurissoire is an equally good guide if we want to follow the astonishing ins and outs of the imbroglio.

Fleurissoire leaves for Rome filled with consternation and
in a spirit of total sacrifice. He is a dedicated man with a
lofty objective: to put an end to the martyrdom of the True
Pope and to the reign of the False Pope. After three sleepless nights, each with its own ordeal of fleas, bedbugs, and
mosquitoes, the demoralized man is an easy prey for Protos,
who lures him into a dreary brothel where he loses his vir-
ginity in the arms of Carola, now allied with Protos. For
the first time he is overcome with doubts as to his own
worthiness. To doubt is to come under Protos's sway. Suddenly much that he had accepted as true and right seems
strangely ambiguous, if not false. Things he had disapproved
of no longer seem reprehensible. He begins to wonder whether
Julius, whom he meets, is the real Julius and whether, indeed, he himself is the real Fleurissoire. Step by bewildered
step, he who had set out so wholeheartedly to re-establish the
True Pope and unmask the False, is fast becoming Protos's
unwilling agent. And by the time Lafcadio runs across him
on the train, he is about to compromise his and Julius's respectability in order to carry through one of Protos's more
shady financial deals. The Pope's champion ends as one of
the Centipedes.

Lafcadio, until the episode in the train, instinctively acts
generously: a model hero and at first a kind of Theseus, he

saves the lives of two children caught in a fire; he carries the bundles of old women; he is happy when he finds his unknown father; he is attracted by the gentle charm of his cousin Geneviève and likes his stepbrother—all this spontaneously and with no ulterior motives. From this instinctive sense of the freedom and essential gratuity of existence, he derives a notion which he promptly applies: there is in life no moral sanction, no good and evil; he saved lives, why not take a life? Opposite him in the train he sees a grotesque little old man. Why not throw him out? Let chance decide. If Lafcadio can count twelve before a light shows outside, Fleurissoire will be saved. At ten, he sees a light. . . . He throws a hideous old man out the window. But the consequences of his act soon become disturbing, until at last, in a scene of metamorphosis worthy of the surrealists, Protos appears and claims him as one of his own. Protos proposes, as a follow-up to this first act, others basely and contemptibly criminal. Lafcadio has found his master. The pattern underlying the story now begins to appear. Gide is concerned with the quite subtle problems of subversion.

Lafcadio's Adventures does not attack the Catholic Church as such; the story of the False Pope is merely part of a vast hoax perpetrated on the naïve by Protos and his gang. There are, in fact, no Vatican cellars. Gide's title emphasizes the devastating irony of his tale. But Gide certainly anticipated without displeasure the scandalized protestations his casual use of sacred symbols—the Pope, Rome, the Vatican—would occasion. That is precisely why he chose them, with an amusement all the greater since he was thoroughly bored with the righteous and solemn adjurations of his would-be converters, Claudel and Jammes. What Gide was really out to satirize, however, was no one institution as such but rather a certain self-righteous complacency, a form of tranquil stupidity. Claudel himself had furnished Gide with an excellent comment on the True Pope-False Pope dichotomy in a sentence from his play *The Tidings Brought to Mary:* "But of which King are you speaking and of which Pope?" [7]

Since the Pope is God's Vicar on earth, the very notion that two men claim the title is obviously wildly destructive. The notion that a False Pope is seated, undetected, on the Vatican throne while the True Pope is held prisoner somewhere is even more wildly confusing. When Fleurissoire, whose faith was unquestioning, unquestioningly accepts this idea, he accepts, without at first realizing it, its logical consequence: the existence of a plot, diabolical, successful, involving the highest church and state authorities. Satan rears his head victoriously as the idea of the "Vatican cellars" grows on Fleurissoire, a belief in the total subversion of all that used to be, in his eyes, the sign of God's presence on earth. Protos now becomes the infallible source of truth in whom the innocent Fleurissoire puts his trust. Like many an earnest crusader against subversion, baffled but undaunted, he is the unwelcome ally of Protos's gang and their stooge. When Lafcadio throws him out of the train, it is only just in time. As for the other adventurers, Fleurissoire's burlesque demise affects them each in turn, altering their newly adopted course.

By means of this ambiguous True Pope-False Pope proposition, Gide traced with a good deal of wicked humor the curious fluctuations of simple notions of "true" and "false" in relation to the mobile and complex stuff of reality. For most of the characters there is a pope, the absolute, incontrovertible, imperative voice of truth; for Protos and his gang, faith in a pope, of whatever kind, is a wonderful terrain for exploitation. Fleurissoire truly believes in the Pope; Lafcadio has never heard of him. All the other characters come somewhere between the two.

With impeccable skill, in every situation that turns up, Gide introduces through his characters so fine a mixture of true-and-false that reasoning, decisions, motivations and words are all suffused with the same ambiguity. The readiness with which each character plunges into actions motivated by beautiful reasons and relative ignorance gives the whole story its fundamental and restful absurdity as, from semierror to semitruth, they keep the plot rolling.

From Fleurissoire's death Julius immediately infers that his brother-in-law is a victim of the Vatican swindlers. This is true to a certain extent, since had there been no swindle Fleurissoire would never have ventured out of Pau. But Julius's inference is false, first with regard to the real circumstances of Fleurissoire's death and, second, in regard to the personal line of conduct Julius now adopts, actually motivated by his own intellectual timorousness although he attributes it to the noble convictions reactivated in him by Fleurissoire's "martyrdom." Julius, a man who makes use of everything, is deeply impressed by the notion that "poor Fleurissoire perished because he penetrated behind the scenes." Julius now knows "where to draw the line," and draws it. Based on false assumptions, his whole line of reasoning is worthless; but from Fleurissoire's death he has drawn the infallible justification for his own prudent return to orthodoxy, to the novel of psychological analysis and to a future seat in the French Academy. The reader knows that Fleurissoire died as the result of a far more illogical and complex set of circumstances than Julius could ever imagine, and that his death proves nothing whatever about the Pope.

Anthime Armand-Dubois, on the other hand, believed not in God but in the natural laws of the universe. This was his own pope, but one which did not explain his cure. The fact that his cure was inexplicable in his terms is true. But this does not necessarily prove, as Anthime thinks, that he has been singled out for divine intervention. Had he observed his rats with a little more imagination, they might have enlightened him.

For Anthime's rats come to him through a set of chance

happenings over which they have no control but which fatally affect them. They are hunted out, brought to Anthime's laboratory, put into cages, systematically mutilated, starved, blinded, weighed, and otherwise employed in the interests of his scientific research. One day goodhearted Mme. Armand-Dubois happens to cross the room. Moved by their plight, she feeds the rats. A miracle, certainly, for the rats. Then Anthime is converted, after his miraculous cure, and gives up his experiments. Now fat and well-fed, the rats lead a very pleasant life until the day Armand reverts to his old ways. If the rats could reason within the limits of their own universe like Gidian characters in a *récit*, and if they were to attempt logically to explain their fate, what might they not infer? From a succession of accurate facts, they would no doubt deduce a metaphysics tailored to their own small universe just as Anthime does with regard to his. The analogy between the miraculously healed Anthime and the miraculously rescued rats is hardly accidental.

Protos, as soon as he appears, disturbs the fine serenity of the characters, in belief or disbelief, with regard to the Pope. It is he who fabricates the story of the False Pope. Amoral, omnipresent and ruthless, he has the gift of ubiquity. He can assume any human form and dress real bishops as false bishops, libertines as martyrs. He seems to incarnate the multiplicity and ambiguities of life itself, challenging as he does ideas, interdictions and beliefs, injecting doubt and question wherever he passes. But he shows his real visage only to the two characters who genuinely commit themselves to actions inspired by their beliefs, Lafcadio and Fleurissoire. The others are unconscious victims.

Anthime never suspects Protos's existence. Of all the characters he is closest to the doctrinaire orthodoxy symbolized by Rome. He goes from Pope to Pope and back again in a simple pattern of reaction analogous to the tropisms he discerned in his rats. His rationalism screens him from ever glimpsing the clandestine Protean disorder behind the neat schematization he sets up. Julius, in his novels, caters to the comfortable beliefs of the society to which he belongs. He has his literary pope—psychological analysis with ethical overtones—and his moral tropism, opportunism. Lafcadio gives him a new idea about human conduct, the existence of gratuitous, disinterested, apparently unmotivated acts, a fine literary idea. But, confronted by just such an act, the one involving Lafcadio and Fleurissoire, Julius hurriedly discards a hypothesis dangerous for his own tranquillity. He comes close to the Centipede only for an instant, attracted by the buxom Carola but, terrified by the very suggestion of an unorthodox connection, hastily withdraws. Julius merely plays with ideas. If life disappoints him, he concludes that the Pope has changed, not he; and with great and righteous relief he comes back, like the prodigal son, to the House, in this case, the French Academy. He will never explore the Vatican cellars.

Protos counts two victims, Fleurissoire and Lafcadio, who join the ranks of Gide's two recognizable families of heroes; the idealists: Fleurissoire, Alissa, André Walter; the sensualists: Lafcadio, Michel, Menalcas. Fleurissoire, the man with a faith and a cause, is ready to sacrifice his life without question, unacquainted as he is with the wiles of Protos. His inner commitment to a cause he conceives as worthy never weakens. But the minute he launches into action right and wrong become hopelessly confused, and from farce to burlesque he easily becomes the baffled stooge and devoted tool of his dangerous adversary. Ironically, his concern for truth becomes an obsession with error that leads him to surrender himself into the hands of the fraudulent and unscrupulous Protos.

As for Lafcadio, he has no concern whatsoever for popes, true or false. He acts in reference only to himself. The consequences of his unmotivated murder at first seem negligible: a scratch on his handsome face and the loss of his elegant felt hat. Until suddenly, in one of the most original and enigmatic scenes in the novel, he catches glimpses of perplexing ambiguities in the most apparently innocuous people, and finally discovers that he has played into the hands of his erstwhile friend Protos. Protos, disguised as a nearsighted professor called Defoulquebise, is about to blackmail him into collaborating with his criminal gang. At this point, as in a game of billiards, Gide sends his balls rolling in every direction and Lafcadio is saved. Only by a set of *quid pro quos* is Protos arrested, leaving Lafcadio free to spend the night with Julius's beautiful daughter, Geneviève. "Here begins a new book," says Gide, here as in many others of his tales. But Fleurissoire and Lafcadio have played their parts to the very end, showing how dangerous it is to become entangled with Protos. Fleurissoire, who thinks that there is one Pope, one ethical principle governing the natural and the moral universe, and Lafcadio, who thinks that man is a free agent in a nonmoral universe, are the two characters who fare badly at the hands of Protos. At worst, both might have lost their lives, as indeed Fleurissoire does; at best, both might emerge slightly disfigured, as does young Lafcadio.

With *Lafcadio's Adventures* Gide was seeking a narrative form through which to express a conception of life that later was to become fairly widespread with the vogue of existentialism. In *Prometheus* Gide had played upon the idea of the incongruity of the human being who partakes of the gratuitous nature of a purposeless universe and yet is motivated by moral and rational exigencies. But where Sartre sees a conflict between a "sticky" existence and a "freely committed" life, Gide accepted the incongruous coexistence of both modes of life in every individual, discovering an inexhaustible source of laughter in their very incompatibility. If both popes exist, what can be done? Do away with all the Vaticans, those illusions of the absolute, answers an amused Gide.

In this sotie Gide also enjoyed manipulating complex series of consequences, inconsequences, motivations, chance events, and errors that any individual, in his relativity, precipitates with every one of his acts. Relativity in position and in vision, hence in reasoning, multiplies the hazards already abundantly prepared at every step by life itself.

Gide spoke of this sotie as a fable, a tale with its own morality, the morality that Lafcadio learns at his own expense, plus another, more comprehensive ethic that Gide was to develop further in *The Counterfeiters*. The ethic proposed is one of limited commitment. Badly shaken up after his experience, Lafcadio modifies his point of view and conduct, but emphasizes his freedom with regard to his past. He commits a crime, he looks Protos straight in the face and admits his responsibility; but he refuses to be drawn for the rest of his life into further illegal acts. He refuses to be committed by his past. The fact that Lafcadio escapes punishment is irrelevant to the problem Gide raises. For Lafcadio punishment could never be, as for Dostoevsky's Raskolnikov, an expiation. His act cannot be effaced whether its social consequences are eluded or not. It has left a mark on his face and given Protos a weapon that Lafcadio might have found hard to take back.

The idea of the free, or gratuitous, act, an idea Gide had been toying with since *Marshlands*, is developed more fully and more subtly than before. Lafcadio's act has no rational motivation, but it can be explained. The young man had failed to distinguish between two orders of value, the human and the cosmic, Prometheus and Zeus. On the other hand, his act is certainly gratuitous in its effects on Fleurissoire, just as Anthime's acts would also so appear to the rats. Gide considers gratuitous acts, then, as those which strike people by chance, from the outside through a set of circumstances that completely escape their control: Anthime's cure; Fleurissoire's death. Here Gide's irony enters into play, for such events are the only ones whose inexplicability his characters never accept, the only ones they always try to explain and justify. On the other hand, on a human level, there can be no gratuity in human intentions. There are good and bad intentions which involve the character's integrity and for which he is responsible. In life one cannot decide with impunity to throw the Fleurissoires out of train windows.

Gide was neither boasting nor yielding to a form of self-doubt when he wrote: " 'Soties' or 'récits,' up to now I have written nothing but *ironic*—or, if you prefer, critical—books of which this is doubtless the last." The main Gidian characters had all been something like players in a game of basketball, which they play with absorption according to all the rules. But, actually, the game turns out to be football. Gide's récits are accounts of the game as seen by one of the baffled players, while the soties describe the game as seen from the outside. In both cases the whole thing is absurd: explicitly pathetic and implicitly ridiculous in the récit; explicitly ridiculous and implicitly pathetic in the sotie. Thus Fleurissoire is a second Alissa seen from the outside.

Gide had now come to conceive another kind of novel, a *summa* containing a totality of experience as *André Walter* was to have been. Just as Gide had conceived his ethics as the art of making one's way through the hazards of life without losing either one's grasp on life or one's humanity, so he now thought of the novel as a transposition of the dynamics of living rather than, as heretofore, a subtle reorganization of the substance of experience. It was perhaps his rereadings of Dostoevsky's novels that directed his ambition to come to grips with a more complex form of narrative. Yet what Gide had to say about Dostoevsky in his lectures offers little that was not already present in Gide's mind. Gide's new aesthetic ideas, precipitated perhaps by the loud clamor around him for the renovation of the novel seem to follow naturally from the progress of his own thought in every other realm. Neither *Lafcadio's Adventures* nor the future *Counterfeiters* is really Dostoevskian in mood or technique. When Gide constantly reiterated his belief that the choice of subject matters little in art and that the work of art has no purpose beyond itself, he was sincere. None of his works were consciously inspired by an intent to moralize. But Gide could only work with subjects that were rooted in his emotional life, itself deeply affected by questions of ethics.

Gide's thought insistently probes a few great questions raised by his own experience which always baffled him and which, through the medium of fiction also challenge the reader's understanding. Each work at its origin is related to all the others. But from *André Walter* to *Lafcadio's Adventures* Gide became progressively more detached from his subject matter. In his last sotie he could look down upon his creatures from above, working out the mechanics of his plot with an Olympian serenity. He seemed to conceive of this satire as the first outline of a universe in which he would be involved only as an artist, and thus he could affirm in all sincerity that the "real show" was now going to begin.

The sincerity to which Gide so often alluded and which he wanted to achieve should not be confused with mere candor or the attempt to live according to certain ethical principles. All Gide's work asserts that life and rigid ethical systems are incompatible and explores the devious forms of self-deception that lurk beneath the mask of candor. His form of sincerity arises from the requirements of his art which, indirectly, did impose a rigorous moral discipline upon him. Sincerity, as Gide understood it, consisted first in never allowing himself to evade facts, and more particularly those facts which elude reason, in never refusing to go behind the scenes. It required also that he as a writer, without deliberately misleading himself or others, honestly work within the limitations of his own relative point of view, clearly defined through the structural patterns of his work. This sense of relativity led Gide to stress what he called the "devil's share" in life, all that in any existence eludes understanding. Whereas art thrives on its sometimes unconscious connections with the devil's share in existence, those human beings who ignore it in life court disaster. And so the work of art has meaning beyond itself and exercises a salutary influence. Gide's former search for an art "that would liberate the unknown within us" had by now become a search for an art "to liberate us from the unknown."

Gide, who had started out with the mental picture of the Christian universe, had now come to see that the only reality he could honestly deal with was the relative, fallacious and mobile order man creates for himself. He seems to have envisioned life somewhat as it is pictured in the most amiable of the Greek myths. On our generally pleasant and sunny earth it is the task of men to live humanly, eliminating monsters, remaining sharply distinct from the gods, achieving as best they can an ideal human form. Lafcadio, starting out on his adventures, anticipates Gide's favorite hero, Theseus. *Lafcadio's Adventures* is a crucial book, disclosing as it does both the evolution of Gide's thought and the reasons that led him to experiment so drastically with the accepted forms of the novel.

Chapter XIII

Interlude

Il ne croit ni en Dieu, ni au diable.

He believes neither in God nor in the devil.

~~~~~~~~~~~~~~~~~~~~

The period between the publication of *Lafcadio's Adventures* (1914) and *The Counterfeiters*—which came out in installments in the N.R.F. during 1925—is one of the most curious in Gide's life. In these years his fame started to grow rapidly, extending beyond the restricted circles of the Parisian literati. His reading public increased not only in France but also abroad. In addition to publishing *The Pastoral Symphony* in 1919, a work widely read and well reviewed, Gide was republishing most of his previous works which now, for the first time, had many readers. When the war ended and literature once more became a major journalistic attraction, Gide became the subject of violent attacks that only served to enhance his fame. *Lafcadio's Adventures* had provoked the disapproval of Paul Claudel and of the doctrinaire reactionary critic, Henri Massis. But otherwise the book had attracted little attention, and World War I soon imposed more immediate preoccupations upon even the most frivolous minds. No one then knew that young Jacques Vaché had taken Lafcadio to the front as his guide, heralding the generation to come which was to discover in Gide one of its masters.

In 1921 Henri Massis fired a new volley in the Paris press denouncing Gide's "demonic" influence. Shortly before that, Henri Béraud, a journalist and not overscrupulous polemicist, had attacked the "snobbery of boredom" emanating from the *N.R.F.* group, particularly from Gide. Painful as these attacks may have proved to Gide's self-esteem, they helped make him one of the more notorious literary figures in post-World War I Paris. Controversy delighted rather than disturbed a Gide now approaching his fifties and surer of himself, who was not averse in times still rife with moralistic and nationalistic bombast, to playing the role of perturber.

The war of 1914 had found Gide at his Cuverville estate engrossed in his usual occupations: literature, family, gardening. While closely observing a starling he was trying to tame, he was preparing his travel notes on a recent trip to Turkey for publication in the *N.R.F.* Not until July 26, five days before the German ultimatum to Russia and France, does his *Journal* register even the slightest suspicion that something might not be as it should be in Europe. As usual, he was working simultaneously on several projected works. Among them a novel, probably the long-deferred *Counterfeiters*, to which he could apply new ideas about the novel already operative in *Lafcadio's Adventures*. He was thinking of a *Treatise on the Dioscuri*—Castor and Pollux—an outline of which he published in 1919 in the *N.R.F.* under the title "Considerations on Greek Mythology." He envisaged writing a comedy, continued to work on *Corydon*, and was busy with his memoirs. But despite his own creative efforts, his translations of Whitman and Tagore, and a projected translation of Shakespeare's *As You Like It*, once again Gide was restless and bored. It seems that from the time he reached his forties he always needed some external impetus to give savor to his life. He feared the somnolence generated by the orderly family life at Cuverville and the climate of Normandy.

Though it affected him deeply, the war temporarily offered him diversion. At forty-five Gide was too old to be drafted, but he tried to find useful ways to "occupy himself." Between August and November of 1914 his *Journal* abounds with detailed notes about opinions and emotional reactions he shared with his compatriots. Then, for about a year, from November on, he was completely absorbed by his work in the "Franco-Belgian foyer" organized by his friend Mme. Theo van Rysselberghe, to help the numerous Belgian refugees in Paris. Eleven months later, in September of 1915, he turned back to his *Journal* to record his exhaustion under the emotional strain of the foyer, his disgust at the stupid chauvinism of the civilian population, his isolation and his distress at a forced inaction all the harder to bear as he saw the blindness and negligence prevailing everywhere. "The atmosphere," he noted, "is stifling, toxic, deadly!" [1] Gide's inaction seems to have been responsible for a new period of overwhelming depression, which the writing he now returned to did not at first alleviate.

On January 17, 1916, Gide learned of the conversion at the front of Henri Ghéon, a friend of some twenty years' standing and for several years his close companion in travel, literature and debauchery. The news elicited a caustic comment: "Ghéon writes me that he has 'taken the jump.' He sounds like a schoolboy who has just had his first try at the brothel. . . . But he is alluding to the communion table." [2] The next day Gide opened his Bible and started a long meditation on the Scriptures, the various phases of which he noted in an adjunct to his *Journal*, a "green cloth notebook." The notebook was published in 1922, in a limited edition with the cryptic title *Numquid et tu . . .* —literally "And are you also . . ."—meaning "Are you also a Galilean?" a disciple of Christ. It was, it would seem, the tedium of 1916, "the year of disgrace," the prolongation of the war, and Ghéon's conversion which reactivated in Gide the grave attitude of his adolescent years. "There was a time," he wrote that year, "when I loathed any literature, any art, which did not spring from joy, from an excess of 'joie de vivre.' Might it not be my present indescribable sadness which now urges me to continue speaking?" [3] Perhaps for want of a better incentive Gide carefully cultivated his sadness, grafting on to the religious theme the moral theme of his sexual "relapses"; the summer months, in 1916, which had been "abominable, devoid of work and completely dissolute," [4] could thus be put to good literary profit. Gide's imagination, easily intrigued whenever occult psychological forces were in question, now seized upon the notion of the devil, suggested to him by a friend—and perhaps by Dostoevsky—as a psychological force actively engaged in human affairs, a new version of his early Prometheus. The devil of rationalization was obviously the power that had duped Michel and Alissa, and a character who might take his place beside Protos in Gide's literary mythology.

Very early in the course of his debate with the Scriptures, Gide concentrated on the literary possibilities of his so-called crisis, reading Pascal to form his style, envisaging a "mystic treatise" to balance *The Return of the Prodigal Son*, [5] in which a Gidian Nicodemus would be a central character, even sketching out a conversation between Nicodemus, Christ and the Devil. The critical phase in his thinking had begun, and as usual Gide was rapidly exasperated with his own "spiritual anxiety," with his projected *Conversations with Nicodemus*, and with himself.

Much has been made of this spiritual crisis, which to some degree seems to have been real. But it was characteristically Gidian in the sense that his tête-à-tête with the Scriptures occupied Gide's mind for some months almost to the exclusion of everything else, until, thoroughly tired of the subject, he turned to other, quite different concerns which he had never really abandoned. A year later he was asked to write a preface to the letters of a young French officer, Dupouey, killed at the front, a convert whose example had led to Ghéon's conversion. For Dupouey's fervent, mystical letters Gide wrote a spiritual and edifying preface. "As soon as I got home," he notes matter-of-factly in his *Journal,* "I wrote at one sitting the preamble to *Corydon* as a reaction to the 'Preface to the Letters of Dupouey,' which I had finished that very morning." [6] He found nothing incongruous in having the second work follow on the heels of the first. They were equally valid in his eyes, and it was simply a question of extending his best effort for the purposes of each. The spiritual crisis if such there was, appears to have been a welcome invitation to return to literature, leaving the rest of the world to carry on the war. Try as he might, Gide could bring himself to believe in deity and the devil only while he had no other literary nourishment. On May 12 he noted:

"Have written nothing more in this notebook for the last fortnight. . . . Can see nothing in it now but a comedy, and a dishonest comedy, in which I convinced myself that I could discern the devil's hand. This is what the demon suggests . . ." [7]—Surely as nice an example of cerebral involution as one can hope to find.

With a parallel *Journal* and *Green Notebook*, Gide invites comparisons from the inquisitive reader, much as he had done in *Strait Is the Gate* with Jerome's tale and Alissa's diary. One can hardly exaggerate the number of literary games Gide sometimes indulged in once he was launched on a topic that intrigued him. From 1917 on, Gide became increasingly impatient with his religious topic.

"It strikes me that I was foolish and guilty of artificially bending my mind in order better to understand Catholic teaching. That is where real impiety lies." [8] "It was when my thought was boldest that it was truest. It was not of my thought I was afraid, but of the fear that some of my friends had of it. O my heart, harden yourself against that ruinous sympathy, counselor of all compromises. Why did I not remain whole and always stick obstinately to my own line!" [9]

There is certainly nothing mystical about *Numquid et tu* . . . Perhaps, had he carried through his project, Gide might have succeeded in creating a mystical Nicodemus; but his own meditations are, above all, exercises in literary expression. In essence, Gide would have liked to believe, could not believe, and was troubled by the questionable side of his eroticism. But what he sought in the Scriptures was the corroboration of his own very personal credo, an authorization to do away with a sense of guilt and to seek happiness "here and now" on this earth, through a "love" free from interdiction. Gide's Christ is always the "son of man," who proposes love in the place of dogma and restraints.

The *Green Notebook* contains only variations on the unorthodox credo which Gide had formulated on its first page —surely from the point of view of any Christian church, whether Catholic or Protestant, a characteristic and old heresy:

"If I had to formulate a credo, I should say: God is not behind us. He is to come. . . . He is terminal and not initial. . . . It is through man that God takes shape, this is what I feel and believe and what I read in the words: 'Let us create man in our image.' " [10] Gide's Christ is a man, a superman, who announces the divine being man could be if he waived all laws in favor of the unique law of love. Gide sees the crucifixion merely as an accident, unrelated to Christ's real message. Christ himself spoke of his "divine mission" only because of a confusion in his own mind concerning his role. The belief in salvation through the cross is, Gide concluded, the invention of St. Paul, whom Gide sees as a false prophet comparable to El Hadj. Gide's Christ thus mainly reflects Gide's personal tendency to seek escape from the burdens of life through love, a form of love in which emotivity and the refusal to take responsibilities have a large share. On this kind of love Gide was later to cast a rather more critical eye with his *Pastoral Symphony.*[11]

The meditations that make up *Numquid et tu . . .* were written over a period of three years, between 1916 and 1919. On May 5, 1917, a very different note was sounded in Gide's *Journal.* Exalting in a new-found joy, he was in a "wild daze of happiness," having fallen in love with a young boy, Marc Allegret, who for some ten years was very close to Gide. The literary idea of Nicodemus still preoccupied him, but much less exclusively. Gide was now tending the "seed" for a *New Fruits of the Earth.* "A clean start. I have swept everything away. Over and done with! I stand naked upon virgin soil beneath a heaven empty and ready for its new gods."[12] In a bad poem entitled "Crossing" Gide now sang of "a heart that made of its inconstancy a sail,"[13] preparing his future *Theseus.* His "Considerations on Greek Mythology" favorably contrasts the rational quality of Greek myths to the unreasonableness of Christian dogma. The epigraph of the *New Fruits of the Earth* could serve as leitmotif for his new mood: "That man is born for happiness, all nature surely proclaims."

Gide had always tended thus to develop parallel and contradictory themes: The *Treatise of the Dioscuri* was to have counterbalanced his *Conversations with Nicodemus.* But in this instance he completed neither work; his new attachment proved too distracting. He wrote a brief sketch of a tale narrated by a certain young "Michel" who travels with an older companion named "Fabrice," a rejuvenated version of Gide in love. Yet Gide's romance almost immediately led to a con-

flict which caused him such pain that he was able to speak
of it only much later. This was the "estrangement" from his
wife who in 1918, without a word of warning or explanation,
burned all the letters Gide had ever written her. Gide eventually discussed this incident in *Et Nunc manet in te*. . . .
Pierre Herbart commented on it at some length in his *A la
Recherche d'André Gide*, suggesting that Madeleine Gide
was jealous because, for the first time, Gide was truly in love
with someone else, a "real" betrayal of his love for her. Real
as Gide's despair was, it did not prevent him from reaping
the benefits of a new sense of freedom accompanied by a
new surge of energy.[14] In any case, Gide no longer suffered
from boredom and felt free to publish *Corydon* openly as
well as *If it die . . . ,*[15] his memoirs. Through Marc Allegret, his protégé, he came into contact with the young Dadaists who now, though temporarily, approved of him. He
had emerged from the "marshlands" of 1916 with a vigor
that was to carry him forward almost to his death.

The 1914-1917 period was really a kind of interlude in
Gide's development. The real orientation of his work was to
reappear with *The Counterfeiters*. *The Pastoral Symphony*
(1919) was a throwback to the past, though it profited from
the preparations for the unfinished *Conversations with Nicodemus* and used some of the thoughts Gide had elaborated
for *Numquid et tu . . .* Even these two works had their origins in the prewar discussions raised by *Strait Is the Gate*.
At that time, in connection with his projected *Pastoral Symphony*, then entitled *The Blind Girl*, Gide had noted:

I shall probably have to write a preface for my *Blind Girl*. . . .
In it I should say: "If to be a Protestant is to be a Christian without being a Catholic, then I am a Protestant." But I cannot recognize any orthodoxy other than the Roman orthodoxy, and if
Protestantism, whether Calvinist or Lutheran, tried to impose its
orthodoxy upon me, I should immediately turn toward the Roman as the only one. "Protestant orthodoxy"—these words have

no meaning for me. I recognize no *authority*; and if I did recognize one, it would be that of the Church.

But my Christianity springs only from Christ. Between him and me, I consider Calvin and St. Paul as two equally harmful screens.[16]

As early as 1893 Gide had planned to write the story of a blind girl rescued and cared for by a pastor whose charitable devotion is imperceptibly transformed into quite an earthly passion. In the 1919 story, Gertrude, the pastor's blind protégée, is the victim of two distortions of the Christian faith: the pastor's inadequate doctrine of pure love and his converted son's doctrinaire reliance on the strict adherence to St. Paul's teaching. So far as Gide himself was concerned, he would seem by 1919 to have dismissed both positions with equal disapproval. Like *Strait Is the Gate* and *The Immoralist*, *The Pastoral Symphony* is a critical, ironic work. Gide wrote it, he said, not because he wanted to, since it was not in line with his current thought, but because it clamored to be written, having slowly developed in his mind since 1893. Unquestionably, what explains its flowering some twenty-five years later was that Gide's initial idea could so beautifully absorb the material he had accumulated more recently in the *Green Notebook*.

Removed as it may seem from Gide himself with its Alpine setting and its clergyman hero, *The Pastoral Symphony* rather curiously reproduces aspects of Gide's life. He wrote his story rapidly, between February and October, 1918. It concerns a middle-aged man who "educates" a young girl with whom, like Pygmalion, he falls in love, just as Gide flattered himself that he was "forming" the young man who so fascinated him. The pastor's jealousy of his son's good looks and his strained relations with his wife are a transposition of some of Gide's own difficulties. But *The Pastoral Symphony* is much less deeply rooted in Gide's life than the two previous récits, Michel and Alissa's, had been.

In this newest work Gide used a slightly modified form of the first-person narrative. The pastor records his adventure through the fiction of two successive notebooks, reminiscent of André Walter's. The first notebook, written between February 26 and March 12, 1891, goes back two and a half years to relate the circumstances which brought Gertrude, the blind girl, into the pastor's home. After a one-month interval, the pastor picks up the thread of the story in the second notebook. But, in the interval, the present has overwhelmed the past. Breathlessly he notes events crowding in from all sides which elude his control, disproving the pious, edifying picture he had so carefully composed, events which precipitate Gertrude, his family and himself into a tragic impasse, where Gide leaves him, alone and emotionally destitute. At the turning point of the story, in the usual central plateau, the pastor's discussion with his son brings out the fallacy in his interpretation of the Scriptures, giving the book its Promethean dimensions.

There is nothing new in the technique Gide employs. The pastor's story is quite simple and straightforward. Called to minister to a dying woman in an isolated part of his parish in the Swiss Alps, he found, crouching by the hearth of the miserable cottage, a blind, misshapen girl covered with vermin, unable to speak since her deaf grandmother had never spoken to the child. Out of pure Christian charity he brings the child back with him to his wife, who is already overburdened with housework and the care of their five children. Inspired by the story of Laura Bridgman,[17] the pastor devotes much care and time to Gertrude's education, which makes great strides as she herself grows in goodness and beauty. Around the clergyman and his charge, absorbed in each other and in the idyllic world he is teaching her to see, one senses the growing disapproval of the family, of his wife in particular. Jacques, the clergyman's eldest son, confides to his father his wish to marry Gertrude, a perfect situation,

which should ensure Gertrude's happiness, supposedly the
pastor's main concern. But the young man's proposition is
firmly refused. Irritated and tyrannical, the pastor sends his
son away, and Gertrude too, innocently admitting her attachment to the pastor, rejects Jacques.

Here the second notebook starts, and Gide subtly develops
the symbolism of sight and blindness suggested in simple
fashion in the first part. The pastor who now knows the nature of his feeling for Gertrude, seeks and finds his moral
justification. But retribution is on the way: an operation re-
stores Gertrude's vision. She discovers Amelia's weary and
anxious expression, the pastor's wrinkles and Jacques's youthful, handsome face. When she turns to Jacques, now a
priest, he knows only how to teach her the meaning of sin.
Gertrude, who personifies love, goes down to the river, like
Ophelia, and tries to drown herself, dying of the consequences.

Essential to the understanding of the story is the form
Gertrude's education takes at the hands of the pastor. Emotionally exalted by his own Christian charity, the pastor gives
his exaltation the language of Christian fervor and, a disciple
of Rousseau, derives from the beauty of nature and the harmony of music—especially Beethoven's Pastoral Symphony—
a mystical credo which he teaches the blind girl: God's creation is harmonious, directed to the fulfillment of man's happiness, through love. Only men's blindness to this Will of
God leads to their unhappiness. Nothing in the novel is better conveyed than the pastor's unsuspecting appreciation of
Gertrude's response to his teaching. Natural beauty, he tells
her, implies divine intention just as aesthetic beauty proves
the existence of an ethical perfection. Beethoven's Pastoral
Symphony symbolizes that universal harmony which is God's
world. Sin is the refusal of love and so he and Gertrude are
without sin. It is only when Gertrude's new-found vision reveals the real world around her that this harmonious universe falls to pieces.

In spite of the perfection of its writing, *The Pastoral Symphony* suffers from Gide's detachment from his theme and the limitations inherent in his récit, not the least of which is the moralizing, clerical style, studded with evangelical texts, which he fabricated for the pastor. The sense of the story is conveyed through the incidents the pastor describes and it is rather hard to assume that he could so long remain unaware of their meaning, while so clearly describing them. The very title, *The Pastoral Symphony*—a rather facile pun—and the contrast between bitter tragedy and the glorious rebirth of an Alpine spring are charged with rather too obvious an irony. On one level *The Pastoral Symphony* is a brilliant play with words.

Convincing and penetrating though it undoubtedly is, the pathetic fallacy of the clergyman's confusion of two forms of love, Christian charity and sensual desire, is weakened by the fact that it has to be conveyed by the victim himself. The use of subtly emphasized key words, ambiguous biblical texts, tendentious conversations, and covertly hypocritical rationalizations, all become rather tiresome. Blindness and lucidity; spiritual and mental blindness; inner and outer darkness; good and evil; love and the law; the creative audacities of the heart as opposed to the routine security of the well-worn traditions—all Gide's themes reappear. The two young people, Gertrude and Jacques, are often unconvincing, speaking and acting like the puppets they are. In contrast, the slow, almost imperceptible warping of the pastor's initially pure, genuinely Christian feelings and the accompanying changes in the atmosphere of his home are accomplished with genuine mastery.

Certain truly excellent passages suggest Gide's new concern to project his story more objectively, to create for his characters less schematic and symbolic circumstances and settings than in the past. The pastor's ride through the snow, Gertrude's arrival in his home, the scene in which the pastor observes Gertrude and Jacques at the harmonium; the crucial conversations between Jacques and his father; Gertrude's arrival in the church after her operation—all these scenes are so superbly described that they inspired a successful film, so far the only film ever drawn from a Gidian work.

It is hardly surprising that *The Pastoral Symphony* was something of a best seller, nor that it disappointed the young avant-garde who had delighted in *Lafcadio's Adventures.* Even while writing it Gide himself had not taken his book seriously, admittedly cutting short its conclusion. He had felt an obligation to write it, but already he was much more preoccupied with his memoirs and with the new novel he had in mind. Not until ten years later was he again to use the récit form.

Chapter XIV

Genesis of a Novel

*Le monde réel me demeure tou-
jours un peu fantastique.*

The real world has always seemed
to me a little fantastic.

~~~~~~

"What is the use of doing over again what other people
have done already, or what I myself have done already, or
what other people might do?" [1] Although Edouard, the novelist in *The Counterfeiters*, blushes at this rather pretentious
declaration, his point of view is pretty close to what Gide's
own was when he started work on this first "novel." The
novel as genre had generated much discussion since the
1910's, particularly in the N.R.F. group. The successful post-
symbolist novelists—Barrès, Bourget, Loti, Anatole France—
and the neonaturalists all seemed to Gide's friends outmoded
and tedious. In the N.R.F., Copeau and the brilliant young
critic Jacques Rivière, both very close to Gide, had attacked
the prevalent types of novels, calling for a modern form of
the "novel of adventure." A whole new generation of young
novelists had started to publish their first works just as Gide

brought out *Lafcadio's Adventures* on the eve of the war, among them Giraudoux, Martin du Gard, Mauriac, and Romains. In 1913 *Swann's Way*, the first part of Proust's monumental *In Quest of Time Lost*, appeared. Awarded the Prix Goncourt in 1918, it drew a good deal of attention. Gide, who was rereading Dostoevsky as well as various English novelists, including Dickens, with renewed interest, was anxious himself to renew the genre. He had always felt Valéry's avowed contempt for the novel as something of a challenge. At the time that he wrote *Isabelle* and *Lafcadio's Adventures*, when he had retrospectively reclassified his earlier novels as soties or récits, he had also outlined a general theory of what, in his eyes, a novel should be. For the first time, he had spoken not in general of "art" or "literature" but of a specific genre: the novel.

Unlike Proust, Gide naturally thought in terms of novels and not of *the novel*, although at one point he seemed tempted by the idea of a single definitive work "to concentrate in one novel all that life offers and teaches me." But when he started to work on *The Counterfeiters* he found that the idea inhibited rather than inspired him:

"My book will not come out well until I have done away with the conviction that it is my last book, that I shall never write any others." [2] By the time Gide really began to make headway on *The Counterfeiters*, in the postwar years, the situation with regard to the novel had changed. When he spoke of contemporary novelists as "coasters," afraid to move out into the open sea, he could surely not have been alluding to Proust, Joyce, Kafka, or Virginia Woolf, to say nothing of the surrealists. Gide, who wanted all his books to herald the future, must have sensed that he was being outdistanced.

Although he was now in his fifties, his own life had radically changed. His friendship with young Marc Allegret had brought him into touch with a precocious group of postwar writers, a good thirty years younger than himself. His wife's silent disapproval, her slow though never completed evolution toward Catholicism, in opposition to his own spiritual inclinations, held Gide in a constant state of tension from which his work benefited. Paradoxically this bound him still more closely to the woman from whom, occasionally, he thought he was now detached.

It was hardly surprising that among other things he felt like adding new variations to his youthful *Fruits of the Earth*. In the detached pages of *New Fruits of the Earth*, which began to accumulate, he proclaimed with unabashed lyricism the "obligation to be happy," "the astonishing miracle of life," the beneficent power of "great Pan": "Who was it said that great Pan is dead?" [3] Happiness is love, the power to let oneself be carried forward on a great tide of love, going wherever it might lead, with a "so be it." Gide now put aside the somber figure of his Saul "dispossessed" by his own demons. Love, he proclaimed, was the highest form of self-forgetfulness and freed the individual from his limitations. He now saw this power of depersonalization as the source of all his creative work, past and future. "I become the other, I get away from myself—and so be it. This is the key to my character and work." [4]

"To push abnegation all the way to total self-forgetfulness" is a fine moral precept. However, its application where Gide's life was concerned is open to question. When applied to literary effort the precept could serve him well, but it served him equally well as an authorization to lay aside some of his human responsibilities: "My mind balks at the word 'consequence.' The consequence of our acts. To be consequent with oneself. Am I to expect nothing from myself but a sequel? Consequence; compromise; a road traced beforehand." [5]

Ever since *Marshlands* and *Fruits of the Earth*, Gide had been playing with the related notions of "consequence"—a form of predetermination—and freedom, as illustrated by the gratuitous act. "Inconsequence," combining the two notions, now became the focus of his thought. The gratuitous act appears merely as an extreme example of inconsequence, more apparent than real, as Gide had been at some pains to show. "There is no act, however absurd or prejudicial, which is not the result of a concurrence of causes, conjunctions, and concomitance."

Gide's old friends Zeus and Prometheus were still at work in his universe and by their very incompatibility were responsible for the thousand inconsistencies that went into the conduct of the life of his fictional characters. The concept of the gratuitous act had served Gide well as a creative device in plotting the generally disastrous but unforeseeable careers of his characters. The new guiding principle he now adopted, the principle of inconsequence, was rather amusingly the logical outcome of his point of view: life never conforms to the patterns conceived by the human mind; but it is impossible for a human being to live without referring, consciously or not, to some such pattern; the only safe and sane course open to human beings therefore is perpetually to modify their idea of life in line with their experience, while elucidating experience through thought. Inconsequence is, then, the supple state of mind which allows the individual to maintain a sane balance between Zeus and Prometheus.

The Dadaists, who set great store by inconsequence, and the surrealists, who violently attacked as illusory the so-called consistency of a logically ordered view of existence, brought Gide a welcome corroboration. But it was probably Blake—whom he had discovered in 1914 and to whom he returned in 1922, translating *The Marriage of Heaven and Hell*—who suggested to Gide the solution of the Prometheus-Zeus impasse. In his preface to *The Poems of William Blake*,[6] Yeats briefly analyzed the conflict of Los and Urizel, the two life principles which preside over the fate of the world in Blake's prophetic poems. Urizel, comparable in a sense to Gide's own Zeus, represents law, while Los, more powerful than Prometheus, is the formative principle that shapes substance itself, directing creation toward ever higher forms. Gide, always fascinated by the idea of "formation," an aesthetic principle essentially, now saw how to go beyond the "deformations" to which previously he had limited his attention.

He also felt the inadequacy of the two basic aesthetic patterns he had evolved, both of which hark back to his *Prometheus*. When Gide wrote: "*Strait Is the Gate* is the criticism of a certain mystic tendency; *Isabelle*, the criticism of a certain form of romantic imagination; *The Pastoral Symphony*, of a form of self-deception; *The Immoralist*, of a form of individualism," [7] he was unjustly reducing these works to the dimensions of the "moral problem" novel. It is true that in them Gide had played with loaded dice. He had condemned his characters in advance. But in the writing Gide never himself intervened between character and reader. So plausible and personal are the circumstances described that the reader seems to participate in the characters' errors. In each récit the main character is so individual that no general moral precepts can be infallibly deduced from his story; it is always open to discussion. If the character erred, where and how did his mistake arise, and how inevitable does it appear to be? The "devil's share," the unsuspected inner forces at work beneath the surface, which Gide so carefully emphasized in each case, always diminishes the human responsibility of the character. An element of chance comes into play—Gide called it "novelistic fatality," [8] excluding from his work some of the more irritating limitations of the time-honored edifying "thesis-novel."

In his récits Gide had worked hard at realizing what he called an aesthetic justice, an inner balance and cohesion defining the organic and aesthetic unity of the whole, comparable to the "verisimilitude" sought by the French seventeenth-century dramatists. But Gide had really succeeded only when dealing with characters whom he considered "re-

jected fragments" of himself, who were in fact "lyric creations." When, as in *Isabelle* and *The Pastoral Symphony*, he
attempted to move further afield he turned out skillful, sophisticated, but not very significant fables.

In the three soties, on the other hand, he had set in motion mechanisms which from inside and outside impose limits on the inner aspirations and understanding of the characters: routine, habits, laws—whether natural or social. Fundamentally more original than the récits, the soties are mobile, four-dimensional structures, which Gide preferred to the
linear structures on which the novel had so long relied. Reducing character and plot to their bare essentials, he had
experimented with structures suggested to him by modern
conceptions of relativity and simultaneity. But in line with
his own ethical point of view, the patterns he evolved served
almost exclusively to reveal the "idols and bugaboos" which
cause human beings to blunder. Thus the soties are quite as
devastating as the récits. All Gide's characters seemed to
come out as quixotic dupes.

"All those who turn man away from life become my personal enemies," [9] Gide wrote. Yet after *Fruits of the Earth*
one might conclude that Gide himself had been engaged in
turning man away from life. In the majority of his books
human efforts to make sense of life had always ended in absurd or tragic dead ends. But, in fact, Gide's works had in
the past always developed in counterpoint with his own ethics
and life. Through his characters Gide had been punishing the
"other" that he might have become had he not at some point
stopped short. Aesthetic justice and self-justification had gone
hand in hand. Gide's humorous and slightly superior attitude
toward Fleurissoire, to some extent a caricature double of
himself, is exactly opposite to Stendhal's idealizations of himself, Julien Sorel and Fabrice del Dongo. The first-person
narrative in the récit and the patent absurdities of the sotie

are distorting mirrors reflecting an image which the reader should redress. Starting from life, the récit takes off into the imaginary, whereas in the sotie the absurd mechanisms of events and the caricature figures end by becoming almost human. Hence the ambiguity which gives both these Gidian genres their elusive and poetic atmosphere.

Récits and soties necessarily emanate from a more general, broader point of view—the author's. It is he who sets up the perspectives, introduces the distortions, and imposes a strong family resemblance upon each work. Gide always insisted that his stories should all be read at once and not evaluated separately. It is true that considered as an ensemble the impression they leave is rather different from what each successively seems to say. As in a fresco, behind the separate groups clearly outlined and emphasized there is a rather pleasing, optimistic background which gives the whole its underlying equilibrium.

Nonetheless, Gide felt his work had been fragmentary and perhaps misleading and now decided he must "illuminate the whole landscape." His article on Dadaism, a misinterpretation so far as the aims of Dada were concerned, was an expression of his own new aspirations.[10] Gide, a disciple here of Nietzsche and even more possibly of Blake, thought that subversive energies were essentially creative. "Dada" seemed to him useful and interesting because it was blazing the way for new forms of literature, a most heretical interpretation from the Dadaists' point of view. "Yes, every form has become a formula and conveys unspeakable boredom. . . . I believe that every new need should create its new form." He was so convinced of this that he wrote about the new form of his novel before he had started work on it: "I have become rather clearly aware of the use I can make of this new form." [11] Five years before, in his outline for a preface to *Isabelle,* Gide had briefly described the kind of novel he was then thinking of:

The novel, such as I know it or imagine it, calls for a variety of viewpoints, dependent upon the variety of the characters brought into action. It is essentially a deconcentrated work. Anyway, formulating a theory about the novel is much less important to me than writing novels.[12]

The novel he described in this way would seem to be a combination of the récit and the sotie, a rather paradoxical notion. But in the postwar years Gide seemed to have become sensitive to a certain lack of vitality in his work and to have wondered whether the forms which had satisfied him so far had not become "formulae."

At the instigation of his friend Rivière, he had started to read Proust again.[13] He was now deeply impressed by the richness of Proust's still uncompleted book; struck with genuine admiration but also, as he honestly admitted, with envy. He often had Proust in mind during the period in which his own novel was taking shape. After 1916 he occasionally saw Proust and read the volumes of *In Quest of Time Lost* as they came off the press. He noted in the *Journal of the Counterfeiters*—not, interestingly enough, in his own *Journal*—a curious dream he had had concerning Proust in March, 1923. "I was sitting on a plain stool beside a low coffee table, almost in the center of a large, dimly lighted room. The person I was talking to, his face half hidden by the wings of a large armchair, was Marcel Proust."[14] Noticing a bookcase containing some precious volumes and a string dangling from the shelf close at hand, in his dream Gide deliberately pulled the string in order to make the volumes fall to the floor—a symbol of Gide's guilt and remorse no doubt at his initial rejection of Proust's manuscript but also perhaps of his wish to surpass him.

Gide wanted to make a fresh start and to surprise the public by his audacity. The brief definition he had given of the novel in his "Outline for a Preface to *Isabelle*" was curiously abstract and referred only to structure, not to plot, characters or content. Gide does not ever seem to have been interested merely in telling a story; what he had always wanted to express was the intricate but abstract interplay of personal relationships. His imagination seemed to work backwards. He did not start out with a concrete imaginary world to be projected by means of a narrative. He seems always to have started with an abstract diagram to which he then had to adapt the traditional components of the novel. This was no easy task.

When Edouard, the novelist in *The Counterfeiters*, after some beating about the bush formulates the subject of the book he is writing he is as abstract as Gide himself. His book is to show "the rivalry between the real world and one's representation of the world"; [15] then developing his idea further he declares: "The *manner* in which the world of appearances imposes itself upon us, and in which we try to impose on the outside world our own *interpretation*, makes the drama of our lives." [16] Edouard is pretty close to the prewar Gide. But much later in the game, when Gide defined what he himself was attempting, he was still no less abstract than Edouard: "On one side, the event, the fact, the external datum; on the other side, the effort of the novelist to make a book out of it all." [17]

That, of course, was not the real subject of *The Counterfeiters*, but the remark does point out Gide's peculiarly intellectual bent. His fiction all deals in part with some of the psychological effects caused by the discovery that there is an autonomous outer reality. In his own life, adventure for Gide seems to have been inseparable from a sense that he had at last emerged from his own inner world and glimpsed, behind "trompe l'oeil" façades, a reality that habitually eluded him: "The real world has always seemed to me a little fantastic. I began to realize this a long time ago. . . . It seems to me that we are all moving about in a fantastic show and that what others call reality, their external world, has not much

more existence than the world of *The Counterfeiters* or of
The Thibaults." [18] One whole aspect of Gide's own personality, disconcerting for his friends, can be accounted for by
this tendency to equate outer reality and fiction: his way of
going through life, his nose stuck in his Vergil, leaving all
practical problems to others, amused rather than irritated if
anything went wrong; the boredom that came over him when
the "fantasic show" offered too little distraction; and, more
serious, his incapacity to see what part he himself played in
the real world of others, his wife's particularly.

Gide's feeling of estrangement from the real world naturally limited his scope as novelist. It would be difficult for
any author to convey the sense of a reality he himself did
not take seriously. But the limitation had its advantages—his
almost uncanny sense of the incomprehensible nature of life
and his capacity to detect the suspect and fictional element
in most representations of reality, including his own.

The Gidian sense of life is based on his conviction that
what *is* is more exciting than any form of fiction and his belief that human beings elude facts by clothing them in fiction or "representation." The characters in Gide's novels have
in various degrees this same capacity for distorting the events
that concern them; even as they relate and interpret them
they tend to fictionalize. His characters are in a sense novelists themselves, transforming experience into fiction. Only
a very few of them are willing to abandon their fictions when
they come face to face with events that do not fit their interpretations.

Gide, fascinated by the elusive nature of experience, sees
the real novelist as the man who strips away these distorted
representations of life. As far as he was concerned, the most
realistic novels and the most exciting, rather than stressing
the rivalry between a real situation and its transformation in
one or many minds, would little by little disclose a real sit-

uation despite its fictional, one might almost say mythic, transformation in the characters' minds.

Gide may have lacked a certain sense of reality, but he had both a sense of life and a great love of life. As he started out on *The Counterfeiters* everything in his own private life seemed to heighten his feeling that life held in reserve for the responsive individual inexhaustible funds of unforeseeable joy. With *Lafcadio's Adventures* he had at last openly asserted his own intellectual and ethical point of view. Now his once rather limited horizons had been considerably enlarged. He wanted to create something entirely new. Although *The Counterfeiters* was, of course, linked to the works that preceded it, it did turn out to be both new and surprising as a novel. Gide, who had wondered whether he should not use a more traditional form, was struck by the "strangeness" of what he had accomplished. *The Counterfeiters* is by far the most original of his works. For the substance of his story he did not go far afield but continued to exploit his own rather narrow area. What was new was the outlook, intent and technique. And with *The Counterfeiters* his capacity for renewal came to an end; except for occasional flashes of his former brilliance, his work steadily deteriorated.

Gide had always played with the idea of inviting his readers to collaborate in the creation of his novels; not the lazy readers of course, but the superior, curious ones, interested in penetrating behind the scenes. Along with his novel he published *The Journal of the Counterfeiters* (1926), the notebooks in which he had kept a record of the creation of the novel. But he was quite unsystematic as a writer and many other notes concerning the novel were tucked away in his own *Journal*. He was actually far too canny a writer to hand over to future critics all his materials and abortive attempts. He refers to rough sketches which he rejected, separate filing cards and loose pages, which seem to have disappeared: "I am writing on a separate page the first vague outline of the plot." Though he wanted his readers and critics to follow his progress, he obviously published only such materials as he deemed fit. Nonetheless, a simultaneous reading of the two journals clarifies Gide's method of work and his intentions.

The Counterfeiters, like all Gide's major works, had occupied his mind for many years—at least twenty. In 1906, 1907 and 1909 he had collected and filed together a number of newspaper clippings connected with this or other projects. Of these items, two concern separate gangs of counterfeiters while a third describes the death of a high-school boy, who, following the rules of the secret suicide gang to which he belonged, had been drawn by lot to commit the first suicide. Even though Gide may at first have planned two separate books, the themes of counterfeit and adolescent suicide are central to his story and from its inception were closely linked in Gide's imagination.

The two gangs of counterfeiters brought Gide certain embryonic suggestions. One of the gangs operated in the Luxembourg Gardens, which Gide used for the opening scene of the novel. As a youngster he had often played there; it was a kind of annex to the Ecole Alsacienne, the Protestant private school he had attended. But more especially, perhaps, it was the moral tone of the articles that caught Gide's attention: the reporter noted with consternation the presence of young prep-school students among the counterfeiters, two of whom belonged to respectable bourgeois homes, sons of a responsible magistrate and an important civil servant. The first reporter's distress was echoed in the clipping concerning the suicide pact: how could boys from good families in a respectable school indulge in such scandalous diversions? This was all grist to Gide's mill; these gangs of teen-agers carrying on clandestine activities in the very heart of the bourgeois citadel have their counterparts in the novel. All Gide's youngsters are from good bourgeois families. And as for the school, killing two birds with one stone Gide made it a Protestant establishment concerned with the religious as well as the intellectual formation of its charges.

The Luxembourg gang offered further rich suggestions. Under questioning one of the young leaders had blandly insisted that the motivation of the gang was entirely disinterested. They were not criminals but anarchists, intent on attacking a social order that they considered corrupt. One of their answers was to echo all through Gide's book. Questioned by the judge as to the nature of his gang, a young counterfeiter said: "Let's call it 'the coterie,' your Honor. . . . It was a group that dealt in counterfeit money, I don't deny that; but we were primarily concerned with questions of politics and literature." [19] Gide's novel is exclusively populated with just such counterfeiters and for a while, rather surprisingly for him, he even thought of developing the theme of political counterfeit, a theme he eventually suggested only in the last pages of his book. Gide finally decided rather to explore the more familiar ethical implications of the young counterfeiter's answer.

He could hardly have hoped for more congenial materials. There, in fact and not just in Gide's imagination, were subversive forces at work beneath the complacent moral fictions of a willfully nearsighted society. All his favorite themes could develop around the central symbol of the counterfeit coin taking on new and positive values. In *Lafcadio's Adventures* the mere concept of a "False Pope" destroys the notion implicit in the word "Pope." On the other hand, a counterfeit coin can circulate only when it passes for the real coin it imitates, whose value is not open to suspicion. Gide must have reveled in the creative possibilities furnished him by this ambiguous symbol.

Despite his early settling upon this basic material, Gide's major work progressed very slowly. He started *The Journal of the Counterfeiters* on June 17, 1919, and finished his novel six years later, on June 9, 1925. Gide was no Flaubert or

Proust, working without cease on one single opus. During those six years he sometimes let a month go by, or even a year, without adding a single line. "I spend long periods of time without writing, in traveling, observing, living. I consider it good to put some air and distance between my books," [20] he wrote. And he also seemed to put air and distance between the various parts of any one book.

As usual, too, Gide did not concentrate all his effort on *The Counterfeiters* to the exclusion of other works. In those years he completed and published *Corydon;* worked on his "memoirs," parts of which appeared in the *N.R.F.* in 1920, 1921, 1924 and 1925; and occasionally added pages to *New Fruits of the Earth.* In addition to the usual array of prefaces, reviews, articles of criticism and translations, he gave six lectures on Dostoevsky which he published in a volume, *Dostoevsky,* in 1923. His *Journal* records a whole set of those lightning moves and journeys which seem to have become more and more characteristic of him as he grew older. He was a hard worker but not a methodical one, picking up in turn the various projects he had on hand. *The Counterfeiters* lay fallow as Gide worked on his autobiography; and, in fact, it could hardly have progressed otherwise. Gide never outlined any over-all plan for his book but occasionally jotted down a vague idea for dividing it into two or three parts, which he then never troubled to implement. He claimed, truthfully it seems, that he never knew beforehand exactly how he was going to proceed. Hence his need for time to allow the work to mature, to "ventilate the subject and infuse into it the reality of daily life." [21] His habit of reading portions of his unfinished book aloud to his friends helped him in this work of ventilation. Gide noted several times that when he reached the point of writing the words flowed from his pen. The long years during which he had imposed on himself the obligation of writing every day in his *Journal* now seemed to be paying dividends. The writing of the novel itself, once Gide reached that stage, seems to have offered none of the difficulties he recorded at the time he was struggling with *Strait Is the Gate*.

The autobiography Gide was writing concurrently served as an antidote to his novel. There Gide, an old hand at discerning the imperceptible distortions inherent in any recounting of facts, attempted to cut his own story down to the bare essentials he needed to lead up to his discovery of what he called "the inner proposition of my being," his particular form of eroticism. The neutral tonality of *If it die* . . .[22] and its strict adherence to fact, allowed Gide by contrast to give free rein to a certain fantasy and spontaneity in the writing of *The Counterfeiters*. One has the feeling that the adventurous adolescents of the novel owe much of their audacity to their long tête-à-tête in Gide's imagination with the solemn and inhibited youth he was describing in his memoirs. Between Gide's description of his own school and its counterpart in *The Counterfeiters*, the Pension Azaïs, Gide introduced a number of distorting mirrors, a different tonality. The tonality of a Gidian work is one of the very elusive factors in its genesis, always of the utmost importance to its author:

"I am like a musician striving . . . to juxtapose and overlap an andante theme and an allegro theme. I think I have enough material for two books, and I am starting this notebook in an effort to distinguish between elements of widely differing tonality,"[23] he noted in the opening paragraph of the *Journal of the Counterfeiters*.

For some time Gide was perplexed by an apparently minor problem: he thought of his novel as belonging to the postwar era but he could not separate the plot from its generating symbol—the gold coin. Some of the connotations of the symbol could also apply to bank notes, but not all. There were no gold coins in postwar France. Afraid of "losing [his] footing,"[24] Gide prudently decided to write so that, reading the book "at any time, one could say today." Actually, the question was purely academic. Gide's work could in any case have had a historical value only indirectly and in the realm of ideas. Each work of Gide's took a long time to mature, absorbing immense quantities of material accruing to it over the years. Books, experience, observation were all slowly distilled and fused into the transparent substance of his novels which did not lend themselves easily therefore to historical accuracy. The twenty years of slow distillation behind *The Counterfeiters* would, of itself, have imposed on Gide a novel "without historical perspective."

Although Gide tended to think of his life in terms of his novel as he wrote *The Counterfeiters*,[25] the novel itself actually drew very little directly from his outside circumstances. It seemed to have a will of its own. Gide's hesitations, notes and rejections all refer to its "invisible mass" which he was not able to "clearly discern." "Nevertheless there is filling out and taking form the book I should like to write if . . . But the vastness of the amorphous substance crushes me; I don't know where to seize hold of it and wonder how I shall manage it," he wrote on October 7, 1915. As late as 1921 he was still mentioning "that enormous novel I must begin to block out." [26] Gide's notes never give the slightest clue to what he might have had in mind, what characters, plot or setting. He mentions a "subject" he never describes and when he writes that his novel is to be a "crossroads of problems," the remark is hardly helpful.

Much the longest phase in the genesis of the book consisted in the patient notation of outer incidents observed by Gide, which furnished him with concrete details that he thought might enrich his story. Gide seems really to have worked at random, in turn collecting, selecting and rejecting. He recorded at length an encounter with a schoolboy he caught stealing books, an incident which later appears in the novel. But he made no use of other, carefully noted incidents. Among other materials eventually used in the novel is a conversation with his old piano teacher drawn from Gide's personal *Journal*. However, the bulk of the material he was to use was drawn from his own memory as direct observation and is never mentioned in his notebooks.

Gide, unlike Balzac, could not start off with situations and characters more real to him than any reality. He had to borrow from reality to give substance to his imaginary world, but the elements he borrowed underwent great changes before they could find their place in a novel which is very far from being, as has been suggested, a "roman à clef." [27] "The best parts of my book," he noted, "are the parts of pure invention." Of one of his characters, La Pérouse, he notes: ". . . too close to reality . . . will not really come to life . . . until he completely displaces his original." [28] The original to be displaced was, in this instance, Gide's old piano teacher. But so it was in every case. The real schoolboy who stole books got in Gide's way when, transferring the incident to one of his own characters, young Georges, Gide stuck too closely to the original episode.

Gide had great trouble visualizing his characters. He could hear them speak,[29] but in order to give them a physical existence, to *see* them, he had to borrow from the people around him. All his characters, however, originated in his inner world before moving out into their own fictional universe. "What today is called 'objectivity' is easy to achieve for novelists without an inner landscape. I can say that I was interested not in myself but in the conflict of certain ideas of which my soul was only the theater and in which my function was not so much that of actor as of witness." [30] He had great difficulty in finding the "objective correlative" for this inner spectacle, a great handicap which left him with the impression that he was "groping in the clouds for hours on end." "This effort to project an interior creation outside oneself," he wrote, "to objectify the subject (before having to subjectify the object) is really exhausting. For days and days one can distinguish nothing at all." [31]

As a result, what took Gide longest was his search for the needed characters. They refused to take shape. Gide had first thought of borrowing Lafcadio ready-made from his sotie and using him as spectator-narrator in his new novel, suggesting later that Lafcadio could also play the role of perverter, but of whom or of what? Gide then briefly considered a vague assortment of characters or rather types, a gambler, a seducer, a novelist.[32] Until 1921 Gide's novel seemed to contain only two characters: Edouard, the novelist, always one of the key figures in the book, and Lafcadio, whom Gide eventually discarded. In 1921 Gide toyed with the idea of a third character, the devil. One could hardly conceive of a more fantastic trio. In the meantime, in the *Journal of the Counterfeiters,* Gide mentioned vaguely a conflict between young people and the generation that preceded them, surely not a very new or promising theme. He sketched out short scenarios involving X, Y, and Z, unnamed and undescribed. A clergyman's family, Gide noted, would be corrupted deliberately by Z, who hates the narrow, puritanical ethics they represent.

Only on August 20, 1922, three years after Gide had started work, are certain characters at last named in the *Journal.* These are, with Edouard, the principal characters in *The Counterfeiters:* Bernard, Olivier, Robert de Passevant, and Vincent, with brief indications as to their psychological make-up. Bernard seeks to define himself in opposition to others; Olivier and Vincent allow themselves to be corrupted, deviated from their natural path. At one point Gide demonstrates through Edouard some of the difficulties his characters were giving him.

Make Edouard say, perhaps: "The bore, you see, is having to condition one's characters. They live powerfully within me and I should say even that they live at my expense. I know how they think, how they speak; I distinguish the most subtle intonations in their voices. I know that they are to commit certain acts, and that others are forbidden them. . . . But as soon as I must clothe them, decide on their place in the social scale, their careers, the amount of their income; above all, as soon as I must invent relationships, parents, a family, friends, I throw up the job. I must admit that I see each one of my characters as an orphan, an only son, unmarried, and childless.[33]

By 1921 the voices had succeeded in becoming people, but it was to take Gide another year to invent families for his heroes, who tend to come to life as picaros, adventurers unattached to any family or social circle. Only when he had his characters in hand did Gide really start to write. Between July 6, 1919, when he read "the still tentative opening of the book" to Roger Martin du Gard, and December 7, 1921, when he wrote: "During the thirteen days I have been here, I wrote the first thirty pages of my book," Gide had been marking time. It was not until 1924, six months before the completion of the novel, that Gide felt "the book now sometimes seems to have a life of its own." [34]

If the characters gave Gide trouble, the plot apparently was of no concern whatsoever. He hesitated, however, over the technical problem of deciding what type of narrative to use. In true Gidian style he first thought of presenting the story indirectly through Lafcadio, a far from omniscient observer, ". . . to avoid the artificiality of a 'plot'; but *events* should fall into a pattern independently of Lafcadio and, so to speak, behind his back." [35]

This relativity in the point of view of the major witness, in itself more essential to the work than any given character, was eventually transferred to Edouard. Gide also considered the feasibility of introducing three successive spokesmen, or intermediaries, who would in turn describe what was going on from their point of view, or of having various characters narrate the events that concerned them. He stressed his interest in using certain techniques of the detective novel which he felt were particularly suited to his subject. It was, in fact, probably the influence of the detective novel that in the end led him to use a direct form of narrative, constantly relayed by journals, letters, dialogues and soliloquies. But the finished novel kept traces of what obviously cannot be attributed to mere fumbling. The alert narrator in *The Counterfeiters*, having reported the events of the first section of the story, stops unexpectedly, in Pirandellesque fashion, to examine and discuss with his readers where the story may be leading. None of his hypotheses apply to the most important event in the making at the very heart of the novel, the semisuicide semimurder of the young prep-school boy, Boris.

Gide's narrator-spokesman, discovering events only as they occur, is obviously no further ahead than the reader. Gide realized his initial plan, "the whole story of the counterfeiters is to be discovered only in a gradual way," [36] and come fully to light only at the end.

Gide had always wanted to rid the novel as a genre of the "parasitic elements" that superficial realism had burdened it with. When he discussed the "pure novel" [37] and the necessity for working toward the "erosion of contours" in fiction he was working out the formula best suited to his own intellectual bent. This was to discover, beneath the complicated network of appearances, the deeper outline of a story in the making. When Gide spoke of "purging the novel of all the elements that do not specifically belong to the novel," [38] this rather vague statement referred quite exactly to what he was attempting to achieve in *The Counterfeiters.* He wanted to subordinate characters and plot to their often episodic role in the formation of one underlying pattern. "I am trying to wind the various threads of the plot and the complexities of my thoughts around the little living bobbins that are my characters." [39]

If the little living bobbins were to become characters, unwinding on their own the threads of a plot indistinguishable from themselves, Gide had to make a great effort at stylization. He had in fact to create characters both "new" and "invented" who could live and breathe only in terms of the novel he had abstracted from reality. It was not a new psychology he was experimenting with but rather a new architecture, a new way of projecting his characters into space: "First study the source of light; all the shadows will depend on that. Every form rests on and finds support in its shadow." [40] The bulk of the novel does indeed remain in the shadow, while Gide brings the greater part of his effort to bear on certain brilliantly lighted surfaces, so much so that these are the ones critics have tended to see to the exclusion of all others. This new architecture accounted for Gide's heroic efforts to avoid a sustained narrative. "With each chapter I must start anew. *Never take advantage of the momentum gained*—such is the rule of my game." [41] He wants each facet of the whole to appear to the reader independently, no single one revealing the pattern of which it is a part. It is not astonishing, therefore, that Gide often worked out his novel, as he said, in reverse, perpetually strengthening the hidden lines whose ultimate convergence would reveal a hidden, guiding intent. But what events? What grouping? The novel is there to elucidate this point and it does not always correspond to what Gide says about it in *The Journal of the Counterfeiters*. For example, he starts the second notebook of the *Journal* with the following statement:

Properly speaking, there is no single center to this book, around which my various efforts converge; it is in relation to two foci, as in an ellipse, that they become polarized. On the one hand, the event, the fact, the external datum; on the other, the very effort of the novelist to make a book out of it all. That effort is the main subject, the new center that throws the plot off its axis, drawing it away toward the imaginative. [42]

But Edouard never really tries to "make a book" out of what he observes, or, at least, Gide shows us two brief and very mediocre passages of a book that, he warns us, Edouard will never write. It is Gide who writes the book, and if he does not really let us into his secrets, it is perhaps because he himself was not clearly conscious of what they were. *The Journal of the Counterfeiters* is quite enlightening on this point. Up to almost the last instant, until May, 1925, Gide thought he was writing a novel in two parts. At the last moment it inevitably became a novel in three parts; the first and last, each with eighteen chapters, are situated in Paris, while the seven central chapters take place in Saas-Fée, in Switzerland. As usual, the novel had taken shape as an ascending curve, a plateau, a descending curve, ending with the disintegration of the main themes rather than a conclusion. Instinctively Gide had worked out the structure which was fundamentally his "own" and which seen from without might appear contrived and artificial:

"I hold that the composition of a book is of the first importance and I hold that it is through a lack of composition that most works of art sin today. . . . It is best to let the work compose its own order, and above all it is best not to *force* it." [43] Apparently this is how all Gide's works took shape. They are fashioned from the inside out. Gide's form, or *design*, for each, perfect as it may seem, even to the point of artificiality when completed, is the end result of a long fumbling and groping. That is why his novels are not merely "thesis-novel" demonstrations. From the fictional debate instigated in the novel about the novel, certain principles do emerge most subtly. This is true too of his ethics. Abstracted from his novels, however, Gide's thought often seems vague, closer to common sense than to wisdom. He sometimes even pontificates, and in rather facile fashion. Fiction alone provided him the means of transmitting in its entirety the inner climate of sensitivity from which his ideas drew their singular and persuasive force.

There is something truly admirable in the discipline Gide imposed upon himself in the writing of *The Counterfeiters*. The creation of a novel was for him adventure par excellence, a veritable Odyssey. He succeeds in projecting something of the excitement and poetry of his creative experience into the very prosaic and mediocre world which the novel sets in motion. It took all Gide's intelligence and vast experience as a writer to make of this strange novel a work of great scope. He succeeded, because he imposed upon his material a form as restrained and controlled as the fugue.

Chapter XV

The Novel

The combats of truth and error
is eating of the Tree of Life.

—William Blake, *The Marriage
of Heaven and Hell*

~~~~~~

The *Journal of the Counterfeiters* is neither a guide to
Gide's novel nor an explanation of it. At most, it can raise
certain questions in the reader's mind concerning Gide's intentions, the merits of the techniques he used, and the scope
of the book itself. On the whole, it stresses those characteristics of fiction which Gide wanted to do away with: (descriptions in the realistic manner, a plot around which to drape
his story, motivational analysis explaining the characters' behavior, the kind of narration so smoothly organized that it
carries the reader along on a kind of conveyer belt, and the
traditional sort of conclusion.

Yet all these customary habitual ingredients have a place
in *The Counterfeiters*. Gide provides a geographic and social
setting, a main plot, and several subordinate plots. The succession of events is carefully timed and the novel is brought

to a conclusion by means of two, perhaps even three, successive denouements, the first two partially happy endings, the third tragic.[1] All the energies set in motion in the first part of the novel come to a temporary rest at the end, an equilibrium on which the book closes.[2]

Gide situates his story carefully: in the Luxembourg section of Paris and in Saas-Fée, Switzerland—a narrow geographic area but with ramifications in France, England, Corsica, Poland, America and Africa. The effect is of a small brilliantly lighted stage beyond which the entire world extends. Lady Griffith's America, the Africa of Vincent, the Poland of La Pérouse's son are the faraway frontiers of a region in which even Pau, in southern France, is considered a place of exile. The setting of *The Counterfeiters* resembles the universe of the ancients: a small flat space surrounded by the vague masses of mythical continents. Gide had wanted the setting of his novel to be "saturated with myth," his Luxembourg Gardens to be as imaginary as Shakespeare's Forest of Arden in *As You Like It*. Actually one may feel rather constrained by the naïveté and narrowness of the Gidian perspective. The borders of the known world in *The Counterfeiters* are rather quickly reached.

The small coherent group of characters belong to a part of the respectable Parisian bourgeoisie, shut in upon itself and limited in its contacts. The foreigners who happen to intrude are promptly thrown out: little Boris, from Poland, commits suicide and Lady Griffith is assassinated by Vincent.

The Protestant milieu, as always, furnishes the main contingent of characters, the family of the Vedel-Azaïs, the Moliniers and the novelist Edouard; but a variety of so-called Protestant righteousness even hangs over the Catholic Profitendieus.[3] Gide did not wish to raise the denominational issue as he had done in *Strait Is the Gate*. What the four families most actively involved in his story have in common is their connection with liberal professions: they are magistrates, professors, pastors, writers. On the fringes, the aristocratic Passavants and the politically inclined Adamantis suggest further upper-middle class connections. Quite late in the story there appears a character who seems out of place in such a respectable group, the counterfeiter Strouvilhou. The social setting, like the geographic, stretches farther than is at first apparent. What shuts the characters in is their own limited point of view, whereas in truth they are "imbricated," as Gide would say, in an apparently unlimited social world.

Gide may have had trouble initially in attaching his heroes to definite families and "relating" them to each other. Nevertheless, he did so with the greatest care, although he leaves it to his reader to spell out the relations that operate implicitly through the story. M. Profitendieu and M. Molinier are magistrates. The wealthier Profitendieus have four children of whom only one, the illegitimate son Bernard, plays a part in the novel. Gide winds the main threads of his plot around the three sons of the Moliniers: Vincent, Olivier, and Georges. The Vedel-Azaïs family, educators and pastors, people the novel with their five children: Rachel, Laure, Sarah, Alexandre and Armand. Boris, the grandson of the music teacher, La Pérouse, attends the Azaïs school as does the nephew of Strouvilhou, Ghéridanisol. All the characters are thus interconnected in a thousand ways and from generation to generation. Gide stresses the continuity within which the opposition of the generations will operate. The friendship of Olivier and Bernard is echoed in the mutual esteem of their fathers. Ghéridanisol goes to the Azaïs school because his uncle went there before him. The web of connections stretches backward in time, giving the story temporal dimensions rather than the more traditional spatial ones.

At the center of the web is Edouard, Mme. Molinier's half brother. He is connected to the Vedel-Azaïs family through his halfhearted love affair with Laure and by having boarded in their school, where he met Strouvilhou and had La Pérouse as his music teacher. He knows Count Passavant, who is one of his literary colleagues, and he will greatly influence Bernard and Olivier. All the events of the novel, in some way, direct or indirect, move within Edouard's orbit. Incidental characters cross his path, wending their way in and out of the main stream of the story, suggesting further perspectives that Edouard's limited attention cannot encompass.

The fabric of the novel is not pieced together to fit the dimensions of the story; the story, Gide implies, stretches beyond his novel in space, time, and human connections. The characters fall into two main groups: the parents and grandparents; the younger generation, all under forty. Edouard, who is just thirty-six when the story begins, moves between the two groups. The conflict between the generations and yet the continuity of the heritage that binds them together is an integral theme.

The young group initiates the action, their parents being immobilized in a sort of social and mental status quo. Some of the lively characters under forty are young adults, already "committed," engaged in life—Edouard, Count Passavant, Vincent, Rachel, and Laure. Others—Bernard, Olivier, Armand, and their friends, all around eighteen—are uncertainly poised between their dependence as schoolboys and their passage into adult life. The baccalaureate, the terminal high-school examination in France, symbolizes this transition, which is one of the major themes in the novel. The younger teen-agers—Georges, Boris, Ghéridanisol, and Phiphi—are at the difficult stage between childhood and adolescence. As the novel progresses, the spotlight moves from group to group, concentrating sometimes on one and sometimes on the other. But whether they are at the center of the stage or in the wings, all the characters are present and active in the novel from the very beginning.

When the story begins one intrigue, involving Edouard, Vincent, Laure, and her husband Douviers, is coming to its

which then initiated action

end; a second involving Bernard, Olivier, Edouard and Passavant is shaping up; a third is vaguely suggested: the illegal, clandestine activity of the high-school boys which preoccupies the two magistrates. It will emerge fully only in the third part of the book.

The characters are tied to their milieu and few break away. When Bernard Profitendieu decides to be adventurous and break with his family, he does nothing more hazardous than to become secretary to Edouard, the uncle of his closest friend, Olivier, and then subsequently to find a job at the Azaïs boarding school. Laure Vedel, in love with Edouard, ventures as far as Pau, only to be seduced there by Edouard's oldest nephew, Vincent.

The professional ambitions of the characters are equally limited. The most arduous profession these young men envisage is literary journalism; the most violent political commitment, joining a right-wing party. Aside from usual and less usual love affairs, the main cause of excitement is the launching of an avant-garde review; the most fascinating adventure of the year is a literary dinner; and the greatest trial is the baccalaureate. Even the reprehensible activities of the boys, which so gravely concern the two magistrates, are cut to scale. They are merely those of a group of schoolboys, cynically indulging with prostitutes in their first sexual experiences.

The rare "explorers" like Vincent Molinier and Alexandre Vedel, who take off for darkest Africa, are deliberately relegated to the periphery of the novel. They come to a bad end or disappear in those obscure regions that extend beyond the boundaries of Gide's stage. The small world Gide chose to depict has nothing very glorious to recommend it. It is ethically and socially refined almost to the point of effeteness.[4] Yet it has the characteristic traits of the well-to-do and well-meaning upper-middle class in Western Europe, as it was before the series of brutal wars which disrupted its righteous tranquillity.

Gide's approach to this world may seem surprising, but the people with whom he deals are quite recognizably related to those also depicted in novels as different from Gide's as Proust's and Martin du Gard's. Galsworthy and Meredith treat their English counterparts and Mann describes their German equivalents in those "people of the plain" whom Hans Castorp rejects in *The Magic Mountain*. Gide merely eliminated from his story all economic or social considerations. His characters interest him only in so far as they are connected with the self-appointed guardians of the ethical values in their society, those values embodied in the law, the church and the educational system.

Nothing in *The Counterfeiters* suggests that the earth is not peopled entirely by persons of this type, and this is perhaps a weakness. Rare are the novels with characters so far removed from the concerns of average human beings. Toward the end of the novel, as Bernard hesitates at a sort of crossroads in his life, Gide imagines that an angel takes him by the hand and leads him "into the poor sections of the town, whose wretchedness Bernard had never suspected. Evening was falling. They wandered for a long time among tall, sordid houses, inhabited by disease, prostitution, shame, crime and hunger." [5] Bernard's angel turns aside to weep, but the reader is tempted rather to shrug his shoulders. It is all too obvious that for Gide the "sordid crimes" perpetrated by the poor are not of the same kind as the more elegantly reprehensible activities of his young heroes.

Gide's human world, in spite of his good will, was limited. The only dramas that flourish in this milieu are the casual, carefully concealed complications of adultery. At worst, the pious pastor Vedel is inwardly tormented because of his addiction to masturbation, to which he alludes in secret code in his journal. The taboo concerning sex is total and on the whole Freud is still almost unknown in the fictional universe described. Yet Gide's characters are all involved in a web of trite clandestine loveaffairs which keep them on the go: Laure's adultery; Vincent's liaisons; the brief encounter of the two adolescents, Bernard and Sarah; Edouard's and Passavant's seduction of Olivier. Edouard, attracted by Olivier, forgets his love for Laure. Laure, disappointed with Edouard, marries Douviers and has a liaison with Vincent. Vincent abandons Laure for Lady Griffith. Bernard leaves home when he discovers he is illegitimate. Armand contracts syphilis in some sordid adventure.

The love affairs are handled casually. Sex plays a role in all these lives, but it is a role neither glamorous nor mysterious. Fortunately Gide does not intend to make it a source of romance; otherwise his novel might have foundered in the embarrassing honeyed sweetness of Edouard's love for Olivier. Sex in *The Counterfeiters* merely opens the way for more disruptive, dangerous and perturbing forces. It sets the characters in motion and its omnipresence suggests that all, in some vital fashion, are governed by its exigencies.

This undercover sexual activity, general though it is, is carefully concealed by everyone. The children would never guess that their parents had ever yielded to erotic impulses were there not to inform them of what goes on behind the scenes the secret letters and locked drawers dear to eighteenth-century fiction which quite naturally find their place in Gide's novel. The parents, in turn, pretend not to notice the love affairs of their children: Oscar Molinier, for example, dwells at some length on the edifying aspects of his two sons' most questionable friendships. Only at the end does Olivier's mother admit the truth concerning her son's homosexual affair, an indirect and reluctant admission.

The clandestine activities of Georges Molinier and his teenage gang are more brutal. They involve not only current concepts of morality but also the law, and they culminate in what is in fact a murder. Gide used to advantage the insights he had gained into adolescent crime when he was a member of the jury in the Assize Court of Rouen. The gang psychology and brutality of his teen-agers are depicted clearly and forcefully. At the beginning of the novel M. Molinier and M. Profitendieu, we learn, are concerned about a vice ring which M. Profitendieu is investigating, which he now knows implicates schoolboys with respectable backgrounds. These are no longer the "scissor thieves" of *The Immoralist*, the picturesque little Arabs whose exoticism accounts for their untoward actions. But the investigators whose job it is to detect crime and make it inoperative cannot tolerate the thought that it has infected their own social class. Silence is preferable to truth. Like the illicit sexual relationships of their elders, the teen-ager antisocial activities are hushed up.

While the love intrigues in *The Counterfeiters* give the novel its picaresque atmosphere, the hidden criminal activity is a source of mystery. The reader, rather like Profitendieu, the investigating magistrate, comes upon certain clues and coincidences and begins to glimpse a rather alarming reality beneath the quiet surface of the story, as Strouvilhou and a counterfeit coin make their simultaneous entrance toward the middle of the book. The mystery attached to both, at first intriguing to the reader, soon becomes sinister. A menace hangs over Gide's pleasant and insignificant set of characters, so full of good will and so self-absorbed. Georges Molinier's trail leads to the mysterious Strouvilhou, but so do many others. As soon as he puts in an appearance it becomes clear that Strouvilhou's influence is all pervasive, that Gide's whole cast of characters is connected with him. They are all prevaricators and, to varying degrees, counterfeiters. All proffer their false coins in the hope that they will be accepted as real, or at least that no detective will appear to investigate their origin.

This is the heart of the novel. Gide's characters and their

concerns may seem insignificant. The narrative tone, rapid, detached and slightly mocking, emphasizes the picaresque quality of the story. But the real subject Gide is handling is neither commonplace nor slight. It brings to light a deep-seated equivocation governing the relationships in the group, exemplified in the acts of all the characters.

"The combats of truth and error," wrote Blake, "is eating of the Tree of Life." Eating of the Tree of Life is what Gide's adolescents do, as their parents have done before them. But nothing prepares them for the flavor of the fruits they taste. Of their educators one could say with Blake:

They take the two contraries which are called qualities, with which
Every substance is clothed. They name them good and evil.
From them they make an abstract which is a negation
Not only of the substance from which it is derived
A murderer of its own body, but also a murderer
Of every Divine Member.[6]

Wherever they turn the youngsters find good and evil inextricably mixed, yet their elders righteously proclaim that good alone reigns around them.

In contrast, Gide's novel is conceived to bring out a deeper pattern and truth as Gide sees it. The intrigues of the counterfeiters notwithstanding, the "combats of truth and error" are fought in the novel on all levels by each character. They give the story the hidden epic value with which Gide strove to suffuse his tale.

Each character follows his own path, journeying through temptations and dangers. Bernard is a winner in this contest, but the novel is strewn with those who are defeated, temporarily or permanently; those who wander around aimlessly; and those who, somewhere along the way, were taken captive or joined the wrong faction. There is a kind of "pilgrim's progress" involved, particularly for the adolescents. Their struggles at this level take place in solitude. Social institutions, family, justice, schools, religion all league together to maintain the righteous fiction of social and moral order. The love affairs secretly weld individuals to one another in a conspiracy of silence. The teen-age delinquents band together to challenge the restraints imposed upon them. The counterfeiters are linked together by their defiance of the law. But nothing binds the Gidian pilgrims to anyone else. Entangled as they are, they can either accept the struggle between truth and error or join the ranks of the counterfeiters, thus alienating themselves from the "substance" of life.

At different levels, therefore, Gide's characters go through solitary trials and adventures through which they are led to an active organic participation in the fight with or against the counterfeiters. In these encounters their spiritual solitude gives them a freedom untrammeled by the tight social bonds which link them to each other. This freedom, the empty space that surrounds each one, is a device whereby Gide emphasizes the inner quality that determines their respective orientations.

At one point Bernard says that he would like his life "to ring true, with a pure, authentic sound." Gide has endowed each character with his own sound. The most serious source of counterfeit is the attempt, whether individual or social, to reduce all dissonance in favor of that universal and wholly theoretical perfect and continuous chord which haunts the imagination of the old piano teacher, La Pérouse. For the sake of some form of harmony all the characters in the novel, at times and more or less deliberately, indulge in counterfeit. The theme is taken up in turn by each instrument in Gide's human orchestra.

Certain characters are centers of emission of the false coin; in varying degrees what they put forth can be deceptive and dangerous. Passavant is a counterfeiter from vanity, from the need to cut a figure in the world: through counterfeit literary pursuits, counterfeit sentiments, and a counterfeit wit.

He deals in small coin and deceives no one except, temporarily, young Olivier. The Englishwoman, Lady Griffith, more dangerous, perverts Vincent, a promising young doctor, to the extent that Gide eventually throws him out of the novel, literally "to the devil." At the very end of the story we learn that Vincent, by this time having killed Lady Griffith, has gone mad and thinks he is the devil in person—a very moral ending. The sense of his adventure is pointed up in the well-known anecdote told by Lady Griffith at the beginning of the novel. Once shipwrecked, Lady Griffith, herself safely hauled into one of the lifeboats, saw the sailors cut off the hands of those unlucky survivors who tried to clamber on after the boat had been filled to capacity. Since then luck and an unscrupulous ferocity had appeared to her perversely romantic eyes to be the only safe guiding principles in life. In a few quick stages she teaches Vincent to gamble on his luck and to cut off all restraining hands, Laure's the first among them. Vincent's unbridled commitment to his appetite is self-destructive, but destroys him alone, not others. Vincent is not, as he thinks, the devil but merely one of the devil's victims.

The master "counterfeiter" and his mint are a good deal more dangerous: pious old Azaïs and his establishment. Strouvilhou, the real-life counterfeiter, is only one of its by-products. All the major characters in the book wander through the precincts of the school. It is the Vatican of the novel. Just as Profitendieu, on the trail of crime, is gradually led back to Strouvilhou, so the story inevitably leads to the school where the major plot is hatched that brings about the one irreparable event, the death of young Boris. There in his study old Azaïs reigns as though he were God. Azaïs, himself, has a certain pleasing innocence that "rings true." But everyone around him must echo back to him his own sound. Systematically he acknowledges only the purest good around him, every day casting the serpent out of Paradise. He is an unbearable burden upon his family and students, who are forced to conceal or overlook all that does not jibe with Pastor Azaïs's "perfect chord." Their only resort is lying, and prevarication teems around the old gentleman. The insigne that young George wears in his buttonhole, the insigne of his teen-age gang, becomes in Azaïs's eyes the emblem of an association for moral improvement. All his children live under the shadow of guilt, unable to grapple with the ambivalence in their own motivations and impulses. In the Azaïs boarding school, the combats of truth and error are impossible. Evil thrives unchallenged, and Strouvilhou has no trouble recruiting his accomplices there.

Strouvilhou is the natural complement of the old headmaster. He is bitterly aware of the illusory nature of Azaïs's idyllic view of things. A nihilist, he sees only the lie beneath the façade and, revolted, openly declares war on the lie. He has become a perverter out of a disappointed idealism akin to Azaïs's own. Detecting everywhere only the counterfeit, he cynically decides to live on it. Morally speaking, the other characters fall somewhere between Azaïs and Strouvilhou. On the headmaster's side there is society, the myth of harmonious family life, the myth of childish innocence, the myth of punishment and reward, and the myth of parental infallibility —every counterfeit that can help put up a decorous screen between people and the plain truth they all know. On Strouvilhou's side there are the young people, apparently cynical but actually counterfeiters only because of ignorance, bafflement or distress.

Bernard becomes a counterfeiter when he discovers the large crack behind the family façade of perfect respectability. Georges and Phiphi at fourteen become counterfeiters because no other outlet is offered for their violent and unrecognized physical energies. Armand becomes a counterfeiter out of despair, unable to live up to his pious family's exigencies. Boris becomes a counterfeiter out of his great desire for purity and the intimate distress caused by the sense of his own unworthiness.[7] Edouard is a counterfeiter because he cannot face such brutal realities as Boris's death, preferring to bypass them in his novel as in his life. Wherever fiction takes the place of truth, counterfeit coin starts to circulate. Like Edouard, the counterfeiters are bad novelists, peddling their ersatz substitutes for truth.

Azaïs and Strouvilhou both judge on appearances, hence the confusion they generate. "Go," said Blake, "put off holiness and put on intellect."[8] That is just what Gide, humorously, proposes we do. Intelligence regulates the play of light and shadow in the novel, suffusing it with a slightly ironic, nondogmatic form of intelligence. The perceptive moralist in Gide lent a hand to the artist. There may have been in Gide himself a Strouvilhou and, even more, an Azaïs, an Edouard, and a Passavant, but in *The Counterfeiters* he succeeded in keeping them at a distance. The humor which pervades the book gives his characters an autonomous yet recognizably human flavor. Semiallegorical, semireal, they disconcert the dogmatic moralist in Gide's readers, far more prone than he was to reduce novels to reassuring parables. To distinguish truth from error requires a perspicacity incessantly alert to the thousand snares laid by gullibility.

There are no general conclusions to be drawn from any individual situation in *The Counterfeiters*, no ready-made roles to be assumed. At the beginning of the novel Vincent tells Lady Griffith about the surprising discoveries concerning the organism of deep-sea fish. They had been thought to be blind, but it was found that almost all had eyes. "Why eyes with no means of seeing? . . . And at last it was discovered that each of these creatures which people first insisted were creatures of darkness, gives forth and projects before and around it its *own* light."[9] Bernard is a character who learns to trust his own light. But no conclusion can be drawn as to what Olivier should do, for to his fish story Vin-

cent adds another. Each species of ocean fish subsists only
in waters containing certain solutions of salt, varying with the
species. They move in layers. When an individual fish moves
too far up or too far down, it weakens and becomes easy
prey for alien fish. To each, therefore, his own dosage of good
and evil.[10] Gide's symbol thus accommodates an inexhaustible number of connected images and themes with many variations.

The reading of the novel itself is something of an adventure, so finely meshed are the wheels which regulate its movement. Wherever possible, Gide used the present tense for his
narrative, as he had in *Lafcadio's Adventures*, to emphasize
his departure from the traditional "story told in retrospect"
that relies on various combinations of past tenses. The narrator's comments along the way are calculated to give the
impression that things are actually developing as the novel
advances. And yet, somewhat as in a movie, they take place
in a different world, submitting to different necessities and
rhythms. No single point of view directs the narrative. The
narrator, whom one naturally first identifies with the author,
starts to tell the story. Almost immediately he turns it over
to Bernard and thenceforward the point of view travels back
and forth as characters move in and out of the scene. Gide
handles these shifts in perspective with great smoothness, re-
lying mainly on a rapid, conversational tone to give the story
an easy, uninterrupted flow. But the narration projects light
only on the narrow segment of the action that each character
perceives. No one, not even the unidentified first narrator
himself, sees the complete sweep of circumstance relating to
each event.

Bernard runs away from home, steals a suitcase, and by
chance gets a job as Edouard's secretary; Vincent wins heavily at roulette, abandons Laure and becomes Lady Griffith's
lover; Edouard comes back from London, collects Laure and
also Bernard, and promises old La Pérouse to bring his grand-

son, Boris, back to Paris. Olivier meets Passavant and becomes editor of an avant-garde review. Old La Pérouse resolves to commit suicide on a given day: all this occurs within thirty hours or so between a certain Wednesday afternoon in late June and the following Thursday night. But Bernard uncovers a set of old letters, and reads and so does the reader with him—Edouard's *Journal*—so that along the way the reader acquires a sense of continuity and pattern that the characters lack.

Within the novel paths crisscross unexpectedly. The characters, like balls on a narrow billiard table, bump against each other, deflecting each other, continually diverting each other from their original paths. Bernard's intrusion into Edouard's life is just such an unforeseeable diversion. The successive diversions caused by such impacts seem to scatter the balls at random. But from diversion to diversion they finally bring about the culminating event in the novel, Boris's death.

All the events noted in Edouard's *Journal*, which Bernard discovers, touch upon Laure's wedding nine months previously, and mesh in with the random set of events which take place in June. Laure, pregnant and abandoned by Vincent, calls Edouard back to Paris. He is attracted by Olivier but lets himself be persuaded rather to take Bernard as his secretary. Not knowing what to do with himself, he decides, on the spur of the moment, to go and get Boris in Saas-Fée. On his return his real inner concern reasserts itself, he becomes engrossed in Olivier's concerns.

But, as a rebound of all these movements, young Boris meanwhile has been transferred to the Azaïs school. As he arrives there and the third part of the story begins, all the apparently unrelated threads of the action come together, and all the characters, including Azaïs and Strouvilhou. No single character sees what is taking place, though all have their part in it. Gide's deconcentrated plot has a significance and an invisible line of progression reflects his intent. In the third part of the story all the "diversions" are rapidly dealt with. The only love story that really interested Gide, Edouard and Olivier's, ends happily after the latter's attempted suicide. Bernard, like the prodigal son, is on his way back home, and Laure on her way to her husband, Douviers. Armand has joined the counterfeiters. The Azaïs school is quite prosperous. Frightened by the message Edouard relays from Profitendieu, the schoolboy gang seems to have stopped its profitable dealings in counterfeit coins. La Pérouse and his grandson are reunited. All is for the best in the best of all possible worlds.

The schoolboys' secret society of "strong men" now takes the center of the stage. The first suicide victim, Boris, is picked in a fake drawing of lots. The fast-moving tempo suddenly halts as the whole novel plunges into a nightmarish reality. While all the main characters have been absorbed in their own lives, the novel itself, operating in a large framework comprising these individual lives, has been leading up to this single shocking event. Boris's fate develops in the shadow cast by the errors and blindness of the others. When he steps forward in front of his grandfather's desk into the chalk circle prepared by the gang and raises the pistol to his forehead, suddenly, in retrospect, all the characters and actions in the novel appear trivial and singularly irresponsible. Like Lafcadio's tossing Fleurissoire off the train, Boris's death changes the perspectives on the whole story.

Boris is the victim of the counterfeiters. Edouard, when he learns of Boris's death, waves it aside as too brutal for his novel, with a few righteous remarks on how inopportune it was for the poor Vedel-Azaïs family, just as he had waved aside the false coin Bernard had brought to his attention. But so far as Gide is concerned, the counterfeit coin and the schoolboy suicide are the very substance of his novel, its central inner core. A glance backward over the story reveals all the responsibilities at work in Boris's death. Edouard is easily the most responsible. But had Bernard, to whom Boris is entrusted, been less concerned with himself; had La Pérouse not loaded the pistol; had Profitendieu really done his job; had Azaïs, enamoured with his image of innocent childhood, not emboldened the gang; had the psychiatrist to whom Boris had been entrusted not put Boris's secret into Strouvilhou's hands; had his little friend Bronja not died . . .

Gide planned his novel so that it might approximate his view of how a great many events come about, *not* through a straight, relatively simple interplay of chance, situation and motivation. An event such as the death of Boris combines innumerable chance factors and, in each, a share of human weakness. Boris's fate is not the consequence of any one set of circumstances. It is made possible by the conjunction of several disparate and random series of activities. All the events in the first part of the novel create a pattern of relationships among the characters. But these are not fixed constellations, each character proceeds along his own path. Edouard's *Journal* is not a Proustian plunge into the past. It is a fictional device which allows Gide to enlarge the temporal dimensions of the novel, so that he can plot trajectories in time, orientations which determine new patterns, and future dispersions. Certainly this is the most original part of *The Counterfeiters* and by far the most arresting.

The novel, which begins at an almost frenzied pace, seems to bog down during Edouard's stay at Saas-Fée, and then to break up at random into a series of secondary plots, connected only by one moral theme—the theme of counterfeit. Only at the very end does Gide's scheme become clear. He wanted his novel to be an "imitation" of an action in the manner of a classical play, revealing all the forces, whether visible or not, which determine an act like Boris's: chance, circumstance, motivation, atmosphere, error working through human contacts, intentions, failures. All the events and characters are seen in relation to that act, so that the whole may realize the "erosion of contours" Gide wanted to obtain.

The Counterfeiters has the free lines, the abstract planes, the multiplication of perspectives, the interplay of form and idea as well as the humor characteristic of the soties. But unlike the soties, Gide's novel treats characters who are not mere pawns, and it has a serious, human significance. *The Counterfeiters* seems to convey something life had disclosed to Gide, who is not Edouard.

The second part of the novel, which takes place in the Alpine Saas-Fée, introduces an interval of repose in the story. But Gide's "infernal machine" is in the background all wound up and set for the dénouements. Meanwhile Edouard, Laure, and Bernard discuss Edouard's novel and Boris's cure with Sophroniska, the psychoanalyst. Strouvilhou passes through leaving behind the counterfeit gold piece Bernard finds in a shop and takes to Edouard. At this point the theme of counterfeit coin brings up a more basic problem, the paradox of its resemblance to real coin. When the action again moves forward, in line with Gidian dialectics, truth has become the main concern, not counterfeit. As always during the interval of repose, Gide clarifies and intellectualizes his theme. Sophroniska deals with the same problems as Profitendieu in his criminal investigation, but in the realm of individual psychology. Boris, with his "Yes-No" answers and his nervous furies, shows clear evidences of deep disorder. Observing the symptoms, Sophroniska patiently attempts to track down the hidden ill, to dislodge it, and to free Boris from its grip. Edouard suggests, and subsequent events tend to corroborate his opinion, that Boris's trouble, if mercilessly tracked down, will only change its aspect and take root more deeply in less accessible parts of his psyche. In the same way, when Profitendieu shuts up the house where the schoolboy orgies are held, the boys turn to peddling counterfeit money. Warned by Profitendieu that their activities are known to the police, they turn to sadism and organize a kind of "superman club." Unhappily, Sophroniska has prepared a ready victim for them.

Boris suffers terrible feelings of guilt for indulging in what he calls the "magic" which relieves him of his solitude, and which he somehow connects with a certain talisman. Believing that good always triumphs, Sophroniska attempts to circumvent evil by eliminating it. She takes away Boris's talisman, but makes the error of handing it over to Strouvilhou, who in turn gives it to the schoolboys. Newly enrolled at the Azaïs school, Boris joins their gang, wistfully wanting to be accepted as one of the boys, wistfully anxious to harbor no suspicion of evil intent in their advances. And yet he is well aware that all is not as they describe it to him. Boris's enemy lurks in recesses well out of Sophroniska's reach, in the person of Ghéridanisol, who does evil for the sake of evil. Boris, unprepared for battle, is totally defenseless.

Meanwhile, cozy in his own comfortable realm, the literary Edouard toys with the word "pure." He plagiarizes Gide, imagining a novel whose hero, a novelist, writes the story of the genesis of a novel. Its theme is to be the struggle between reality as observed and the novelist's idea of the nature of that reality. Edouard reads two pages of his book—a kind of parody of *Fruits of the Earth*—to Georges, in the hope of influencing him. He fails completely. Edouard is not Gide's spokesman but, like other of the characters, he introduces those variations on Gide's main themes that apply to his particular profession as novelist. Edouard moves to the periphery of the action as events converge toward the central catastrophe. He ends up as a sort of supernumerary. The range of his vision falls short of the requirements of his art. He wants reality to "ring" exclusively according to a "chord" of his own choosing.

Gide's *Counterfeiters* is a novel of adolescence, a novel of orientation which depicts young people emerging from various forms of myth into the reality of life. For the first time Gide's work has really deep social implications. He portrays the struggle of the young to discover through trial and error the genuine forces and limits of their personalities, in the face of obsolete social forms and ethics which tend to impose stereotyped feelings and attitudes upon them. Experience teaches Edouard nothing, since he ignores it, whereas Georges, shaken by Boris's death, alters his disastrous course. For Gide, to live, as to write a novel, is to undergo the test of reality.

By the time he wrote *The Counterfeiters* Gide had left behind him the ironic, critical novel. For his young people the "trial by life" ends with a return to their own social orbit. From error to authenticity, the way is difficult but open. Each separate adventure in the novel, as well as the novel as a whole, converges toward the discovery of the real and the true as opposed to the false. Bernard gets rid of his silly ideas, while Georges discovers what real monsters lurked behind his revolt. Neither devils nor angels, the characters simply become more human: "As for these antinomies," wrote Gide of devils and angels, "I believe them to be all imaginary . . . but the mere fact of living calls them up, creates them." Gide's novel is oriented away from finding antinomies in life. According to him, life does not long put up with counterfeit. It neither deceives nor disappoints. It is we who disappoint and deceive ourselves:

In this world: real sufferings; imaginary sufferings. The first can be attenuated; the second almost suppressed. They most often result from a belief in *idols*—or in *bogeymen*. The former are constructions that are venerated and do not deserve to be. The latter are phantoms that are feared and do not deserve to be feared.[11]

Gide felt, as did Proust, that the artist is "prompted" by life but that one of the elements given him is an inner orientation and sensitivity to which he must remain faithful; "it is the secret of the depths of his flesh that prompts, inspires and decides," he said of the artist. There is really no possible counterfeit in art; there are only individual limitations, success and failure.

The "given elements" of life on which Gide worked are slight, perhaps, but at least they are authentic. The point of view that molded them into a novel, however, is quite broad in scope and original. Gide succeeded in setting up for his story a form which is complex without being arbitrary. It is highly intellectual, yet permeated with a special poetry, made up of humor, lucidity, and that very mystery which springs from "the depths of the flesh." *The Counterfeiters* has neither the power nor the density of Proust's novel or of Joyce's *Ulysses*, its two great contemporaries. The reader can accept it straightforwardly without ever filling in the empty spaces, re-establishing the perspectives, or being moved to laughter by its implicit humor. It will seem outmoded, slight and artificial, and its curious transparency irritating, when the boldness of its structural movement goes unnoticed.

In *The Counterfeiters* Gide overcame his difficulties and facilities as a writer. The antiromantic yet poetic stylization of all the elements of the novel, the orchestration of the diverse voices, the lively pace of the story, the concern with permanent human values, the stringency of the language—all contribute to make *The Counterfeiters* an unusual book. To the ordinary pleasures of novel reading it adds, for the sensitive amateur, the "pure" pleasure of aesthetic understanding. No novel ever written was more "literary" and yet more free of literary influences. What Gide really investigated in his novel is what happens to all forms of "literature," in contact with life. It was perhaps the only real adventure that he himself had fully lived, and as a result, *The Counterfeiters* is the only one of his novels which fully expresses him.

Chapter XVI

The Last Act

Le dernier acte de la comédie
n'est pas moins beau . . .

The last act of the comedy is not
less beautiful . . .

∽∽∽∽∽∽∽∽∽∽∽∽∽∽∽∽∽∽∽∽∽∽∽∽∽∽∽∽∽∽

"I was like one of those creatures that can only grow
through successive metamorphoses."[1] With *The Counterfeiters* Gide's metamorphoses ended. His busy old age, rather
than a metamorphosis, was a slow progress toward serenity
and a tranquil self-acceptance. His journey to the Congo in
1925 seems to have dulled the sense of urgency which earlier, in spite of barren periods, had always set him on the
track of some new work. On his return in June, 1926, after
nearly a year in Africa, with obvious boredom and solely out
of a sense of obligation, Gide prepared two long articles, on
his "Travels in the Congo" (1927) and "Return from the
Tchad" (1928), which exposed certain malpractices of com-
mercial companies operating in those regions.[2] His reports
had political repercussions and led to the investigation and
correction of some of the more glaring abuses. Reluctantly

but conscientiously he carried through the further action and correspondence which his testimony elicited. In his *Journal* he complained endlessly about the good reasons he found for his "laziness." He cursed the outside distractions that disturbed him but added to them himself. Never did Gide travel so much nor so far as in the quarter of a century that followed. "A sort of inner trepidation shakes my being," [3] he confessed, and he was haunted by a sense of time wasted.

As he approached sixty Gide began to feel a certain decrease in his creative forces and, honest as ever, he made note of it. "Certainly I am no longer tormented by the imperious need to write. The feeling that 'the most important remains to be said' does not inhabit me as it once did. I persuade myself, on the contrary, that perhaps I have not much to add to what a perspicacious reader can glimpse in my writings." [4] Yet nothing in the rest of the *Journal* is so moving as the fight Gide put up against "the progressive decay of old age" [5] and his attempt to compensate for it through a stubborn will not to give up writing.

Will power alone could do little to compensate for a dearth of imagination and, perhaps in order to combat his "absurd longing to begin the past over again," [6] Gide attempted to launch out into what were for him new unchartered oceans. Until 1931 he had steadily used the *Journal* to express the antimystical and, in fact, the antireligious trends of his thought which had slowly come to light, indirectly, in his works.

"For a long time, for too long a time . . . I tried hard to think that I was wrong . . . it was as if my own thought frightened me, and thence came the need I felt to attribute it to the heroes of my books, the better to detach it from myself." [7] Now that his thought no longer frightened him, he was inhabited by no new heroes: "I feel I am myself and full of valor only when I am in a state of struggle," [8] which was so highly propitious to his work. Around 1931 he began to take a really serious interest in communism, feeling that the purpose of Marxism coincided with his own, the liberation of men from their "bugaboos." Applauded by new friends, he felt for a while a new fervor and excitement.

From one work to another, Gide's thought had, by indirection, progressively "disclosed" itself rather than evolved. Henceforward Gide often was to say what he thought without hedging. He summed up his general point of view in one of the "imaginary interviews" which he wrote in the forties. In its main lines it had not changed since his *Prometheus,* written half a century earlier. It was a point of view he had since then frequently reiterated, more specially in *Numquid et tu* . . . :

> I am careful, when using the word "God," not to confuse two very different things; different to the extent of being opposed: on the one hand, the whole of the Cosmos and the natural laws that govern it; matter and forces, energies; that is the side of Zeus; and one could indeed call it God, but by removing all personal and moral significance from the word. On the other hand, the totality of all human efforts toward the good and the beautiful, the slow process of mastering those brutal forces and their use in achieving the good and the beautiful on earth; that is the side of Prometheus; and it is the side of Christ as well; it is the full flowering of man, and all virtues. But this God does not inhabit nature at all; He exists only in man and through man; He is created by man or, if you prefer, it is through man that He is created.[9]

For many years Gide had considered that "all living matter is plastic" [10] and that man therefore could be conditioned and transformed. However, he had thought only in terms of individuals, and was still thinking that way in 1930:

> The only conflict that really interests me and that I should always be willing to depict anew is the struggle of the individual with whatever keeps him from being authentic, with whatever is opposed to his integrity, to his integration.[11]

It is the old Gidian theme, the literary possibilities of which he had perhaps by then exhausted with the publication of *Corydon, If it die . . .* , and *The Counterfeiters*.

Communism brought him a new idea; the vision of a collective metamorphosis, of the passage of all humanity to a new and better stage. Gide had never before considered society as anything but static; the capacity to move forward was, in his eyes, the prerogative of individuals only. "It is this glimpse of a possible progress," he wrote in 1931, "which so deeply cut through my thought and changed my former ways." [12] Gide felt that in Russia humanity was perhaps at last emerging from the "mythological age":

> It is no longer a matter of restoring ruins, but of building anew on ground that must first be tested . . . nothing will be accepted that is not authentic and all mysticism is banished.[13]

He felt rather like a St. John the Baptist of the era, a belief which his friends encouraged.

At the same time he acquired a new though rather elementary sense of the "masses." He could hardly be said to have felt at home with them. Though he liked to dwell on the possibilities of man, men in general seemed to him incredibly mediocre. "Humanity's generally accepted value . . . humanity such as it is, not such as it might be" seemed to him "very much exaggerated." [14]

Gide had always been interested in man as he might become in the future, "a product, a work of culture and art." [15] Under the influence of communism he now imagined future new "heroes": "What our present literature most lacks is heroism." [16] Yet all Gide's work since *Fruits of the Earth* had been directed against heroism, against the evils arising out of inner exaltation and social myth. Beginning in 1930, the events of history plunged Europe first into melodrama, then into tragedy, and Gide felt perhaps that his ethic of individual freedom, development and equilibrium did not quite fit the needs of the hour.

In the "heroic virtues" of the Russian people he found a new hope for the future. He felt safe in the new political role he assumed because it allowed him to think and speak in terms of his liberal and optimistic faith in the inexhaustible resources for betterment possessed by human beings.[17] Yet nothing was, in fact, further removed from Gide than the dogmatic cast of Marxist thought and, more especially, of Marxist politics. There was a wide gap between Gide's "future man," a "product of culture and art," and Marx's "new man," conditioned by economic laws. Gide soon balked at an "orthodoxy" so radically incompatible with his own way of thinking. Even before his trip to Russia [18] he had lost interest in the political maneuvers of communism. He had done his best to take his political role seriously as long as he thought the Marxist myth coincided with his own. But he had always felt out of his element in practical politics and doctrines annoyed him. History on a vast scale now began to act like a Gidian récit, precipitating the world into the unknown:

> How can one still write novels? when around us our world is crumbling, when something unknown is being elaborated . . .[19]

After his journey to Russia Gide, ever himself, was not ready to see that "unknown" take the form of Russian Marxism.

After 1931 Gide's *Journal* becomes incomparably richer as his works lose in interest. The picture the *Journal* gives of the elderly and famous writer steadily forging ahead—obstinate, inquisitive and ever questioning, never satisfied to rely on the past, to strike a pose—is in itself a very moving thing. Gide continued to refuse the pathetic fallacies offered him. He remained scrupulous, objective, spelling out his real reactions to Russia, for example, inappropriate as they might seem to his communist friends.[20]

His wife's death in 1938 affected him deeply, but also removed the last obstacle to the full development of his personality. His *Journal*, to the very last lines of *So be it*, written just before he died, is the really important work of his last fifteen years. It hides neither the weaknesses and limitations of the man nor his fine qualities. Even more than Gide's sustained effort to remain serene and clearsighted in his old age, without despair or undue optimism, what the *Journal* shows up by contrast is the pettiness of those detractors who seized upon his private life to attack him once he was dead.

What the *Journal* gained from the new incisiveness of Gide's thought his works seemed to have lost. Only with the liberation, in 1944, carried forward by the wave of joy and relief around him, was Gide able to tap once more a really living source of inspiration and produce his *Theseus*, a charming epilogue to his work.

A cursory glance at the list of publications that followed *The Counterfeiters* would seem to indicate that there had been no falling off in his creativity. One could be tempted to compare it with the first rich spurt of activity in the 1890's. The trilogy of three récits—*The School for Wives* (1929), *Robert* (1929), and *Geneviève* (1936)—relating the same story from three points of view, could be considered together as a single "novel." *Oedipus* (1931), with which Gide now returned to drama was followed in 1933 by the stage adaptation of *Lafcadio's Adventures*. Shortly after, in 1934, at the request of Ida Rubinstein, Gide reworked his *Proserpine* into a three-act opera rechristened *Persephone*. At the instigation of the brilliant avant-garde director and actor, Georges Pitoeff, who had produced his *Oedipus* in 1935, Gide finally wrote a farce he had long had in mind, *The Thirteenth Tree*. In 1933-34 he had also started work on a play with "social significance," *Robert* or *The Common Weal*. His *New Fruits of the Earth*, in 1935, seemed to balance the first *Fruits of the Earth* at the beginning of his career, just as Gide had planned.

But appearances are deceptive. None of the works written

between 1926 and 1935 was really outstanding, and some were even slight. Only *Oedipus,* because of the light it throws on Gide's personal point of view and its connections with the later *Theseus,* really merits attention.

The fate of the three-part novel he began on his return from the Congo is revealing. The outline of *The School for Wives* first appeared in Gide's *Journal,* then in the *Journal of the Counterfeiters* in connection with a theme which had long attracted him, the theme of the "decrystallization" of love.[21] In *The Counterfeiters* Gide had used only one facet of the subject he had in mind: Pauline and Laure, both exceptional young women, are married to mediocre men, Molinier and Douviers. For his *School for Wives,* Gide used the more complex original design: Eveline, the protagonist, falls in love with a young man Robert, whom she places on a pedestal; when some years later, having discovered his mediocrity, she wants to leave him, she meets only with general disapproval and disbelief. *The School for Wives* is one of what Gide called the "discards" of *The Counterfeiters,* but it is hard to believe it was ever connected with that novel. Gide settled back into the old groove of the récit and, to give his dreary characters a measure of credibility, he adopted a style with that unfortunate, dreary quality.

For no particular reason, except perhaps that this was the period in which he felt most at home, he situated Eveline's story between 1896 and 1914, the war furnishing a melodramatic denouement. At one point, while writing *The Counterfeiters,* Gide had thought of showing, as Proust was then doing, that war could do no more than drive individuals further in their own direction. In *The School for Wives* the theme is simplified to the point of absurdity. Robert, the mediocre and selfish husband, who turns everything to his own advantage, gets to the front in spite of himself and wins a military award; whereas Eveline, devoting herself completely to the care of contagious cases, dies obscurely in the military hospital where she is a nurse.

Gide finished Eveline's story almost in spite of himself at the insistence of the American *Forum* to which he had promised it. "To tell the truth, the book hardly interests me at all and my mind does not of itself go back to it" [22]—an oft-repeated refrain which accompanied the writing of the book. But the Gidian rhythms of creation were so peremptory that, almost in spite of himself, by a sort of spontaneous parthenogenesis his novel produced two sequels, *Robert* and *Geneviève*, which he had not planned to write and which were not called forth by any inner necessity. At first published separately, the three tales when taken together have hardly the dimensions of a short story.

The initial theme is simple. Eveline, the only child of wealthy parents, falls in love with Robert, a promising young man. At his request, after their engagement, she starts to keep a journal, breaking it off just before their marriage when she discovers that Robert has failed in his promise to keep a diary destined to her, as hers was to him. The diary starts again twenty years later when Eveline finally revolts and leaves her husband. Gide seemed to have had in mind a modern Ibsenian heroine. As Eveline paints the two conflicting portraits of her husband she also, in true Gidian fashion, traces the limits of her understanding. Robert begins to attract the interested sympathy of the reader.

Almost automatically Gide felt the need, as usual, to contrast Eveline's point of view with Robert's, although this was hardly necessary. The reader could read between the lines all that Robert would have to say, and said. More than Robert's defense, it is the unfinished confession of their daughter, Geneviève that gave Gide so much trouble,[23] and that adds a little life to the whole. With his new social concern in mind Gide had proposed boldly to take up the whole question of feminism.[24] But, by the mid-thirties, feminism was no longer a very exciting topic. Gide seems to have realized this and, after many attempts, made Geneviève's story a brief one. It was only fairly late that Gide, finally abandoning the social problem, by a sudden stroke of inspiration tied his three stories together and so saved them from foundering. It was then that they really formed a triptych, three points of view on a private domestic conflict. Geneviève becomes a detective in the manner of Lacase and discovers the hidden bonds attaching her mother to one of the secondary characters in the novel, a doctor. Gide's feminist novel turns into a bourgeois novel of manners.

Gide admitted that no exigency drove him to the writing of the three récits. Not so with *Oedipus* or *New Fruits of the Earth*. Gide's evaluation of the latter is therefore all the more pertinent. "Of all my books it is the most uneven, the least good." [25] Begun in 1917 and not completed until 1935, *New Fruits of the Earth* is a hybrid. In 1917 Gide was highly elated and in love; in 1935 he was conscientiously trying to express a communist-inspired social message. The book fluctuates indecisively between two antithetical states of mind. After the 1917 surrender to the gospel of joy and love, Gide, in the fourth part of his book, prescribed a new litany of collective progress: "that men have not always been what they are, that they have slowly made themselves" [26] was his new refrain. "The idea of progress has taken root in my mind. Related to all my other ideas, it dominates them all," [27] Gide declares for the benefit of a new Nathanael, the "comrade" of his book. The great lyrical surge of the first pages is now only a prelude to the coming of "the man announced," [28] and with him a future golden age, the product of human efforts. "Most of our ills have nothing inevitable or necessary about them, and are due only to ourselves." [29] In 1917 Gide had written: "It is toward voluptuousness that all nature's efforts tend," [30] a sentence he did not strike out of his 1935 volume.

Gide forced two successive and incompatible themes into one book, whereas in the past each would have developed separately and organically by itself. He tried to create a pattern to give the book an appearance of order with alternating lyrical passages and "encounters." The encounters prepare the way for the social gospel Gide later grafted onto the book and contain some of the better pages in it. As for the lyrical passages, they are among the worst Gide ever wrote, including the poems he later transferred to his *Persephone*, and advisedly so, since they were better suited to the artificial charm of an opera-ballet.

There may be, as has been suggested, a social message in *Persephone*,[31] but if so it is hard to detect and certainly not convincing. But there is undoubted charm in this scenario that Gide wrote for the Ida Rubinstein-Stravinsky ballet. Tightening and transforming the *Proserpine* he had written some thirty years before, Gide followed the main lines of the Homeric legend: Persephone's capture by Pluto, her descent into the underworld kingdom where she is made queen; the great grief of her mother, Demeter, goddess of harvests; Demeter's search for her daughter as the neglected earth suffers great famine; the return of Persephone at the request of Zeus —only a partial return, because the six pomegranate seeds eaten in Hades bind Persephone to her husband's underworld kingdom. In his "Considerations on Greek Mythology" Gide had explained that in Greek mythology he sought psychological truths. He took care to characterize his Persephone psychologically: before Pluto ever appeared, Persephone, sniffing a narcissus blossom, sees mirrored in the flower the sufferings of the shades in Hades. Irresistibly she is drawn to share their pain. In Hades she catches a glimpse of the denuded earth. The pity that opened her way to Hades now sends her back to earth.

Gide's unorthodox Persephone, like the first characters in his plays, is really guided by her inner fidelity to her fate, the *amor fati* Gide culled from Nietzsche. Voluntarily sacrificing her joy to alleviate suffering, she is a kind of social heroine with a Christian feeling for humanity, while the damned in Pluto's kingdom, the Shades, are there for very Gidian reasons, punished because on earth they failed fully to do what Persephone did: they failed fully to accept their destiny. In Persephone's closing speech Gide suggests that the suffering of the Shades symbolizes all human misery, but that stretches the implications of his charming opera with its Grecian nymphs and choruses.

However Gide may have felt about it, the stumbling block of social consciousness alone can hardly account for the insignificance of his late novels, the weakness of the *New Fruits of the Earth* and the slightness of *Persephone*. The failure of the problem play, *Robert* or *The Common Weal*,[32] shows that Gide, now over sixty, had, in spite of his admirable obstinacy, really run out of inspiration—and not merely because he felt the old world "crumbling around him." "I spent as much time," he remarked, "spoiling *The Common Weal*, and then *Geneviève* . . . as I did successfully completing *The Counterfeiters*."[33] Yet he couldn't let his play be. He went back to it, worried at it, read it aloud to friends in the hope that it would meet with their approval. It stubbornly remained a failure, an old-fashioned social propaganda play. Gide realized this and attempted to substitute a comedy of character for the social conflict he had first envisaged. Like the Robert in *The School for Wives*, Robert Dormoy, the main protagonist, is a man who, under cover of concern for the "common weal," is out to make his own fortune. No part of Gide's own personality responded to anything in Dormoy's. Painstakingly Gide plods through the most hackneyed conflicts with never a trace of his usual semi-ironic, semi-humorous detachment.

The plot could come straight out of a comic strip: in one camp the bad, self-seeking employers, the Dormoys; in the other the good, honest workers, typified by the Orlovs, although M. Orlov is, strangely enough, Dormoy's illegitimate brother. The younger of the Dormoy sons, Michel, falls in love with Orlov's daughter, whose brother, a labor leader, organizes a strike against Michel's father. A jealous foreman turns traitor and Michel is killed in the front ranks of the workers' demonstration. Gide could hardly have been less inspired. He was not much luckier with the stage adaptation he made of Lafcadio's Adventures. The Thirteenth Tree,³⁴ a light farce fared better without adding much to his works.

Of everything Gide wrote in that period, only Oedipus is a work of some stature, and even that is not a truly good play. Gide grafted onto the Oedipus story a set of brilliant dialogues which were no substitute for drama, let alone tragedy. Oedipus as a character had lived in his mind since 1896. He is, Gide had noted, the only character in legend who willingly tears his eyes out, hardly the gesture to endear him to Gide, the prophet of clearsightedness. Oedipus's final act in fact really irritated Gide, who takes it no more literally or seriously in his play than he took Prometheus's famous vulture in his early sotie. The Theban plague, the murder of Laius, and Jocasta's suicide are not given any dramatic weight or value in Gide's play. Indeed, Oedipus is not far removed from a sotie. Gide's hero, for whom he had little sympathy, is stripped of the sacred horror with which Sophocles had endowed him.

"The palace of faith. You find consolation, assurance, and comfort there. Everything in it is arranged to protect your laziness and guarantee your mind against effort. . . . One enters there with eyes closed; with eyes blinded. This is indeed the way Oedipus enters. Oedipus, or the triumph of ethics." ³⁵ And again: "Not The New Oedipus—but rather The Conversion of Oedipus." ³⁶

In the third part of the play, Gide explained, Oedipus's submission to Tiresias symbolizes the sacrifice of the best to mediocrity. Gide was again fighting his old enemies, organized religion and stereotyped ethics. Any kind of doctrinal persuasion now made him feel ill at ease and seemed to him tainted with voluntary blindness and "bad faith." Gide used a number of devices to detach his Oedipus from the awesome Sophoclean image, especially anachronism and every possible variation on the Freudian Oedipus complex, which in his play covers all the relationships in Oedipus's household, producing a number of unexpected and burlesque situations. He thus carefully deflated the premises of the myth and simultaneously took a dig at Freudian thought. He doesn't seem to have realized that it is hard to see a symbol of spiritual complacency in Oedipus. Irony is an inadequate response to the Oedipus legend.

As Gide realized, he had strangled his play. He reproached himself for having made everything in it too "intentional, motivated, necessary," and for having "reduced God's part to nothing." [37] As a matter of fact, he had, rather, allowed Gide's part to get out of hand, so that the play took on the appearance of a set of Gidian "variations on the theme of blindness." Oedipus is rather ungraciously accorded some superiority over Tiresias as suffering from a less abysmally reprehensible form of blindness. But at no time does Gide consider his Oedipus admirable, the basic weakness of the character he conceived coming out in his last, irresponsible gesture.

A bitter and slightly grotesque fantasy presides over the other characterizations: the mother-wife Jocasta, a Freudian and yet typically Gidian figure, the woman who draws Oedipus back into the past, quite unconcerned about a truth she has always known; Creon, the amusing opportunist; the Freudian sons, Eteocles and Polynices; Antigone, the mystic who thinks she wants to become a nun but finally succeeds in her real desire to dominate her father. The father-daughter relationship complements the mother-son and brother-sister ones which Gide introduces into the already involved relationships of the family. The underlying theme of the play is that "Under whatever form it appears, there is no worse enemy than mysticism." [38] The sin of Gide's Oedipus is that he fell prey to mysticism.

Gide expected his audience to be familiar with Sophocles's play, and drew most of his humorous effects from the contrasts which he exploited. Only the sustained debate between Tiresias and Oedipus that runs through the whole play gives it a consistency of its own. Oedipus, the surprisingly happy man who swaggers onto the stage when the curtain rises, is little more than a mask. Gide deflates his legend, which veers toward the burlesque. As Creon reminds him, Oedipus was conceived one festive night when Laius, drunk, forgot the usual precautions he and Jocasta had been taking since the oracle had predicted that their son would kill his father and marry his mother. The fruit of drunkenness and inconsequence, Oedipus is therefore impulsive and inconsequential. And so is the act whereby in the end he blinds himself: a gesture of rage at the bad faith of the gods, by which he merely plunges from one form of blindness into another, a familiar Gidian disaster.

But Gide's play also suggests another more interesting theme which he seems either not to have clearly grasped or not to have clearly worked out. Gide's *Oedipus* is a man intent on moving forward, who really moves only backward, marrying, with Jocasta, his entire past. He who had given the answer "Man" to the Sphinx's riddle, ends by joining Tiresias and the camp of the gods. Gide's Oedipus, like his Vincent in *The Counterfeiters* is, in fact "diverted"—an interesting idea, but the play and characters lack consistency. Ideas and attitudes, often wittily debated in amusing dialogues, and the whole atmosphere of the play—all seem dated. It took Theseus, the favorite son of Gide's old age, born unexpectedly almost twenty years after Oedipus, to save that elder hero from oblivion.

Once again, as in his youth, Gide seemed to be haunted by certain mythological figures. Dismissing all other interpretations, Gide wanted to see in Greek legends only their human suggestions. He could rid Theseus more easily than Oedipus of the weight of an awesome fate, humanizing his story without too much inconvenience. His Theseus could walk freely upon an earth empty of gods.

Theseus is made to order for Gide: his successes and trials, his amorous adventures and devotion to the public cause, his tolerance, and the freedom and strength of his life and personality. Gide had first been charmed by the less edifying sides of his hero's life. In *Fruits of the Earth* Theseus is cited among the famous lovers who have known how not to be faithful. Theseus' impertinent good luck in his love affairs and his infidelities become, in Gidian language, the refusal to "get stuck." The slight connotation of vulgarity in the expression suggests the almost imperceptible vein of indecency with which Gide handled the erotic episodes in the tale. He lingered perhaps a little insistently on the voluptuous pleasures of Crete, taking an altogether too special joy in depicting a heterosexual Theseus, a barbarian in Cretan eyes, who, instead of falling in love with the King's son Glaucus, as expected, prefers the charms of the young princess, Phaedra: a completely gratuitous episode invented by Gide for his own delight. But the legendary Cretan atmosphere authorized the nonchalant eroticism with which he endowed his story.

At the time when he was thinking of his "Treatise on the Dioscuri," Gide had already expressed his preference for the benevolent Theseus over the more heroic Hercules. Daedalus, in the récit, explains to Theseus that same preference, inherited from Gide:

At one time I saw quite a lot of your predecessor, Hercules. He was a stupid fellow, and I could never get anything out of him but heroics. What I did appreciate in him, and what I appreciate in you, is a sort of absorption in the task at hand, an unrecoiling audacity, a temerity even, which thrusts you forward and destroys your opponent. . . . Hercules took greater pains than you do; was more anxious, also, to do well; and was rather melancholy, especially when he had just completed a great exploit. But what I like in you is your joy; that is where you differ from Hercules.[39]

Theseus, as compared to Oedipus, is an entirely sane and healthy hero. The parallel Gide established between the two men is rather amusing: Theseus and Oedipus are both kings' sons, whose births are shrouded in mystery. Both, as young men, start out on the road to adventure and both, at first, perform the same acts: they rid the earth of monsters. Both succeed to the thrones of their fathers under rather ambiguous circumstances. Here Gide gave the legend a slight Freudian twist: On his way back from Crete, the legend tells us, Theseus "forgot" that he had promised Aegeus, his father, to put up a white sail if he had vanquished the Minotaur; the shock of the black sail kills Aegeus—a revealing incident in Gide's eyes. Theseus, therefore, is less innocent than Oedipus, who kills his father Laius by chance, without knowing who he is. Oedipus marries his mother, to be sure, but Theseus is responsible for the death of his son Hippolytus. The two heroes reigned successfully for many years, each over his own city. The balance of crime, ambition, self-sacrifice, service and success is just about even for both. But at this point their fates diverge. Oedipus plunges into disaster and his people undergo a cruel war. Theseus' kingdom prospers and develops in peace. Oedipus is the destroyer of Thebes, Theseus the founder of Athens.

It was particularly pleasing to Gide's imagination that the two legendary heroes lived during the same years, that their paths crossed, that Oedipus died peacefully under the protection of Theseus and that, because of this, Athens obtained the special favor of the gods. Actually Gide saw in the two myths two récits. Theseus and Oedipus could complement each other as had Tityrus and Menalcas in Gide's youth, Michel and Alissa a little later. Gide's Oedipus helped to create Theseus, just as Theseus in turn, when he came into being, modified the figure of Oedipus, which Gide treats much more sympathetically in the récit than he had in the play.

To think of Theseus merely as a projection of Gide himself would limit the scope of the tale. Yet the comparison at times is both pertinent and amusing, as when Theseus declares, surely with Gide in mind:

"No one can deny it: I have, I think, performed some notable services. . . . I've cleaned up certain dangerous byroads on which even the bravest could not venture without trembling; and I've cleared up the skies in such a way that man, his head less bowed, may be less afraid of the unexpected." [39] But Theseus is not Gide, nor is the story a Gidian apologia. Brought up in the manner of Lafcadio, but in a fabulous age, Theseus with his fine equilibrium and limited good sense is no more Gide than are Daedalus and Icarus, whom Theseus encounters in the récit. Gide was particularly fond of this last of his heroes, but treated him with the same affectionate irony as any of his earlier creations.

For *Theseus* Gide used the spoken narrative he had adopted for *The Immoralist*. The Athenian king speaks in a warm, engaging voice for which Gide easily found the right tone, re-creating his own myth for his listeners. The juxtaposition of the mythical universe of ancient Greece and Theseus' familiar matter-of-fact vocabulary is a rich source of poetry and humor. Theseus is as at home in his world as we are in ours, and his feelings, very similar to our own, give our everyday contemporary world a kind of poetic extension into the fabulous. The directness and musicality of Theseus' language acts as a sort of charm and touches the imagination. He comes to life immediately with his first sentence: "It was for my son Hippolytus that I had wanted to tell the story of my life so that he would benefit from it: but he is no more, and I shall tell it just the same." [40] For this story-telling Gide forged a deceptively simple style, rich in controlled modulations. Theseus' description of his arrival at Cnossos, for example, combines the wonder of what he saw with the simple reality of what he felt. For the first, Gide used the long incantatory sentence he had tried out fifty years before in *El Hadj*; for the second, in brilliant contrast, the flat declarative statement with a strong anachronistic flavor:

I was so overwhelmed by fatigue that I could hardly feel due astonishment at the great courtyard of the palace, or at a monumental balustraded staircase and the winding corridors through which attentive servants, torch in hand, guided me to the second floor, where a room had been set apart for me. All but one of its many lamps were snuffed out after I arrived. The bed was scented and soft; when they left me, I fell at once into a heavy sleep which lasted until the evening of the following day, although I had already slept during our long journey; for only at dawn, after traveling all night, had we arrived at Cnossos.

I am by no means a cosmopolitan. At the court of Minos I realized for the first time that I was Greek, and I felt very far from home.[41]

Theseus uses to good purpose all the resources of style Gide had mastered over the years.

His narrative falls into three parts: the hero's childhood, his journey to Crete and victory over the Minotaur, and the founding of Athens. All Gide's themes appear successively in the various episodes—the sensuous plenitude of childhood, the disciplines necessary to adolescence, the struggle against monsters, and so forth—but are condensed and nourished by the wisdom of a now elderly Theseus, the wisdom of Gide's old age. And it is Gide's voice that breaks through directly in the conclusion with no trace of irony or doubt:

If I compare my lot with that of Oedipus, I am content. I have fulfilled my destiny. Behind me I leave the city of Athens. It has been dearer to me even than my wife and son. My city stands. After I am gone, my thought will live on there forever. I draw near to a solitary death willingly. I have enjoyed the good things of the earth, and I am happy to think that after me, and thanks to me, men will find that they are happier, better and freer. I worked for the good of those who are to come. I have lived.[42]

All Gide's thought leads to Theseus, and it was a Theseus within himself that he had striven so long to perfect. "I remain a child of this world," says Theseus, "and I believe that man, be he what he may, and whatever his faults, is duty-bound to play out his hand to the end." Many others contribute to this wisdom of Theseus: Aegeus, Minos, Pasiphaë, Ariadne, Daedalus, Icarus, Pirithoüs, and Oedipus all in turn talk with him as a young man, revealing something of importance for him to learn. But the meetings with Daedalus, placed in the center of the story, and the last conversation with Oedipus, at the end, are the two great "moments of truth" for Theseus.

Daedalus, a sculptor, has freed the gods from their traditional hieratic positions, representing them in motion and thereby bringing Mount Olympus down to earth. A man of science like Prometheus, Daedalus has tried to penetrate the secrets of the gods so that, "with the aid of science" he could "mold mankind to the likeness of the gods." [43] Such a twofold ambition to realize a meeting of gods and men had, in fact, presided at the birth of Theseus, who is himself half-god, half-man. Daedalus thus formulates the idea that Theseus illustrates: man fashioned in the image of humanized gods.

Among all the voices that merge in Theseus' without ever diverting him from his task of founding the city of Athens,

there is one that differs from all the others, Oedipus's. Theseus tolerates and even welcomes the man whom Gide had
treated so harshly some years before. But he does not understand him, hence the irony and yet the respect in his account
of their conversation:

I am surprised that so little should have been said about the
meeting of our destinies at Colonus, about that moment at the
crossroads when our two careers confronted each other. I consider
it the summit and crown of my glory. Till then I had forced all
life to do obeisance to me, and had seen all my fellow men bow
in their turn (excepting only Daedalus; but he was my senior by
many years. Besides, even Daedalus gave me best in the end). In
Oedipus alone did I recognize a nobility equal to my own.[44]

At the very end of his life Gide thus gave the mystical, even
Christian Oedipus entrance into his world, though a little reluctantly and only under the aegis of Theseus. Gide had come
a long way since The Notebooks of André Walter.

It was Theseus' resolution to carry through his task to the
very end without getting lost in any labyrinths. This had also
been Gide's task as a writer. Like his hero, he had gone his
way, conversing with many others yet pushing ever forward
on his own. What his own work could not encompass someone else's might, someone whom he would welcome with the
same respect that Theseus offered Oedipus. For Gide, an artist, is committed, like any other man, only to his own work,
as Theseus was to his, or Daedalus and André Gide to theirs.
What is most engaging perhaps about Gide's writing is the
Theseus-like manner through which he "obtained," as he
would say, the writer he became, molding him a little more
with each work, from the tormented André Walter to a serene and tranquil Theseus.

Notes

All quotations refer to works mentioned in the bibliography.

Whenever possible, the reader is referred to the edition of the *Oeuvres complètes* of André Gide, published by the N.R.F. and designated in the footnotes by the abbreviation O.C., followed by the number of the volume.

CHAPTER I

1. Letter to Raymond Bonheur, March 12, 1900. *Le Retour* (Neufchatel and Paris: Ides et Calendes, 1946), p. 56.
2. *Feuillets d'Automne* (Paris: Mercure de France, 1944), p. 277. It is interesting to note in this respect young Paul Valéry's account of his discussions with Gide around 1890: "In a word, I think— and these are my metaphysics and ethics—that God exists and the *Devil* too, but inside us. . . . That is my belief: God is our private Ideal, Satan everything that tries to divert us away from it." Paul Valéry, *Lettres à quelques-uns* (Paris: Gallimard, 1952), p. 41.
3. *Pages de Journal* (1939-1942), ed. by Jacques Schiffrin (New York: Pantheon Books, Inc., 1944), p. 75.
4. *Journal* (1942-1949) (Paris: Gallimard, 1950), p. 177.
5. *Journal*, p. 890.
6. *Le Journal d'André Gide* (1889-1939), Ed. de la Pléiade (Paris, 1939), p. 890; hereafter referred to as *Journal*.
7. *Feuillets d'Automne*, p. 44.
8. O.C., IX, 444 and 430.
9. "He is the most attractive, the most meditative, the most *secretly musical*, the most affectionate young man." Paul Valéry, *Lettres à quelques-uns* (Paris: Gallimard, 1952), p. 43.
10. Letter to Raymond Bonheur, March 12, 1900, *op. cit.*, p. 56.
11. *André Gide et notre temps* (Paris: Gallimard, 1935).
12. *Retour de l'U.R.S.S.* (Paris: Gallimard, 1936).
13. We have no intention here of reopening the discussions of Gide's

religious position, his communism or his homosexuality. These topics have been dwelt upon endlessly. The scholarship on these subjects was for many years conspicuous neither for its objectivity nor for its common sense. The French psychiatrist Jean Delay's book on Gide's youth (*La Jeunesse d'André Gide*, 2 vols. [Paris: Gallimard, 1956-1957]) has made most earlier studies obsolete. Several critics seem to think that there are only two "Protestant" writers in the world: Rousseau and Gide. Harold March's conscientious and well-documented book, *Gide and the Hound of Heaven* (University of Pennsylvania Press, 1952), defends in our opinion a simplified and questionable thesis. Pierre-Henri Simon's essay "André Gide . . . et Dieu," in *Témoins de l'homme* (Paris: Librairie Armand Colin, 1951), is a commendable effort toward impartiality but remains, as Gide would have said, "incliné," i.e., biased.

As for the question of homosexuality, prior to Dr. Delay's book it seems to have been most impartially treated first by Léon Pierre-Quint in his *André Gide* (Paris: Stock, 1952) and then by Dr. Henri Planche: *Le Problème de Gide* (collection "Notre Monde," [Paris: Téqui, 1952]). Without bringing anything new to the discussion, Henri Planche restated the problem clearly. See also: Ramón Fernandez, *André Gide* (Paris: Ed. Corréa, 1931).

On the subject of Gide's communism, Maurice Lime's book, *Gide tel que je l'ai connu* (Paris: Julliard, 1952), is infinitely too colored by a personal quarrel to be of any use whatever, while Ilya Ehrenbourg's *Vus par un écrivain d'U.R.S.S.* (Paris: Gallimard, 1934), is interesting. In addition one might wish to see Claude Naville, *André Gide et le communisme* (Paris: Librairie du Travail, 1936), and W. Drabovitch, *Les Intellectuels français et le bolchevisme* (Paris: Les Libertés françaises, 1938). See also Jean Guéhenno's article in *Europe*, Nov. 15, 1930. The best over-all study is George Brachfeld's *André Gide and the Communist temptation* (Geneva: Droz, 1959).

The political and religious opinions of those of Gide's critics who are not primarily scholars cannot be overlooked. At the time of his death the "shower of insults" from the extreme right and the extreme left make in themselves a rather curious document. In *Homage à André Gide* (Paris: Gallimard, 1951), see: Jean Paulhan, "La Mort de Gide n'a pas été si mal accueillie," p. 155.

14. François Derais and Henri Rambaud, *L'Envers du journal de Gide* (Paris: Le Nouveau Portique, 1951).

15. In the unproductive years that followed the publication of *The Immoralist*, Gide had planned to write a documented study on North Africa. Instead, he brought out his charming collection of subjective impressions and notes, *Amyntas*. See the preface to *Le Renoncement au Voyage*, O.C., IV, 241.

16. Letter to Marcel Drouin, May 10, 1894, quoted by Davet, *Autour des Nourritures Terrestres* (Paris: Gallimard, 1948), p. 65. See Charles Du Bos, *Le Dialogue avec André Gide* (Paris: Au sans pareil, 1929), and the preface to *Les Lettres de Charles Du Bos et réponses d'André Gide* (Paris: Corréa, 1950).

17. André Rouveyre, *Le Reclus et le Retors* (Paris: Crès, 1927), p. 200.

18. Letter to Rouveyre, O.C., XII, 560.

19. O.C., XII, 561.

20. *Journal*, p. 984.

21. *Journal*, p. 1237.

22. "Lettres à Angèle," O.C., III, 214.

CHAPTER II

1. *Journal*, p. 782.

2. *Thésée* (Paris: Gallimard, 1946), p. 74.

3. *Numquid et tu* . . . , in *Journal*, p. 603.

4. *Journal*, p. 651.

5. *Dostoeïvsky*, O.C., V, 61.

6. *Renoncement au voyage*, O.C., IV, 301. Italics are mine (G.B.).

7. Letter to Bouhélier, 1897. Quoted by Davet, *op. cit.*, p. 14.

8. 1926 preface to *Les Nourritures Terrestres*, O.C., II, 229.

CHAPTER III

1. *Les Poésies d'André Walter*, O.C., I, 190.

2. *Si le grain ne meurt*, O.C., X, 301-302.

3. *Les Cahiers d'André Walter*, O.C., I, 68.

4. *Ibid.*, O.C., I, 95.

5. *Ibid.*, O.C., I, 94.

6. *Si le grain ne meurt*, O.C., X, 301. Bussy, p. 217.

7. "At night, I lean out of the window, air! Oh! I suffocate; —air! I am feverish; Oh, for some cold air to refresh my throbbing heart!" O.C., I, 145. Some characteristic mannerisms of Gide's writings are already present in *André Walter*. He seems to start from certain familiar rhythmic groups of words which carry the tonality

he wants. He avoids the banal by slightly shifting the usual order of the words. His prose therefore borders upon clichés but never exactly reproduces them: adverbs are slightly displaced; pronouns omitted; the sentence broken unexpectedly by curious procedures of punctuation.

8. *Si le grain ne meurt*, O.C., X, 302.
9. *Ibid.*, O.C., X, 321.
10. Mallarmé, "Variations sur un sujet." *Oeuvres complètes*, ed. de la Pléiade (Paris, 1945), p. 365.
11. The Narcissus myth, a favorite with the symbolists, was treated simultaneously in very diverse fashion by André Gide and his then newly acquired friend Paul Valéry.
12. *Le Traite du Narcisse*, O.C., I, 208.
13. *Ibid.*, O.C., I, 211.
14. *Ibid.*, O.C., I, 215.
15. *Ibid.*, O.C., I, 217.
16. Gide "Feuillets," *Journal*, p. 343.
17. *Narcisse*, O.C., I, 219.
18. *Ibid.*, O.C., I, 220.

CHAPTER IV

1. *Les Poesies d'André Walter*, O.C., I, 181-182.
2. *Ibid.*, O.C., I, 198.
3. *Le Voyage d'Urien*, O.C., I, 281.
4. *Ibid.*, O.C., I, 284.
5. *Ibid.*, O.C., I, 327.
6. *Ibid.*, O.C., I, 349.
7. *Ibid.*, O.C., I, 350.
8. *Ibid.*, O.C., I, 362-363.
9. Albert J. Guérard (in *André Gide* [Cambridge, Mass.: Harvard University Press, 1951], pp. 58-67) offers an interesting interpretation of "unconscious" sexual symbolism. Nonetheless, at this early period in his development Gide's images are so obviously culled from literature that a psychoanalytic interpretation can only be applied with extreme caution.
10. *Ibid.*, O.C., I, 344. For this phase see a letter to Marcel Drouin, March 10, 1894. "For me, who had squeezed out my soul like a sponge to extract from it the *Notebooks* (of André Walter) which you know, the habit of keeping a journal had given me enough self-knowledge to make any further introspection insipid from the day it ceased to surprise me." Quoted by Davet, *op. cit.*, p. 66.

11. *Ibid.*, O.C., I, 364.
12. *The Amorous Attempt*, O.C., I, 239.
13. *Ibid.*, O.C., I, 240-241.
14. *Ibid.*, O.C., I, 223.
15. *Journal*, p. 40.
16. *The Amorous Attempt*, O.C., I, 241.
17. *Ibid.*, O.C., I, 231.
18. *Ibid.*, O.C., I, 231.
19. *Journal*, pp. 40-41.
20. *Urien's Voyage*, O.C., I, 365.
21. Preface to *The Amorous Attempt*, O.C., I, 223.

CHAPTER V

1. *Les Poésies d'André Walter*, O.C., I, 184.
2. "Projet de conférence pour Berlin" (Outline for a Berlin lecture) (1918), O.C., XV, 513.
3. Letter to Marcel Drouin, quoted by Davet, *op. cit.*, p. 55.
4. *Si le grain ne meurt*, O.C., X, 386.
5. Letter to Drouin, March 18, 1896. Davet, *op. cit.*, p. 46.
6. *Si le grain ne meurt*, O.C., X, 387.
7. Letter to Jacques Doucet, January, 1918. Davet, *op. cit.*, p. 21.
8. *Marshlands*, O.C., I, 391.
9. *Ibid.*, O.C., I, 371, 401, 404, 405, 454. Cf. Holdheim: "Gide's *Paludes*, the Humor of falsity," in *The French Review*, April, 1959, pp. 601-609.
10. *Ibid.*, O.C., I, 379.
11. *Ibid.*, O.C., I, 379.
12. *Ibid.*, O.C., I, 396, 428.
13. *Ibid.*, O.C., I, 377, 382, 388, 391.
14. *Ibid.*, O.C., I, 377, 382.

CHAPTER VI

1. *Les Nourritures Terrestres*, O.C., II, 173.
2. "These are the fruits which nourished us on the earth," Koran, II, 23. Used as epigraph for the book, O.C., II, 56. Italics are mine (G. B.).
3. *Les Nourritures Terrestres*, O.C., II, 205.
4. *Ibid.*, O.C., II, 98.
5. *Ibid.*, O.C., II, 161.
6. *Ibid.*, O.C., III, 220-221.

7. *Ibid.*, O.C., II, 166.
8. *Ibid.*, O.C., II, 167.
9. *Ibid.*, O.C., II, 105.
10. *Ibid.*, O.C., II, 69, 71.
11. *Ibid.*, O.C., II, 74.
12. *Ibid.*, O.C., II, 76, 77.
13. *Ibid.*, O.C., II, 81.
14. *Ibid.*, O.C., II, 91.
15. *Ibid.*, O.C., II, 92.
16. *Ibid.*, O.C., II, 107.
17. *Ibid.*, O.C., II, 63.
18. *Ibid.*, O.C., II, 137. The story of Menalcas was first published in the review *l'Ermitage* in January, 1896. *See:* Davet, *op. cit.*, pp. 83-87.
19. *Ibid.*, O.C., II, 138.
20. *Ibid.*, O.C., II, 151-155.
21. *Ibid.*, O.C., II, 147.
22. *Ibid.*, O.C., II, 183-184.
23. O.C., II, 192.
24. "I have always had a horror (or fear) of freedom." *Journal*, p. 739. Gide often insisted on his fear of freedom.

CHAPTER VII

1. O.C., IV, 215.
2. Nietzsche's influence is felt in all these works: Cf. "Letters to Angela." See Holdheim: "The young Gide's reaction to Nietzsche," in *PMLA*, June, 1957, pp. 401-409.
3. O.C., III, 70-71.
4. L. Martin-Chauffier, "Notices," O.C., III, VIII.
5. *El Hadj*, O.C., III, 94, 95.
6. Even before he wrote *El Hadj*, Gide had been moving away from his adolescent faith. "The history of God can only be the story of what men have thought Him to be." ("Littérature et morale," *Journal*, p. 88.) See also the letter to Drouin, March 18, 1893: "Today your friend . . . is a pagan—or not much else. The 're-ligious question' exasperates me; and I can't bear to talk about it." Quoted by Davet, *op. cit.*, p. 44.
7. *Le Prométhée mal enchaîné*, O.C., III, 101.
8. *Ibid.*, O.C., III, 102.

9. "What makes us laugh is the sense of the atrophy of something which could have developed fully." *Journal*, p. 39.
10. *Le Prométhée mal enchaîné*, O.C., III, 142.
11. *Ibid.*, O.C., III, 103.
12. "We played the flute. You didn't listen to us." *Marshlands'* "Envoi." The "flute player" links together the two satires. In *Prometheus* Angela leaves Tityrus, the hero of *Marshlands*, to follow the carefree Meliboeus. Writers are sometimes ironically called "joueurs de flutes," i.e., those concerned only with frivolities.
13. *Le Prométhée mal enchaîné*, O.C., III, 120. See Holdheim: "The dual structure of the *Prométhée mal enchaîné*," in *Modern Language Notes*, December, 1959, pp. 714-720.
14. *Ibid.*, O.C., III, 138.
15. *Ibid.*, O.C., III, 104.
16. *Ibid.*, O.C., III, 109.
17. *Ibid.*, O.C., III, 140-141.
18. *Ibid.*, O.C., III, 130.
19. "But I know that I should like to consider the work of an artist as a complete microcosm, completely strange, in which, nonetheless all the complexity of life is reflected. I should like to feel it contains a special philosophy, a special form of humor." *Letters to Angela*, O.C., III, 165.
20. *Le Prométhée mal enchaîné*, O.C., III, 116.
21. *L'Evolution du Théâtre*, O.C., IV, 214.

CHAPTER VIII

1. *Letters to Angela*, O.C., III, 166.
2. Written in 1898, published in 1899. The original tale as dramatized by Sophocles runs as follows: Philoctetes left with the Greeks for Troy. He volunteered to land on the island of Chrysea to consult an oracle as the gods required. There he was bitten by a serpent. Because of the stench which emanated from his wound he was left at Lemnos. An oracle later decreed that Troy would not fall until Philoctetes and his famed bow and arrows were brought to Troy. Odysseus (Ulysses) went with Neoptolemus to fetch the hero back. Nothing could persuade him to join the Greeks until the gods themselves gave him the order. Gide's play was inspired, most certainly, by Sophocles's.
3. Gide wrote his play in 1897-1898. Several scenes were published in 1898, but the entire play was published only in 1903. The play

has obvious reminiscences of Shakespeare, and borrows its materials from the Books of Samuel, in the Old Testament.

4. Written in 1899, *King Candaule* was published that same year in one of the neosymbolist "little reviews," *l'Ermitage.* It is based on an anecdote told by Herodotus, of which Plato gave a different version, introducing the magic ring which makes its wearer invisible. See McLaren: *The Theater of Gide,* p. 27.

5. *Le roi Candaule,* Preface, O.C., III, 294.

6. *Philoctète,* O.C., III, 17.

7. *Ibid.,* O.C., III, 23.

8. *Ibid.,* O.C., III, 25-26.

9. *Ibid.,* O.C., III, 31.

10. *Ibid.,* O.C., III, 34.

11. *Ibid.,* O.C., III, 38-39.

12. *Ibid.,* O.C., III, 59. See Sartre's mention of Gide's *Philoctetes* in *L'Etre et le Néant* (Paris: Gallimard, 1943), pp. 554-555.

13. *Théâtre Complet,* 1, 184. Letter to Christian Beck, Dec. 21, 1907, quoted by Heyd.

14. *Saül,* O.C., II, 248-249.

15. *Ibid.,* O.C., II, 249.

16. *Ibid.,* O.C., II, 345.

17. *Ibid.,* O.C., II, 351.

18. *Ibid.,* O.C., II, 400.

19. *Le roi Candaule,* O.C., III, 350.

20. *Ibid.,* O.C., III, 314.

21. *Ibid.,* O.C., III, 300.

22. *Ibid.,* O.C., III, 299.

23. *Ibid.,* O.C., III, 319.

24. *Ibid.,* O.C., III, 321.

25. *Ibid.,* O.C., III, 331.

26. *Ibid.,* O.C., III, 334-335.

27. *Ibid.,* O.C., III, 354, 355.

28. *Ibid.,* O.C., III, 370.

29. *Ibid.,* O.C., III, 383-384.

30. *Ibid.,* O.C., III, 394.

31. Cf. "But the one I used to be, that *other,* Ah! How can I ever become him again!" *Les Nouvelles Nourritures,* O.C., II, 216.

32. O.C., III, 292.

33. *Candaules* was first produced in 1901, by Lugné-Poë; *Philoctetes,* privately in 1919, and *Saul* by Gide's friend Jacques Copeau at the Théâtre du Vieux Colombier. See McLaren, *op. cit.,* pp. 95-96.

CHAPTER IX

1. *L'Immoraliste*, O.C., IV, 10.
2. *Ibid.*, O.C., IV, 10.
3. *Ibid.*, O.C., IV, 15.
4. *Ibid.*, O.C., IV, 169.
5. *Ibid.*, O.C., IV, 169.
6. Preface to *L'Immoraliste*, O.C., IV, 6-7.
7. *L'Immoraliste*, IV, 18.
8. *Ibid.*, O.C., IV, 20, 21.
9. *Ibid.*, O.C., IV, 22.
10. *Ibid.*, O.C., IV, 28.
11. *Ibid.*, O.C., IV, 34.
12. *Ibid.*, O.C., IV, 36-43.
13. *Ibid.*, O.C., IV, 50.
14. *Ibid.*, O.C., IV, 52.
15. *Ibid.*, O.C., IV, 62.
16. *Ibid.*, O.C., IV, 76.
17. *Ibid.*, O.C., IV, 93.
18. *Ibid.*, O.C., IV, 119.
19. Preface to *L'Immoraliste*, IV, 7.
20. *Ibid.*, O.C., IV, 7.
21. *L'Immoraliste*, IV, 112, 113.
22. *Ibid.*, O.C., IV, 102.
23. *Ibid.*, O.C., IV, 170.
24. Albert J. Guérard, *André Gide*, Chap. III.
25. *L'Evolution du Théâtre*, O.C., IV, 218.
26. *Ibid.*, O.C., IV, 217.

CHAPTER X

1. Written in 1902-1903; published in the review *Vers et Prose*. See McLaren, *The Theater of André Gide*, pp. 41-42. To the story as told in II Samuel, Gide added the story of the dove which his young friend Athman had told him as part of the Arabic version of the episode.
2. *Bathsheba*, O.C., IV, 231.
3. Written in 1904, later transformed into an opera scenario, *Persephone*. See McLaren, *op. cit.*, p. 67.
4. *Proserpine*, O.C., IV, 350.
5. See McLaren, pp. 44-47.

6. "Lettres à Raymond Bonheur," *Le Retour* (Neuchâtel et Paris: Ides et Calendes, 1946).
7. *Quelques livres*, O.C., V, 271.
8. *Journal*, p. 244.
9. *Journal*, p. 211.
10. *Ibid.*, pp. 226-227, 228.
11. *Ibid.*, p. 220.
12. *Ibid.*, p. 255.
13. *Ibid.*, p. 253.
14. *Ibid.*, p. 219.
15. *Ibid.*, p. 157.
16. *Ibid.*, p. 257.
17. *Ibid.*, p. 240.
18. *Le Retour de l'Enfant Prodigue*, O.C., V, 5.
19. *La Porte étroite*, O.C., V, 186, 221.
20. See Pierre Lafille, *André Gide* (Paris: Hachette, 1954), pp. 30-33.
21. *La Porte étroite*, O.C., V, 75.
22. *Ibid.*, O.C., V, 223.
23. *Ibid.*, O.C., V, 93.
24. *Ibid.*, O.C., V, 95.
25. *Ibid.*, O.C., V, 156, 157, 158.
26. *Ibid.*, O.C., V, 160.
27. *Ibid.*, O.C., V, 165.
28. *Ibid.*, O.C., V, 167.
29. *Ibid.*, O.C., V, 187.
30. *Ibid.*, O.C., V, 187-188.

CHAPTER XI

1. Originally entitled *La Mivoie* Isabelle was written in 1910, with ease. Gide published it first in the *Nouvelle revue française* and it was one of the first books to appear later in the *N.R.F.* editions.
2. *Journal*, p. 359.
3. *Ibid.*, p. 300.
4. *Ibid.*, p. 385.
5. *Ibid.*, p. 670. This remark, made after the war when Gide was preparing a new and complete edition of *Corydon*, seems to apply equally well to his point of view at the time he first wrote it.
6. *Ibid.*, p. 365.
7. *Ibid.*, p. 260.

8. *Ibid.,* p. 323.
9. *Ibid.,* p. 182.
10. Prefaces he planned for *Strait Is the Gate* (1909), *Isabelle* (1912), and *Lafcadio's Adventures* (1913).
11. Letter to Jacques Copeau dated July 12, 1914. O.C., VII, 407.
12. "Propositions," O.C., VI, 351.
13. "Feuillets," O.C., VI, 359.
14. "Propositions," O.C., VI, 353-354.
15. *Journal,* p. 388.
16. *Ibid.,* p. 388.
17. *Ibid.,* p. 392.
18. Gide visited Formentin in 1898 with his two friends, the poet Francis Jammes and the critic and future playwright Henri Ghéon. The visit inspired Jammes's "Fourth Elegy," published in *Le Deuil des Primevères* (1901). But as early as 1892 Gide had mentioned the abandoned estate in a letter to Paul Valéry, and thus it may also have some connection with the "closed park" described in Gide's own early work, *The Amorous Attempt.*
19. Gide noted in his *Journal* (p. 387) the "preciosity" of certain passages in *Strait Is the Gate* as opposed to Alissa's journal and letters, which he felt were convincingly written in a style appropriate to the character. Lacase still says, rather preciously: "J'ai presque peine à comprendre aujourd'hui l'impatience qui *m'élançait* alors vers la vie" (O.C., VI, 174), a rather precious use of the word "s'élancer." But such mannerisms are rare in *Isabelle.*
20. *Journal,* p. 323.

CHAPTER XII

1. Written principally between May, 1912, and June, 1913, Gide's *Les Caves du Vatican* has been variously translated into English as *The Vatican Swindle, The Vatican Cellars* and *Lafcadio's Adventures.* The last title has been the most popular and the most usually adopted.
2. A sotie is a medieval farce in which the players freely mocked the powers that be, more often than not the Church.
3. In 1895 a scholar named Jean de Pauly published the facts of the real story in a book called *The False Pope,* which Gide never read. See Yvonne Davet's notes in André Gide, *Romans, récits et soties, Oeuvres lyriques* (Bibliothèque de la Pléiade, pp. 1567-1568).
4. *Lafcadio's Adventures* was adapted for the stage in 1933 in two

versions. The second and better adaptation, Gide's own, is still presented from time to time by avant-garde groups, although a production at the Comédie-Française in 1950 did not meet with much success.

5. Allusion to Jacques-Louis David (1748-1825), leading exponent of the classical reaction in European painting, a portrait painter who also painted historical scenes. David always drew his figures first in the nude, and only afterward clothed them.

6. "Tropism" is a biological term referring to the involuntary response of organisms to external stimuli.

7. Claudel, very much upset by the parts of *Lafcadio's Adventures* he had read, asked Gide to omit this quotation, which Gide did.

CHAPTER XIII

1. *Journal*, p. 559.
2. Ghéon was six years younger than Gide. A jovial "bon vivant," after 1916 he turned his talents to pious literary endeavors, particularly to the theater. For the series of conversions among Gide's friends in those years see O'Brien, *Portrait of André Gide* (New York: Knopf, 1953), pp. 225-235.
3. *Journal*, p. 569, 570.
4. *Ibid.*, p. 565.
5. *Ibid.*, p. 554.
6. *Ibid.*, p. 641.
7. *Ibid.*, p. 598.
8. *Ibid.*, p. 619.
9. *Numquid et tu . . .* in the *Journal*, p. 603.
10. *Journal*, p. 533.
11. See O'Brien, pp. 263-265.
12. *New Fruits of the Earth*, O.C., IX, 94.
13. "Traversée," O.C., IX, 157.
14. In 1923 Gide's daughter, Catherine, was born. Her mother was Elizabeth van Rysselberghe, the daughter of Gide's very devoted friend, Mme. Theo van Rysselberghe. Madeleine Gide was then doubly betrayed.
15. In both these works Gide frankly presented the facts concerning his homosexuality, or what Dr. Delay has called his "pediphilism."
16. *Journal*, p. 300.
17. Laura Dewey Bridgman (1829-1889) was an American girl who was born deaf, dumb, and blind; her education, first described in 1881,

caused considerable interest and was often referred to in educational circles.

CHAPTER XIV

1. *Les Faux-Monnayeurs,* O.C., XII, 267.
2. *Journal,* p. 709, and *Journal des Faux-Monnayeurs,* O.C., XIV, 5. The novel in question is already an embryonic form of *The Counterfeiters* as certain comments in both *Journals* indicate.
3. *Les Nouvelles Nourritures,* O.C., X, 457, 458, 477.
4. *Journal des Faux-Monnayeurs,* O.C., XIII, 48, 49.
5. *Les Nouvelles Nourritures,* O.C., X, 461.
6. *Poems of William Blake,* ed. by Yeats, the edition in which Gide first read Blake.
7. "Feuillets," O.C., XIII, 439-440.
8. *Journal,* p. 444.
9. *Ibid.,* p. 796.
10. "Dada," O.C., X, 18-21.
11. *Journal des F.-M.,* O.C., XIII, 9.
12. *Projet de Préface pour Isabelle,* O.C., VI, 361.
13. In 1912 Gide had read at least the first pages of the manuscript of *Swann's Way* and it was he who was mainly responsible for its rejection at the time by the N.R.F., one of the few major artistic mistakes he made.
14. *Journal des F.-M.,* O.C., XIII, 45-46.
15. *Les Faux-Monnayeurs,* O.C., XII, 297.
16. *Ibid.* Italics are mine (G. B.).
17. *Journal des F.-M.,* O.C., XIII, 31. Italics are mine (G. B.).
18. *Journal,* pp. 799, 801; *The Thibaults,* Roger Martin du Gard's Nobel Prize-winning novel.
19. *Journal des F.-M.,* O.C., XIII, 11.
20. "Feuillets," O.C., XIII, 445.
21. *Journal des F.-M.,* O.C., XIII, 10.
22. Some of the pages of "Souvenirs" which Gide wrote later have a lyrical quality and charm that he eliminated from *If it die . . .*; written at different intervals these reminiscences were collected in the volume *Feuillets d'Automne* (Paris: Mercure de France, 1949).
23. *Journal des F.-M.,* O.C., XIII, 5-6.
24. *Ibid.,* O.C., XIII, 15.
25. On Jan. 13, 1921, for example, he decides to include a whole section of his notebook in the novel. He thinks of his lectures on Dostoevsky as "confessions" somehow connected with *The Coun-*

terfeiters and he notes that reading *Tom Jones*, his brief contact with Fielding, is having repercussions on his own novel. See O.C., XIII, 51.

26. *Journal*, pp. 510, 688.
27. In his *André Gide* (Arthur Barker, Ltd., 1950), George Painter equates Passavant with Cocteau, Dhurmer with Camille Mauclair, etc. No doubt there are connections between Gide's invented characters and some of his acquaintances, but certainly not a one-for-one identification.
28. *Journal des F.-M.*, O.C., XIII, 48.
29. *Ibid.*, O.C., XIII, 36.
30. *Journal*, p. 783.
31. *Ibid.*, O.C., XIII, 15-16.
32. In the novel Vincent is a gambler and seducer; Edouard, a seducer and novelist.
33. *Journal des F.-M.*, O.C., XIII, 36.
34. *Ibid.*, O.C., XIII, 9, 27, 50.
35. *Ibid.*, O.C., XIII, 11. Italics are mine (G. B.).
36. *Ibid.*, O.C., XIII, 18.
37. *Ibid.*, O.C., XIII, 40, 41. The term "pure novel" was suggested to Gide by the controversy then raging among the literati concerning "pure poetry."
38. *Ibid.*, O.C., XIII, 40.
39. *Ibid.*, O.C., XIII, 14.
40. *Ibid.*, O.C., XIII, 19.
41. *Ibid.*, O.C., XIII, 50.
42. *Ibid.*, O.C., XIII, 31.
43. *Journal*, p. 716.

CHAPTER XV

1. Bernard returns home, intellectually matured; Olivier, in Edouard's charge, has rejected the enticement of the literary counterfeiter Passavant; Boris is dead.
2. As in *Lafcadio's Adventures* Gide wanted his novel to give the impression that it could be continued. It is true that, having come through the particular set of events recounted in *The Counterfeiters*, the characters are ready to go on living, as in life itself. The book closes with Edouard's remark concerning his interest in Caloub, Bernard's young brother, a rather impertinent and not really necessary fillip at the end to stress the continuation of life.

But the particular events with which the novel is concerned have spun out their course by its conclusion.

3. Gide sometimes unblushingly puns when giving his characters their names: Profitendieu = Prospers-in-God; Passavant = Gets there first.

4. The actual activities of Gide's gang, increasingly dangerous though they tend to become, seem relatively harmless compared to the widespread battles of teen-age urban gangs since World War II. Nonetheless, Gide raises most pertinently the whole question of adolescent delinquency.

5. *Les Faux-Monnayeurs*, O.C., XII, 489.

6. *Poems of William Blake*, ed. by W. B. Yeats (London: The Muses Library), pp. 231, 255.

7. Dr. Delay goes in detail into the connection between Boris's excruciating struggle against masturbation and the shattering experience Gide went through as a child when he was publicly called to task for just the same thing, then temporarily expelled from his school.

8. *Poems of William Blake*, XXXIV.

9. O.C., XII, 223.

10. Passavant notes the "pun," from which Gide drew ample suggestions. In French slang a person who is "déssalé," or "unsalted," is cynically sophisticated. Vincent, one might say, "went off the deep end" or "got into deep water" far too "salty" for him.

11. *Journal*, p. 811.

CHAPTER XVI

1. *Journal*, p. 960.

2. The two articles were published under the English title *Travels in the Congo* (1929).

3. *Journal*, p. 818.

4. *Ibid.*, p. 1014.

5. *Ibid.*, p. 863.

6. *Ibid.*, p. 1074.

7. *Ibid.*, p. 900.

8. *Ibid.*, p. 1095.

9. *Pages de Journal* (1939-1942), p. 164.

10. *Journal*, p. 1138.

11. *Ibid.*, p. 995.

12. *Ibid.*, p. 1027.

13. *Ibid.*, p. 1050.
14. *Ibid.*, p. 904.
15. *Ibid.*, p. 1281.
16. *Ibid.*, p. 1050. The "new generation" of novelists, Malraux and Saint-Exupéry in particular, had turned Gide's mind in this new direction.
17. Gide was very active in the antifascist movements of the thirties, pushed forward by others rather than by his own initiative. He never really felt at home in the public meetings where he spoke. His integrity was never in question, however, for, genuine liberal that he was, he was deeply opposed to fascism. His main speeches and essays from this period were collected in a volume called *Littérature engagée* (Paris: Gallimard, 1950).
18. Gide went to Russia in the summer of 1936 at the invitation of the Soviets, to speak at the meeting of the Association of Soviet Writers.
19. *Journal*, p. 1128.
20. Gide's *Return from the U.S.S.R.* came out in November, 1936. His "left-wing" friends, by that time already involved in the Spanish Civil War, had vainly tried to persuade him not to publish the book. Gide was from then on, naturally, steadily under attack from the communist press and his reputation was systematically depreciated by the Marxists as it had been before by the militant Catholics. (See O'Brien, *op. cit.*, pp. 329-334.) The vulnerable side of his life, his pederasty, which had formerly been overlooked, was now systematically ventilated by his opponents on both sides.
21. Gide was an admirer of Stendhal, whose essay on love analyzes the various phases of what he called the "crystallization" of love, that is to say, the accidental circumstance in which someone in a highly receptive, subjective emotional state meets a person around whom his or her emotions "crystallize." Gide and Proust, both post-Stendhalians, found a very good theme for their novels in the reverse phase of this process, i.e., the "decrystallization" of love.
22. *Journal*, p. 887.
23. *Geneviève* was published in 1936, but Gide had been working at it since 1930, and often referred to it in his *Journal*.
24. *Journal*, p. 972.
25. *Journal* (1942-1949), p. 168.
26. *Les Nouvelles Nourritures* (Paris: Gallimard, 1942), p. 282.
27. *Ibid.*, pp. 282-283.
28. *Ibid.*, p. 286.

29. *Ibid.*, p. 294.
30. *Ibid.*, p. 255.
31. *Persephone* was performed on April 30, 1934, at the Paris Opéra with a measure of success. Gide used the outline of the "dramatic symphony" *Proserpine* he had worked on in 1904. Proserpine is the Latin equivalent of the Greek Persephone. See McLaren, *op. cit.*, pp. 67-69.
32. Published first in *l'Arche*, a literary magazine in 1944-1945, *Robert* was performed in Tunis in 1946 by a small amateur group. Gide wrote a first draft of the play between 1934 and 1936, at the height of his enthusiasm for communism, but after his return from Russia he reworked the play and completed it in 1940. See McLaren, *op. cit.*, pp. 76-83.
33. *Journal* (1942-1949), p. 305.
34. *The Thirteenth Tree*, a farce, was written in 1935 and performed that year by an amateur avant-garde group in Marseilles. It is an amusing spoof on psychoanalysis.
35. *Journal*, p. 837.
36. *Ibid.*, p. 840.
37. *Ibid.*, p. 1050.
38. *Ibid.*, p. 860.
39. *Thésée* (Paris: Gallimard, 1946), pp. 56-57.
40. *Ibid.*, p. 9.
41. *Ibid.*, pp. 39-40.
42. *Ibid.*, p. 123.
43. *Ibid.*, p. 58.
44. *Ibid.*, pp. 115-116.

Works of André Gide

Les Cahiers d'André Walter. Paris: Librairie de l'Art Indépendant, 1891.

Les Poésies d'André Walter. Paris: Ibid., 1891.

Le Traité du Narcisse. Paris: Ibid., 1891.

La Tentative amoureuse. Paris: Ibid., 1893.

Le Voyage d'Urien. Paris: Ibid., 1893.

Paludes. Paris: Ibid., 1895. (*Marshlands* and *Prometheus Misbound.* Translated by George D. Painter. London: Secker & Warburg, 1953.)

Les Nourritures terrestres. Paris: Mercure de France, 1897. (*Fruits of the Earth.* New York: Alfred A. Knopf; London: Martin Secker & Warburg, 1949.) *

El Hadj. Paris: Mercure de France, 1899.

Le Prométhée mal enchaîné. Paris: Mercure de France, 1899. (*Marshlands* and *Prometheus Misbound.* Translated by George D. Painter. London: Secker & Warburg, 1953.)

Philoctète. Paris: Mercure de France, 1899. (*Philoctetes* in *My Theater.* Translated by Jackson Mathews. New York: Alfred A. Knopf, 1951.)

Le Roi Candaule. Paris: La Revue Blanche, 1901. (*King Candaules* in *My Theater.*)

L'Immoraliste. Paris: Mercure de France, 1902. (*The Immoralist.* New York: Alfred A. Knopf; London: Cassell & Co., 1930.)

Prétextes. Paris: Mercure de France, 1903. (*Pretexts.* Selected, edited, and introduced by Justin O'Brien. New York: Greenwich Editions, 1959.)

Saül. Paris: Mercure de France, 1903. (*Saul* in *My Theater.*)

Amyntas. Paris: Mercure de France, 1906.

* Unless otherwise indicated, all translations are by Dorothy Bussy.

289

Le Retour de l'enfant prodigue. Paris: Vers et Prose, 1907.
La Porte étroite. Paris: Mercure de France, 1909. (*Strait Is the Gate.* New York: Alfred A. Knopf; London: Martin Secker & Warburg, 1924.)
Oscar Wilde. Paris: Mercure de France, 1910. (*Oscar Wilde.* Translated by Bernard Frechtman. London: Kimber, 1951.)
Isabelle. Paris: Gallimard, 1911. (*Isabelle* in *Two Symphonies.* New York: Alfred A. Knopf; London: Cassell & Co., 1931.)
Nouveaux Prétextes. Paris: Mercure de France, 1911. (In *Pretexts.*)
Bethsabé. Paris: Bibliothèque de l'Occident, 1912. (*Bathsheba* in *My Theater.*)
Les Caves du Vatican. Paris: Gallimard, 1914. (*The Vatican Swindle.* New York: Alfred A. Knopf, 1925; or *Lafcadio's Adventures.* Ibid., 1927; or *The Vatican Cellars.* London: Cassell & Co., 1925.)
Souvenirs de la Cour d'Assises. Paris: Gallimard, 1914. (*Recollections of the Assize Court.* Translator anon. London: Hutchinson & Co., 1941.)
La Symphonie pastorale. Paris: Gallimard, 1919. (*The Pastoral Symphony* in *Two Symphonies.*)
Morceaux choisis. Paris: Gallimard, 1921.
Dostoïevsky. Paris: Plon-Nourrit, 1923. (*Dostoevsky.* London: J. M. Dent, 1925; Secker & Warburg, 1949; New York: Alfred A. Knopf, 1926; New Directions, 1949; trans. anon.)
Incidences. Paris: Gallimard, 1924.
Corydon. Paris: Ibid., 1924. (*Corydon.* Translated by Hugh Gibb. New York: Farrar, Strauss & Co., 1950.)
Les Faux-Monnayeurs. Paris: Gallimard, 1926. (*The Counterfeiters.* New York: Alfred A. Knopf, 1927; or *The Coiners.* London: Cassell & Co., 1927.)
Journal des Faux-Monnayeurs. Paris: Gallimard, 1926. (*Logbook of the Coiners.* Translated by Justin O'Brien. London: Cassell & Co., 1952.)
Numquid et tu . . . ? Paris: Editions de la Pléiade, 1926. (*Numquid et tu . . . ?* in *The Journals of André Gide*, Vol. II. Translated by Justin O'Brien. New York: Alfred A. Knopf; London: Secker & Warburg, 1948.)

Si le grain ne meurt . . . Paris: Gallimard, 1926. (If It Die . . .
New York: Random House, 1935; London: Secker & Warburg,
1950.)

Dindiki. Liège: Editions de la Lampe d'Aladdin, 1927.

Voyage au Congo. Paris: Gallimard, 1927. (Travels in the Congo.
New York: Alfred A. Knopf, 1929; London: Secker & Warburg,
1930.)

Le Retour du Tchad. Paris: Gallimard, 1928. (In Travels in the
Congo.)

Essai sur Montaigne. Paris: Editions de la Pléiade, 1929. (Montaigne. Translated by S. H. Guest and T. E. Blewitt. New
York: Horace Liveright; London: Blackmore Press, 1929.)

L'Ecole des femmes. Paris: Gallimard, 1929. (The School for
Wives. New York: Alfred A. Knopf, 1929, 1950; London: Cassell & Co., 1950.)

Robert. Paris: Gallimard, 1929. (Robert in The School for Wives.)

Un Esprit non prévenu. Paris: Editions Kra, 1929.

L'Affaire Redureau. Paris: Gallimard, 1930.

Lettres. Liège: A la Lampe d'Aladdin, 1930.

La Sequestrée de Poitiers. Paris: Gallimard, 1930.

Divers. Paris: Gallimard, 1931.

Œdipe. Paris: Gallimard, 1931. (Œdipus in Two Legends: Theseus and Œdipus. Translated by John Russell. New York: Alfred A. Knopf; London: Secker & Warburg, 1950.)

Œuvres complètes. Paris: Gallimard, 15 vols., 1932-9.

Perséphone. Paris: Gallimard, 1934. (Persephone in My Theater.)

Les Nouvelles Nourritures. Paris: Gallimard, 1935. (New Fruits
of the Earth. New York: Alfred A. Knopf; London: Secker &
Warburg, 1949.)

Le Treizième Arbre. Mesures, No. 2, 1935.

Geneviève. Paris: Gallimard, 1936. (Genevieve in The School for
Wives.)

Retour de l'U.R.S.S. Paris: Gallimard, 1936. (Return from the
U.S.S.R. New York: Alfred A. Knopf; London: Secker & Warburg, 1937.)

Retouches à mon Retour de L'U.R.S.S. Paris: Gallimard, 1937.
(Afterthoughts on the U.S.S.R. New York: Dial Press; London:
Secker & Warburg, 1938.)

Journal, 1889-1939. Paris: Gallimard, Editions de la Pléiade, 1939. (*The Journals of André Gide.* Translated by Justin O'Brien. New York: Alfred A. Knopf; London: Secker & Warburg, 1947-1951.)

Théâtre. Paris: Gallimard, 1942.

Attendu que . . . Algiers: Charlot, 1943.

Interviews imaginaires. New York: Pantheon Books, 1943. (*Imaginary Interviews.* Translated by Malcolm Cowley. New York: Alfred A. Knopf, 1944.)

Pages de Journal, 1939-1942. New York: Pantheon Books, 1944; Paris: Gallimard, 1946. (*Extracts from the Journals, 1939-1942.* In *The Journals of André Gide.*)

Robert ou l'Intérêt général. Algiers: L'Arche, 1944-5.

L'Enseignement de Poussin. Paris: Le Divan, 1945. (*Poussin.* London: *The Arts,* No. 2, 1947.)

Jeunesse. Neuchâtel: Ides et Calendes, 1945.

Deux Interviews imaginaires suivies de Feuillets. Algiers: Charlot, 1946.

Le Retour. Neuchâtel: Ides et Calendes, 1946.

Thésée. Paris: Gallimard; New York: Pantheon Books, 1946. (*Theseus* in *Two Legends.*)

Poétique. Neuchâtel: Ides et Calendes, 1947.

Théâtre complet. Neuchâtel: Ides et Calendes, 8 vols., 1947-9.

Préfaces. Neuchâtel: Ides et Calendes, 1948.

Eloges. Ibid., 1948.

Correspondance Francis Jammes et André Gide, 1893-1938. Paris: Gallimard, 1948.

Rencontres. Neuchâtel: Ides et Calendes, 1948.

Feuillets d'automne. Paris: Mercure de France, 1949. (*Autumn Leaves.* Translated by Elsie Pell. New York: Philosophical Library, 1950.)

Correspondance Paul Claudel et André Gide, 1899-1926. Paris: Gallimard, 1948. (*The Correspondence between Paul Claudel and André Gide.* Translated by John Russell. New York: Pantheon Books; London: Secker & Warburg, 1952.)

Journal, 1942-1949. Paris: Gallimard, 1950. (*Journal, 1942-1949.* In *The Journals of André Gide.*)

Lettres de Charles Du Bos et Réponses d'André Gide. Paris: Corrêa, 1950.

Littérature engagée. Edited by Yvonne Davet. Paris: Gallimard, 1950.

Et nunc manet in te. Neuchâtel: Ides et Calendes, 1951. (*Madeleine.* New York: Alfred A. Knopf, 1952; or *Et nunc manet in te.* Translated by Justin O'Brien. London: Secker & Warburg, 1953.)

Ainsi soit-il ou Les Jeux sont faits. Paris: Gallimard, 1952. (*So Be It,* or *The Chips Are Down.* Translated by Justin O'Brien. New York: Alfred A. Knopf, 1959.)

Correspondance Rainer Maria Rilke et André Gide, 1909-1926. Edited by Renée Lang. Paris: Corrêa, 1952.

Journal 1939-1949, Souvenirs. Paris: Gallimard, Bibliothèque de la Pléiade, 1954.

Romans, Récits et Soties. Edited by Yvonne Davet and Jean-Jacques Therry. Paris: Gallimard, Bibliothèque de la Pléiade, 1958.

The Correspondence of André Gide and Edmund Gosse, 1904-1928. Edited by Linette F. Brugmans. New York: New York University Press, 1959.

Selective Bibliography

Ames, Van Meter. *André Gide*. Norfolk, Conn.: New Directions Books, 1947.

Brachfeld, Georges I. *André Gide and the Communist Temptation*. Geneva: Librairie E. Droz; Paris: Librairie Minard, 1959.

Delay, Jean. *La Jeunesse d'André Gide*, 2 vols. Paris: Gallimard, 1956-7. (*The Youth of André Gide*. Translated and abridged by June Guicharnaud. Chicago and London: The University of Chicago Press, 1963.)

Fayer, H. M. *Gide, Freedom and Dostoïevsky*. Burlington, Vt.: Lane Press, 1946.

Guérard, Albert J. *André Gide*. Cambridge, Mass.: Harvard University Press, 1951.

Hytier, Jean. *André Gide*. Algiers: Charlot, 1938. (*André Gide*. Translated by Richard Howard. Garden City, N. Y.: Doubleday, 1962.)

Lafille, Pierre. *André Gide, romancier*. Paris: Hachette, 1954.

Magny, Claude-Edmonde. "Satanism in Contemporary Literature," *Satan*, ed. by Bruno de Jesus Marie. New York: Sheed & Ward, 1952.

Mann, Klaus. *André Gide and the Crisis of Modern Thought*. New York: Creative Age Press, 1943.

Martin, Claude. *André Gide par lui-même*. Paris: Editions du Seuil, 1963.

McLaren, James C. *The Theatre of André Gide*. Baltimore: The Johns Hopkins Press, 1943.

O'Brien, Justin. *Portrait of André Gide, A Critical Biography*. New York: Alfred A. Knopf, 1953.

Painter, George. *André Gide, a Critical and Biographical Study*. New York: Roy Publishers, 1951.

Pierre-Quint, Léon. *André Gide*. Paris: Stock, 1952.
Savage, Catharine H. *André Gide: l'évolution de sa pensée religieuse*. Paris: Nizet, 1962.
Schlumberger, Jean. *Madeleine et André Gide*. Paris: Gallimard, 1956.
Thierry, Jean-Jacques. *Gide*. Paris: Gallimard, 1962.

Index

Aeschylus, 87

Ajax, 145

A la Recherche d'André Gide (Pierre Herbart), 201

"Allain," see André Walter

Allégret, Marc, 200, 201, 208

Amorous Attempt, The, 31, 37, 42, 45, 53, 62; critical analysis of, 50-52

Amyntas, 75, 143

Anabasis (Saint John Perse), 84

André Walter, 8, 9, 14, 16, 20-23 passim, 52, 53, 125, 148, 154, 191, 192, 270; publication of, 23; critical analysis of, 31-37

Angela, see Letters to Angela

Apollinaire, Guillaume, 165-166

Arabian Nights, The, 52, 68

As You Like It (Shakespeare), 195, 231

Athman, 111

Balzac, Honoré de, 20, 171, 223

Barrès, Maurice, 14, 26, 31, 38, 44, 79, 106, 157, 207

Bathsheba, 57, 143-144

Baudelaire, Charles, 64, 70

Beethoven, Ludwig van, 204

Béraud, Henri, 195

Bergson, Henri, 29

Bible, The, 25, 28, 68, 69, 83, 86, 100, 101, 111, 114, 144,

148, 149, 154, 196-198, 199, 200, 202

Blake, William, 15, 28, 210, 213, 238

Boccaccio, 68

Bonheur, Raymond, 145

Bourget, Paul, 26, 207

Breton, André, 176

Bridgman, Laura, 203

Browning, Robert, 28

Caligula (Camus), 153

Calvin, John, 202

Camus, Albert, 30, 99, 153

Candaules, see King Candaules

Claudel, Paul, 6, 14, 25, 56, 86, 98, 145-146, 151, 163, 164, 178, 184, 185, 194

Cocteau, Jean, 145

Common Weal, The, see Robert ⁻or The Common Weal

Congo, see Journey to the Congo

"Considerations on Greek Mythology," 195, 200, 260

Conversations with Nicodemus, 197, 200, 201

Copeau, Jacques, 22, 25, 163, 207

Corydon, 18, 152, 164, 165, 195, 198, 201, 220, 254; publication of, 25, 164

GIDE

by Germaine Brée

One year after the death of André Gide in 1951, Germaine Brée began work on a book later published in France entitled *André Gide, l'Insaisissable Protée.* Of this work Henri Peyre recently wrote: "There is nothing that equals it. Each chapter is penetrating, rich, subtle and astonishingly right. . . . you are an extraordinary critic."

The past ten years have seen the appearance of a number of stimulating papers on Gide which have assisted Miss Brée in the revisions she made as she completely reworked the original book and rewrote it in English. "And yet," Miss Brée writes, "my basic approach to Gide's work has not greatly changed. I found, when I came back to his work, that the approach was, rather, reaffirmed." An objective and thorough appraisal can now be made of the man who never faltered in the task he had set for himself—to fashion his life and his work by means of a constant intellectual discipline of a very personal kind.

Gide was a man for whom writing was an act of commitment—each stage in his career as novelist, dramatist, and essayist clarifies certain ethical problems to which he gave esthetic expression. Using his writings as her

(continued on back flap)